BELOW THE LINE

Vicki Mayer

BELOW THE LINE

Producers and
Production Studies in
the New Television
Economy

Duke University Press   *Durham and London*   2011

© 2011 Duke University Press
All rights reserved
Printed in the United States
of America on acid-free paper ∞
Designed by C. H. Westmoreland
Typeset in Warnock
by Keystone Typesetting, Inc.
Library of Congress Cataloging-
in-Publication Data appear on the
last printed page of this book.

Duke University Press gratefully
acknowledges the support of Tulane
University School of Liberal Arts, which
provided funds toward the production
of this book.

An earlier version of parts of chapter 3
appeared as "Guys Gone Wild?
Soft-Core Video Professionalism
and New Realities in Television
Production," in *Cinema Journal* 47,
no. 2 (2008), 97–116.

Contents

Acknowledgments

The idea for this book started in listening to what examiners had to say at the defense of my doctoral dissertation on a completely separate topic nearly a decade ago. John Caldwell pressed on me the need to see producers as a cultural formation. Chon Noriega encouraged me to look historically into the cultural geography of my field site, and George Lipsitz asked me to do the same concerning the history of social movements and citizenship. Dan Schiller reminded me of the importance of theorizing labor and communication. In the end, Ellen Seiter asked, "So what do you think about doing an ethnography of media production?" These topics—production, ethnography, labor, and identity—spurred the idea for this book.

Along the way, John and Ellen have continued to be mentors and friends. Toby Miller has given excellent advice, references, and tempered but deserved critiques of my blind sides. I have Nick Couldry to thank for the book's title and for his ability to help me frame my field studies in larger debates. Dave Hesmondhalgh keeps me on my toes. Helen Wood, Diane Negra, Bill Kirkpatrick, Allison Perlman, Sandra Braman, and Des Freedman have given important feedback on individual chapters. I thank the faculty, staff, and students at the University of California, Los Angeles; the University of Southern California; the University of Virginia; and the University of Wisconsin, Madison, for giving me a chance to test out cases and arguments. Countless people at conferences have listened to me stumble through the messiness of my field notes, interviews, and speculations.

The enormous support of Tulane University, its faculty, and students during a difficult time post-Katrina has been without parallel. My undergraduate researchers and assistants Denise Gass, Rachel Applestein,

Candace Boyle, Stephanie Spicer, and Amy Leonard have been stable forces behind each project. The writing group organized by Justin Wolfe, and much appreciated insights by Mauro Porto, Connie Balides, and Michele White have been invaluable. The Roger Thayer Stone Center for Latin American Studies, the Newcomb Institute for Women, the School of Liberal Arts, and the Provost's Office have all provided funding for aspects of this work. Courtney Berger of Duke University Press has been exceedingly patient with me and very helpful in allowing me the time and freedom to work through the manuscript during the various crises in New Orleans.

Special thanks to the people who participated in this project through interviews, observations, and critiques. An even greater thank-you goes to Torbjörn Törnqvist for his invisible and emotional work over the past three years.

Introduction

WHO ARE TELEVISION'S PRODUCERS?

In the digital age, everyone is potentially a media producer, but most of us only recognize certain forms of media production as important. Consider, for example, the twenty-two-year-old woman working the assembly line in an international electronics export zone. Without her nimble abilities to fix a broken solder machine while affixing the hot wires to a chassis, we would never have access to the equipment on which middle-class children in the United States download programs and upload their own TV contents. Conversely, consider another twenty-two-year-old in a local dance club. He loves our moves and our shoes. After some chummy conversation, we receive a business card requesting our presence at a taped audition for a reality program. Such scouts generate talent and viewership for much of the television programming landscape. This book focuses on the people—from assemblers to scouts, from agents to regulators—who produce television beyond the nomenclature of media production and outside the hierarchies assigned to Hollywood industries and their personnel. Their labors, situated somewhere between the "producers" located at the apex of television studio hierarchies and the "everyperson" implied in the rhetoric of digital production, reproduce the identities that support an entire lexicon of production. By looking at the producers betwixt and between these restrictive and expansive notions of production, this book begins to unravel the complex mirroring of producers with political economy, and of identity with labor value.

I use the word *complex* here consciously because my notions of producers throughout this book run counter to the common-sense definitions of who produces television. After all, the young women on the assembly line and the scouts in the club would just as soon blush or laugh if I called them "television producers," even if they wholly recognized the important roles they play in economies of television production. I remember the pride with which a former assembler stated that her husband earned a good living in the informal economy but that her factory job mattered more to her. "I gave the television life," she proclaimed, her eyes shining. Likewise, a casting scout who scoured the U.S. Midwest for a reality program boasted that his company's cast members "made" the program—"Without us, you wouldn't have a good show"—and yet his achievements seemed bittersweet when he was not invited to the wrap party for the official production crew. These are the ironies that workers face in roles as physically remote from each other as the chassis creator and the studio brand sponsor, or as far afield from each other as a civic activist and a freelance videographer. In each scenario I encountered, people defined themselves in relation to the work they did on behalf of television industries, even as they were invisible to *the* television industry itself. Conversely, the industry—itself a euphemistic construction that replaces human activities with a collection of businesses—relies on their invisible labors, even as it denigrates or disavows the workers as outside the creative professionals who construct the industry's narratives about itself.[1] The producers I present here thus do not suffer from a false consciousness of their own conditions but from a historical process of displacements, substitutions, and transformations that anchored the "producer" to forms of labor, sites of production, and identities that were simply not-them.

The recognition of workers who economically support, symbolically reproduce, and thus practically consent to the industry's own construction of the producer has been woefully absent in the otherwise diverse range of research on television production during the past half century. Following in the industry's own footsteps, scholars have most frequently identified television producers as the medium's chief managers and artists, evaluating these unique individuals' abilities to combine roles associated with economic control and creative conceptualization.[2] As these roles have transformed, the paradigm for identifying producers according to these ideals has not. Observers of the shifts in television labor more commonly lament the winnowing of creativity and the hollowness of professionalism among the narrow categories of executives, often laying blame on the incursions of sponsors and on the absence of regulators sitting over media industries. Although this constitutes one story line about the declining state of producers and the television industry, the present book offers an alternative narrative about television production, one in which the industry's political economy expands through its incorporation of invisible labor. This narrative should be of particular concern at this conjuncture at which all of us increasingly define ourselves through our productive work while at the same time industries devalue our agency as producers through abstract quantitative measures, from stock share prices to advertising rates. Confronting this state of affairs, scholars' most damning critique might be one recognizing that, indeed, everyone is a producer in the new television economy, but that the television industry comes away as the primary benefactor of these labors.

My own critique encompasses four case studies: television set assemblers, soft-core cameramen, reality-show casters, and volunteer cable television advocates. Their corresponding labors deconstruct the monopolies of creativity and professionalism that have structured the producer as ontologically different from all the other people who serve the television industry's symbolic and material economies. Their work to construct their own identities and identify others demonstrates the importance of sponsoring and regulating selves in the new television economy. The ethnographic orientation of this book looks into working selves, and material conditions provide their own lessons about the new television economy: its propensity to generate new work spaces and times; its disappearing boundaries between subjectivities and commodities; and its continual incorporation of new people who will work freely on its behalf. More important, though, each case demonstrates how the abstraction of television's value in society relies on the agency of workers not only to produce things that the industry needs, such as a bit of content or a broad policy statement, but also to produce themselves in the service of capital expansion. My project thus advocates for production studies that consider identity and identification as key factors in future labor struggles. As this introductory chapter shows, the exclusionary politics of labor and identity are part of a longer trajectory that predates the formation of the television industry but has taken formations specific to the organization of television labor. Yet this argument begins with a historical materialist reading of industrial labor divisions that give a context for the idealized constructions of the television producer as an embodied creative professional over the past half century.

Production to Producer
FROM THE UNIVERSAL TO THE PARTICULAR FORMATION
OF THE MASS PRODUCER AND THE PRODUCER ARTIST

The use of the term *producer* in media organizations has been ideological, used to justify why some workers command more labor value than
others. After all, all humans are producers in the sense that we make our
material lives and cooperate to reproduce social relations.[3] These relations, in turn, are hierarchical, setting different values on productive
human actions. By the end of the film studio era and at the beginning of
the television age, the different values ascribed to work contributing to
media production separated along a division of labor known as "the line."
Studio accountants used this line physically on their budget sheets to
separate upfront production costs from expenditures made during production. Thus this line indexed the scarcity or surplus of so-called creativity and professionalism, two competing resources for labor value in
industrial capitalism since the late 1800s.[4] Whereas the word *professional*
in this discourse came to separate those who managed themselves from
those who were managed by others, *creativity* more often demarcated
intellectual from manual activities.[5] Professionals located "above the line"
managed themselves and used their intellectual capacities, as opposed to
tradespeople, artisans, and others "below the line," who used their manual
skills under the control of managers. The title of this book points to those
workers whose labors are the structuring absences to this particular formation of the producer and his or her labor value.

The construction of the producer has corresponded to broader political economic changes that have usurped workers' agency and individuated their productive capacities. Since the post–World War II period,
national governments have gradually privileged creativity and professionalism as necessary forms of human agency for a competitive and
individualized so-called enterprise society, which formed the basis for a
neoliberal state driven by market-based policy.[6] In other words, the industrial consolidation of the producer as the embodiment of the creative
professional relied on the bifurcation of spheres of control and skills as
the sources of labor value in production, while isolating them from other
forms of human agency in market mechanisms or state regulation. We
feel these divisions today, as shown by recent meditations on the lost

value of artisanship, the nostalgic need for communal bonds in the workplace, and the acute desire to see the human agency that produced otherwise abstract crises on Wall Street.[7] These feelings of loss for values grounded in the social relationships of production have been the targets of global economic policies and corporate practices during the past quarter-century. Neoliberal trade policies have devalued labor and reduced workers' solidarity by combining labor markets worldwide. Political attacks on workers' agency have been decentered throughout much of the world, which now focuses on inflation indexes, stock market values, and corporate profit margins as the only indicators of a healthy economy.[8] Today the attempt to see the range of workers and labors not recognized in media industries' final product seems completely in line with the erasure of workers' agency and solidarities in other spheres. Yet these alienating shifts were of central concern to early scholars of film production.

Two classic studies of Hollywood film production during the studio era (ca. 1920s–1950s) are forerunners in conceptualizing television producers as either ordinary or extraordinary in terms of their productive agency and collective identities. The sociologist and former screenwriter Leo Rosten conducted what he called a "Middletown" study of the film industry, combining reams of quantitative data on studio expenditures and labor earnings with trade accounts and interviews about the culture of production.[9] A decade later, the esteemed anthropologist Hortense Powdermaker published an insider's look into production processes through fieldwork and participant observation.[10] As the students of Harold Lasswell and Bronislaw Malinowski, respectively, Rosten and Powdermaker attempted to demystify moviemaking as labor, all the while also establishing these laborers' differences from other U.S. workers.

Both researchers concentrated on above-the-line workers, whom Rosten calls the Hollywood elite.[11] In their narratives, the elite emerges as a social grouping of rootless eccentrics, superficial neurotics, and self-indulgent narcissists. Rosten starts his story of Hollywood's residents as if they were the cast for its own movie: "The hordes which flocked to Los Angeles (after 1919) included a generous assortment of the déclassé: hard men and easy women, adventurers, race-track touts, quacks and cranks of every delicate shape and hue. Confidence men exploited many who came to retire; embezzlers fleeced many who came to invest; 'healers' fed on those who had come to recover; evangelists consoling those who had been betrayed. Yogi mystics and swami palm readers, occult fakirs and bold-faced fakirs took hasty root in the City of Angels, and they flourished."[12] Likewise, Powdermaker's pseudonyms for her subjects, such as "Miss Purposeful," "Mr. Qualified," and "Miss Manifest Destiny," identify workers by their roles in the city's culture and political economy. Through the details of daily degradations in the studio and of exclusive nightly soirees, both authors give a human face to the stratification in the cultural geography, including numerous anecdotes of racism and sexism that counter Parker Tyler's claim in 1950 that the "universal church" of Hollywood required individual workers to shed their cultural differences.[13] People may have shed their identities on the screen, but Rosten and Powdermaker revealed that, off-screen, workers' identities could justify unequal treatment and different forms of exploitation. The ironic portrayal of working communities as devoid of group consciousness in a "town of individualists" paralleled other social science accounts of the time, emphasizing the antagonisms in a labor market oriented toward the success of the few while homogenizing or stifling the creativities of the masses.[14] The workers in Powdermaker's and Rosten's research portray the dysfunctionality of a production-based economy that individuated stars while creating a mass of faceless laborers.

Rosten and Powdermaker seemed poised to support the cause of collective labor, though they ultimately endorsed a liberal compromise based on a meritocracy that would privilege the definition of a producer as a creative artist over a mass worker. Their studies, published in 1940 and 1950, respectively, bookended the heights of film labor union struggles with the studios, which had generated their own narratives about production workers as stars. Powdermaker and Rosten countered the idolization of studio-produced celebrities that were common in fan magazines and so-called insider guides to the film industry. Reflecting contemporary fears of the power of propaganda and, then, of the deleterious effects of mass culture,[15] Rosten and Powdermaker offered critical insights into the ways real people's lives were shaped by the industrialization of artistic production. At the same time, their critiques of the industrialization of culture did not extend to a support of unionized workers, particularly those below the line. Focusing on the individuals located from the middle to the top of budget payrolls, these scholars offered no insight into the lives of other individuals engaged in skilled labor or the trades during the era in which

President Franklin D. Roosevelt launched the New Deal's National Recovery Administration (NRA) to safeguard workers' wages. As Danae Clark has noted, scholars that focus solely on stars reify studio power by making it seem that laborers "were readily complicit with their employers' desires."[16] In fact, although writers' and actors' guilds initially supported the NRA, the organization gave the studios carte blanche to keep labor in check in exchange for free government propaganda films.[17] Presumably critiquing this cozy relationship between guilds, studios, and government, Rosten laments that Hollywood films generate the passive acceptance of elite power, creating a society "more respectful of [the NRA leader] Hugh Johnson than John Dewey."[18] The comparison of Johnson and Dewey is revealing. Dewey, a champion of liberal pragmatism, fostered Rosten's ideal Hollywood, one in which the best workers' talents could flourish in opposition to the populist appeals of New Dealers and unions.[19] Powdermaker similarly traces the cause of contemporary social ills back to the producers themselves who disrespect hard work, teamwork, and rational thought.[20] Despite their longings for creative collaboration, both authors imply that creativity must be cultivated and managed in a meritocratic system in which individual talent and skills, like their own as researchers, will simply rise to the top.

The study of media production through its human subjects and their real-life experiences helped bound the definition of the television producer as creative and professional. Whether emerging from organizational sociology, developmental communication, or film and media studies, the collective literature on television production that followed in the Anglo-dominant world was paradoxical in that studies rendered the producer's presence through two competing tropes of identity. In one sense, producers were extraordinary individuals, possessing creative capabilities countering the forces that turned other workers into a faceless mass. In another sense, however, producers were ordinary members of the professional class. Lacking a gender, race, or other cultural features, the professional producer worked in a closed system defined by shared class objectives. Today, the paradox continues through the oxymoron of the *creative professional*, a term that condenses a focus on particular, marked individuals as producers in an unmarked social class. From the identification of auteurs and their relative power over contents or technologies, to the exploration of producers' relative powerlessness in the negotiated realms of capital investments and distribution, policymaking and regulation, studies of television's production ultimately excluded the labors that circumscribed these limited realms for the exercise of power.

The Television Professional and the Producer's Others

By the time television "arrived and conquered" the technological means for mass communication (in the quasi-colonialist language of Paul Hirsch), the conception of the producer as a particular kind of individual in a few select segments of the labor market was unequivocal.[21] Continuing earlier inquiries into the abilities of above-the-line personnel to create art in an industrial setting, scholars of television production conflated laborers' creative abilities with their value to media industries, thus excluding workers not valued for their intellectual inputs into production processes. Studies of television also sidestepped the focus on the antagonism between laborers and their managers that framed this early work on film production. Instead, research into television production delved further into the relationships between different white-collar workers who represented clear economic and political objectives in the market or the state. By focusing on the negotiations, collaborations, and conflicts between these specific workers recognized for their labors, studies of television production framed producers' practices in terms of structural forces that constrained their presumed creativity. The notion of the "television professional" condensed these assumptions about the producer for export precisely as the medium became a tool of foreign development policy and domestic social engineering.

Throughout the 1960s and 1970s, studies of television production conceptualized the industry as a system that included working subjects, their networks, their resources, and their rewards in a relatively coherent and stable organization. The opulence of Tinseltown and the drudgery in the "dream factory" depicted in early field studies of Hollywood now gave way to functionalist approaches that integrated culture, politics, and the economy in explanations of the television production process.[22] These studies resulted in labyrinthine diagrams and convoluted flowcharts (see figure 1), such as Philip Elliot and David Chaney's "A Sociological Framework for the Study of Television" in 1969, which proposed that television

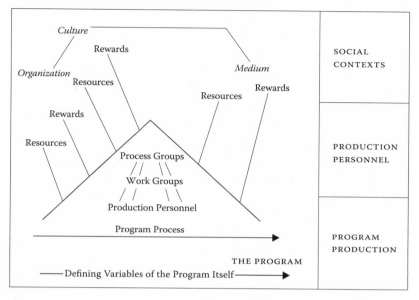

1. The social science approach to studying television production in the 1960s and 1970s often produced more confusion than clarity.

followed from flows of inputs and outputs in a predictable organizational structure.[23]

Groups of above-the-line workers, here named "production personnel," in the base of a pyramid take economic, cultural, and technological resources to gain rewards that perpetuate the production of television genres and their defining variables. This veritable nightmare of heuristic modeling, which referenced the rising importance of behavioral psychology, systems theory, and managerial strategies in the social sciences, placed above-the-line workers at the center of a "production of culture perspective," proposed by the sociologist Richard A. Peterson in 1976 and evident throughout studies of "cultural industries," such as music labels, film and television studios, and television news networks.[24]

This totalizing circumscription of cultural production as a distinct field in which a producer class created television was coterminous with the global spread of television, in general, as a tool of development, and of U.S. media culture, in particular, as a force of modernity. That is, as television researchers looked to how these select personnel created culture to achieve the ideals of television as a system, whether as a public service or a commercial industry, U.S. modernization theorists and Western media industries posited the medium and its professional production as core features of advanced industrial societies. Daniel Lerner, Wilbur Schramm, and Everett Rogers, among others, traced the development of television in mass communication systems as hallmarks of cultural progress in societies that fell within the U.S. sphere of influence during the cold war.[25] Meanwhile, U.S., French, and British media industries moved to establish influence in those markets through the export of managerial assistance in television production, as well as in the related fields of broadcasting and journalism.[26] Although perhaps not in direct correspondence with the studies of television as a system, these activities globally promoted a constellation of meanings around the medium that associated television producers generally with national development projects and the Hollywood producer class in particular as exemplary workers in the most developed television system to which the rest of the world could aspire. Quoting Rogers's work, Armand and Michèle Mattelart have critiqued the implied paradigm: "Development-as-modernization was a 'type of social change in which new ideas are introduced into a social system in order to produce higher per capita incomes and levels of living through more modern production methods and improved social organization.' This implied strategies for research and action, typologies of target populations and the stages through which they had to pass."[27] In other words, television producers in this model did not just aim to produce content but also strove to produce a new citizenry that would exemplify Western modernity.

Indeed, while the international communications intelligentsia evaluated the world's populations according to scales of cultural development, students of television production took a culture-neutral approach to how producers function in the overall organization of television as a system. No longer interested in the eccentrics who broke the social rules emulated in the cultural texts they helped create, academics focused more narrowly on how "occupational identity (defined as a combination of two factors, specialized training and aspirations) determines role performance (the attitudes, beliefs, and at times actual behaviors)," in the words of Muriel Cantor.[28] "Personality plays its part," wrote Manuel Alvarado and Edward Buscombe in a study of the making of a popular British drama from the 1970s; "but our emphasis in looking at the production process has been on the constants rather than the variables—always bearing in mind that the variables are present."[29] These constants—such as chains of command, the resources available to producers, the legal bases for censorship, and the rewards accorded to those deemed success-ful—promised to reveal how these producers, with their shared occupa-tional identity, could be expected to act within a system of economic and legal constraints. To "those who would insist on the role of chance," Alvarado and Buscombe explained, "we would say this is only a name for what is not yet understood."[30]

By focusing on the middle range of occupational norms and on role per-formance as indicators of how television works, media scholars generated an observable realm of empirical data through which the producer class channeled its power as creators. Legal or economic obstacles—to the extent that they constrained the most valuable element of the producer's labor, his or her creativity—could be negotiated through workplace rou-tines, content formulas, and collaboration with other professionals in distinct cultural, economic, or legal spheres of action.[31] Scholars, in other words, confined themselves to questions embedded in the industry's own relatively stable division of labor from the 1960s to the 1980s.[32] The role of the sponsor, once central to the creation of television programs in the United States, disappeared in contemporary studies of the production process, replaced with new forms of advertising and marketing. Similarly, the regulator, once central to the formulation of broadcasting standards across various countries, now operated peripherally to the production process. From the literature the "television professional" emerged as an individual who, as an ideal worker, assumed the economic considerations of sponsorship and the legal standards of regulation in his or her role.[33] The professional as an ideal normalized what Dan Schiller calls a "re-stricted view of human agency," one concerned purely with the intellec-tual means that a white-collar workforce exerted toward instrumental ends, and it neutralized a labor-based critique.[34] During the past three decades the phrase "creativity within constraints" repeatedly expressed a view of television producers as distinct, first, from other workers repre-senting the industry, state, or public; and, second, from all other workers excluded from professional class privileges.[35]

Within this restricted sphere of inquiry, the television professional formed part of a class-based community that stressed collaboration over independence, compromise over conflict. "Whether the subject is news or entertainment, the product is the result of a regularized, collaborative effort," summarized Joseph Turow, referencing the literature on creators in mass media organizations.[36] While labor in other economic sectors clashed with management over declining benefits and diminished futures, and while capital moved in search of more receptive workforces and less stringent legal conditions, conflict in the world of television producers remained comparatively benign. Cantor paints a halcyon picture of the cultural world of the sixty Hollywood television producers in her study of 1971: "These people did not fit the stereotype that I and possibly others had of 'Hollywood.' . . . None lived in the high style usually associated with Hollywood; instead they were raising children in the suburbs of Los Angeles with values little different from their professional and business neighbors. . . . Their parties resembled others in the hills of Los Angeles. When the sexes were separated women talked about children and clothes and men about business and politics. When the sexes were mixed, there was little flirtation."[37] Joined by educational background, shared values, and sex roles, television professionals espoused a normative culture that Cantor, as an academic, identifies with. This community extended to others in the geographically concentrated centers of white-collar power and media capital, while excluding a host of Others beyond.

As scholars normalized television producers as members of an unmarked, professional community, public concerns about the racial and gender exclusivity of labor markets in broadcast television, specifically, and in media industries, more generally, increased throughout the period. In the United States, social groups had long targeted media representations as indicative of social inequalities in the body politic.[38] Yet during the 1960s and 1970s, the conjuncture of social movement demands with integrationist institutional reforms explicitly tied television representations to the composition of film and broadcast production crews and the dearth of diversity in above-the-line guilds. In the wake of the Civil Rights Act of 1964, coalitions of civil rights groups and media reform activists set their sights on social and economic reforms within the liberal framework now guaranteed by the establishment of the Equal Employment Opportunity Commission (EEOC).[39] Meanwhile, the state channeled these long-standing public concerns about derogatory, limited, or discriminatory media representations through a variety of institutional mechanisms, including educational and job training programs, broadcast license renewal procedures, and the establishment of public and public-access television stations.[40] The *Kerner Commission Report* of 1968, which concluded that media representations helped fuel national racial unrest, linked "problematic discourse (stereotypes) not to mass communication per se but to employment within its related industries."[41] An explosion of publicly and privately financed quantitative studies of television contents, employment practices, ownership patterns, and cultivated audience effects buttressed social movement claims that distortions on the screen should be remediated through production practices and broadcast regulation.[42] Judicial rulings allowed "citizen and public interest groups—including African American, Chicanos, gays and lesbians, environmentalists, conservatives, and feminists—" to use unequal employment practices as evidence in broadcast licensing hearings, spurring hundreds of petition-to-deny requests on this basis.[43] Affirmative action standards became matters of federal policy, and, in 1970 the two major organizations representing both above-the-line and below-the-line workers signed agreements with the EEOC to increase the numbers of minorities and women in their ranks.[44] Federal Communications Commission policy supported minority and female broadcast license owners in 1978. Federally funded job training programs and new education programs, supported by state and nonprofit investments, sponsored the first cohorts of nonwhite students in film schools and "are often credited with giving rise to independent film movements based on racial identity groups."[45] Their graduates worked on social issue documentaries and news programs on public television that differed significantly from mainstream programming. New professional organizations, such as Women Make Movies, Women in Film, the National Latino Media Coalition, and the National Asian American Telecommunications Association, dispelled the presumption that the professional television producer class was not already marked by its whiteness and its masculinity.

Henceforth issues of identity in studies of television production seemed tied to the labor that could be held responsible for representations of race or gender on television. Questions of creativity reemerged in the study of the professional class. In a study of television casters' considerations, Turow explained in 1978, "Writers concerned about stereotyped portrayals have speculated that the images are due to personal conscious or unconscious decisions made by those engaged in the creation of characters."[46] While some studies of television production continued to paint producers as average members of a professional organization or a class-based community, others pointed to exceptional individual producers who wielded creative decision-making power.

Studies of directors, writers, and talent agents promised to look behind the scenes into the "decision-making process governing prime-time network television" production, as Todd Gitlin explained in 1983 in his interview-based *Inside Prime Time*.[47] Organizational analyses now intersected ideological studies with the aim of making distinctions between those who simply reproduced ideological messages and those who transformed them: "The individuals we focus on . . . go beyond the basic 'creativity of competence.' . . . They also establish the creative vision of the projects they control. The term vision exceeds 'content,' or 'ideas,' exceeds the notion of a 'message.' The vision encompasses all these things and recognizes the best ways to express them *as television*."[48]

Suddenly Jewish ethnicity or middle-class Midwestern roots, to cite two of Gitlin's examples, could account for why some producers excelled at making television more distinctive or even an art form. Accountable as the creators of representations, Gitlin's producers were the embodiment of the represented: "Network executives are skilled in negotiating the heights of corporate bureaucracy. Their own hard-won skill testifies to the possibility of personal triumph. Their own lives are 'upbeat.' If this sounds like a television movie, there is good reason for it. Men and women of this character gravitate toward the upbeat formula, partially because they believe it's what the mass audience desires, but also because their own experience enshrines it."[49] If the lives of the executives mimicked a movie plot line, then Gitlin's portrayal of individual directors more resembled the white, heteronormative, masculine characters in TV scripts. Two of his subjects, Steven Bochco and Michael Kozoll of *Hill Street Blues* fame, were analogues of the protagonist in the series, the police captain Frank Furillo. All three were driven, edgy, and savvy managers in rough-and-tumble work worlds.[50] Egocentric, ambitious, and instrumental, the producers' managerial attitudes obtained gender, sexual, racial, and class identities through their doppelgänger characters. Alongside a theory of ideological overdetermination, Gitlin's study inferred homologies between above-the-line producers' identities, network television contents, and mainstream audience dispositions.

The collapsing boundaries between producers' identities as workers, the representations they created, and the audiences they served has added significance in the context of the deregulation and liberalization of television markets globally. As international conglomerates such as Disney, General Electric, News Corporation, and Sony entered deregulated U.S. production markets in the 1980s and dominated liberalized television markets throughout the rest of the world in the 1990s,[51] television scholars focused on their internal star systems and on their ability to control creation. Following in the footsteps of the Directors Guild Association (DGA), which secured authorial credit rights for individual filmmakers in the 1960s,[52] U.S. television scholarship in particular developed its own variety of auteurism to evaluate the workers whose names are part of production studios' top billings and marketing campaigns. The "self-conscious creative producer," in the words of Horace Newcomb and Robert Alley, is the *one* who gains "recognition of his peers, the confidence of network officials, and the bedrock on which these measures are grounded—the response of the mass audience."[53] This definition, penned as cable industries fragmented the mass audience, seemed to privilege an auteur as a network-contracted, guild-member professional. Beyond the United States, the Australian screen editor Sylvia Lawson explains that questions of authorship there would hinge on who resisted Hollywood's dominance of the world television and film market.[54] No longer preoccupied with Rosten's and Powdermaker's concerns that capital would crush artistic aspirations, television scholarship has focused narrowly on the subjective perspectives of those who have already been assigned the legal rights over creative production.

Today, the consolidation of a television producer as a creative professional continues to operate in scholarly treatments through a series of equivalences that slip between the bodies of particular humans, the symbolic meanings of the representations that result from their occupational labor, and their class standing in a global economy. Numerous humanistic treatments of television continue to reaffirm the distinctions between those who have authorial status and those without it.[55] The use of trade magazines and interviews with above-the-line stars—for example, directors, writers, and show-runners—has become commonplace to show how these unique individuals negotiate industrial structures to create hit programs, popular genres, and television as a "producer's medium."[56] Their spotlight on particular workers as "special and mysterious," as well as on the latter's struggles to assert their individuality in the medium, often replicates the industry's own modes of reflexivity as publicity while reinforcing the boundaries around this class of professionals as the only ones who create television.[57] In the social sciences, research on television producers often places them among the ranks of other semiautonomous workers in education, the arts, tourism, and design in what Richard Florida has named the "creative class."[58] Unified only by the industries that employ them, producers have been further distinguished by academics based on either a presumably exclusive set of professional skills—such as the ability to manipulate symbols for "symbolic, expressive, or informational production"—or the embodied values, identities, or lifestyles of employed professionals, which then generate creativity.[59] While neither of these distinctions can be determined empirically, the notion of producers as unique, individual creatives who populate an industrially defined professional class continues to permeate scholarly discourse, guiding research questions that evaluate how creative these individuals are or how professional they are as a group.

Meanwhile, some scholars have also begun to interrogate the mechanisms of capital and politics that supplement the exclusive definitions of the producer as a creative professional. Even as studies of media production exempt populations, geographies, technologies, and institutional formations not directly related to the professional hierarchies involved in content creation, critiques of digital capitalism show, paradoxically, the accumulative tendencies of television industries to dominate more technologies with television and to incorporate more people in the production process. The spread of corporate webs and capital investments that capture workers in a global "knowledge economy" commodify increasingly more forms of communication, from information exchange to mediated subjectivities.[60] Policymakers have packaged these communicative commodities as autonomous sources of creative production, when they actually rely on a host of urban development regulations, as well as on transnational agreements for liberalized trade and intellectual property rights.[61] Current scholarly discourses about the creative class can be traced to the labors of political and economic elites in the 1960s who wanted to shift the focus away from the federal support of cultural production toward the self-sufficient generation of culture as capital. Some of this critical work about work laments the lost status of television producers in this new economy, reaffirming producers' ideal roles as creative professionals without deconstructing them.[62] Yet this literature also provides an opening to reconsider the crucial roles sponsorship and regulation play in television production processes, supporting definitions of creativity and professionals in the knowledge economy. Regulators and sponsors should thus be added to a consideration of how producers are defined and should be subject to the same theoretical frames that guide the rest of the present book.

From the Producer to Producers
IDENTITY WORK IN AND THROUGH INVISIBLE LABOR

By broadening the scope for considering workers as producers of television, I aim to evaluate how media work implicitly constructs identities in and through labor. That is, labor—the structural arrangements that extract value from work—contributes to specific social formations that have historically been the basis for establishing differences between populations. The relationship between labor and identity in this book can be summarized through two premises. First, identities create surplus value for television industries. Second, this invisible work encourages subjects to identify themselves and others as members of cultural groups defined by gender, race, class, and nationality. The dialectic between labor structures and identity work captures the dynamic process by which political economies frame subjectivities, producing capital for industries and contradictions for workers identifying with profitable identities. In the chapters that follow, the workers involved in the creative and professional production, sponsorship, and regulation of television invite the reevaluation of these terms by revealing the contradictory ways in which their work promotes identities and encourages identifications as part of television's labor economies. For the deconstruction project, as Mary Poovey aptly explains, "is to problematize the very idea of opposition and the notion of identity upon which it depends."[63]

The relationship drawn here between labor and identity in constructing television producers follows precedents in critical studies of labor that demonstrate the centrality of identity to the constitution of invisible labor in the modern industrial period. In this literature, invisible labor, or nonwaged forms of work, is a precondition of industrial waged labor, giving wage workers labor power by evacuating the value of work outside an employer-employee relationship. Feminist scholars have long cited child care, domestic chores, volunteerism, and prostitution as female-identified work that supports industrial labor relations, both by ensuring the entry of new wage workers into the labor force and by sustaining the artificial relations between employers and employees that form the basis for labor power.[64] In each of these cases, affirms Leopoldina Fortunati, women have been central to the reproduction of use value and exchange value, but this work "appears otherwise," as a natural form of production or a personal service.[65] Similarly, racial and ethnic Others have frequently been denied labor power through their exclusion from the labor-wage relation in industrial societies. Ethnic immigrants and racial migrants were the primary sources of so-called home work, the process by which factories subcontracted piecework in the nineteenth century. Located in their homes, these nonwhite workers remained invisible both to waged workers and on employers' formal payrolls, denying home workers the labor power to demand legal rights or societal respect.[66] Immanuel Wallerstein has coined the term *ethnicization*—the identification of cultural differences between workers—to mark the primary means for maximizing capital accumulation, while minimizing the costs of labor power and the potential for political challenges from outsiders.[67]

Meanwhile, the variety of cultural differences that seem relevant to maximizing capital accumulation through production have multiplied, highlighting new identities in the unwaged surplus value calculus of formal labor markets. Observers of the postwar changes in Italian factories wrought by shifts to export-oriented markets sustained by low wages and high employment amid union fragmentation noted the subsumption of immaterial forms of labor into working-class realities. Writing from within a nascent autonomist-Marxist tradition, Mario Tronti asserted in 1971, "The whole of society becomes an *articulation* of production," meaning that social relations beyond the workplace now followed in the footsteps of factory organization.[68] Subjectivities once associated with leisure and consumption now followed production logics as sites of employer control. Discipline, however, is self-imposed, regulated by the competition for fewer job opportunities of shorter contracts. Maurizio Lazzarato cites affective skills, communicative capacities, entrepreneurialism and volunteerism, and temporal and spatial flexibility as invisible sources of unwaged surplus in this new economic landscape based on precarity. These knowledge and culture inputs drive down the cost of labor power since they precede and extend beyond simple execution processes that form the basis of exchange, even though they contribute value to goods and services globally.[69] Thus as capitalism profits from the invisible labors of identifiable Others whose work can be deemed "natural" or unskilled, it simultaneously profits from invisible inputs into formal production markets generalized across the many labor sectors organized by precarity. In other words, just as capitalism seems to demand stable identity categories to exclude from production markets, it exerts instability by blurring identities associated with a variety of social spheres outside work places or temporalities. There are at least three theoretical considerations following this conjuncture of invisible labors and their constructions of identity.

First, changes in political economy, with its contradictory tendencies toward the ethnicization and universalization of labor subjectivities, signify new relationships between the material and symbolic dimensions of labor, thus opening new possibilities for identities. The mobility of capital and goods, the flows of information and texts, and the migrations of populations in and out of waged work across geographies are hallmarks of the global knowledge economy. New technologies, developed to speed the globalization of communication and transportation, have transformed "how infrastructural 'networks' of different types enable (or inhibit) different modes of activity for different sectors of the population," as David Morley writes.[70] These changes have also altered the composition of labor forces, whose work is now subject to alternative identifications. Men shut out of constrained labor markets have entered sectors previously limited to female workers, such as electronics assembly, secretarial work, and even domestic work. Their increased numbers contest the feminization of work practices once associated with essentialized notions of docility, intuition, or nurturance.[71] Management's discursive appropriation of languages associated with private spheres—such as fandom, leisure consumption, alternative lifestyles, and familial relations—has blurred the values associated with youth, queer sexualities, white bohemians, and mothering, identities all formerly outside formal labor markets.[72] As such, managerial discourse has recalibrated the hierarchies of value assigned to expressions of connection and autonomy, responsibility and freedom, and emotion and affect. David Hesmondhalgh and Sarah Baker emphasize this point by stressing that affective labor may be a feature of many job descriptions but that different job roles stress different emotional competencies.[73] The feelings affected by the factory worker, male or female, register differently from those of the television studio staffer because they have different values in production and supply chains. Conversely, corporate men may engage in exercise rituals designed to show off a controlled and fit body at work, but the range and considerations of body images do not necessarily equal those of women in similar positions.[74] The implication is that political economic changes put the identification regimes associated with labor in flux, but it is not a free-for-all.

Related to this consideration, the emergent subjectivities that capitalism now demands from its laborers continue to draw on the residual identities that have corresponded to invisible labor in the past. Secretaries may now be male, but feminized forms of emotional work and peripheral activities, for example, picking up laundry or choosing gifts, still organize the routines and define the submissive status of the position.[75] Asian Americans may have left the service sectors associated with "servile coolies" in the nineteenth century, yet they continue to be racialized and feminized as more passive or docile than Anglo American workers in information and technology sectors.[76] Above and below the line, gendered and racialized expectations on workers in television and film studio production persist. Miranda Banks's investigations into costume design and stunt work reveal that cutting fabric and falling from a building remain heavily imbued with classed notions of femininity and masculinity, respectively.[77] For network television producers, diversity and inclusion in production connotes the introduction of a racialized body to above-the-line work groups, even though the team as a whole must preserve the normative status of whiteness as the most desirable audience.[78] Despite the seeming opportunities for parity in workplaces today, the continuity of feminized and racialized labors as categories for defining production practices remains a mechanism for presuming and justifying the exploitation of workers' surplus in those roles according to a logic of difference. Understanding the ways in which work retains its symbolic associations with cultural identities establishes the terrain on which workers struggle to define themselves in accordance with or in resistance to this logic.

The role of workers' agency, then, is a third theoretical consideration in evaluating the potency of political economic structures in defining the invisible surplus value of identities in assessing labor power. By examining the invisible labors that modern economies depend on to generate capital, for example, Enda Brophy and Greig de Peuter remind scholars to see how "heterogeneous sectors of labor are *articulated*, albeit implicated in dramatically different manners, along lines of class, gender, 'race', as well as sector and place."[79] This directive implies an interrogation of the role of agency, for, importantly, articulations are communicative acts. They involve people who claim identities and identify others, while others identify them themselves. Articulations are subject to the structures of political economy, but they are not determined by them. These negotiations are apparent in Laura María Augustín's fieldwork with migrant sex workers, who accept, negotiate, and resist the passive and victimized identity categories assigned them by social workers and other well-meaning members of governmental communities, including feminist lobbies. Given limited labor options, migrants "may prefer to sell sex to their other options," but in doing so, they "are treated as passive subjects rather than as normal people looking for conventional opportunities, conditions and pleasures."[80] The dynamics of invisible labor reveal the opportunities and limits that workers have for identity claims at places and times in which others are identifying them, and in the context of political economic regimes that degrade the work and marginalize the worker.

The articulation of identities in and through processes of identification has been central to cultural studies of media consumers, and of television audiences in particular. These studies, conducted since the early 1980s, have treated viewers as producers for the ways they create meanings, appropriate technologies, and form interpretative communities in numerous settings and field sites.[81] They have motivated researchers to explore how producers, in the words of the anthropologist Mark Allen Peterson, "are never only engaged in the production of media texts; they are also always engaged in producing themselves as social persons in relation to others."[82] These researchers—including Barry Dornfeld, Laura Grindstaff, John Caldwell, and a host of others involved in cultural studies of production—have treated production practices as "self-defining activities" that simultaneously construct identities while reproducing various forms of economic, cultural, and symbolic capital in societies.[83] In 1998, Dornfeld's ethnography of public-television documentarists demonstrated the ways in which they constituted themselves as members of an imagined community of liberal-minded, educated professionals, reproducing their own social class and elite habitus: "Though this community aspires to some shared national participation, in the end it remains largely a community based in class and cultural exclusions."[84] Similarly, Grindstaff's participant observation of talk show production reveals a matrix of work practices, as well as dispositions invested in maintaining hierarchies of gender, race, and class.[85] The boundary-maintaining rituals of producers, outlined in Caldwell's examination of workers above and below the line throughout Hollywood film and television industries are never simply about personal prestige; they also extend a universe of production narratives that masculinize skills, techniques, and success.[86] This emerging body of work provides ample illustrations of why the producers of feminized television genres, such as soap operas or children's programs, might stress their identities as women on the job; or why the producers of transnational or diasporic television genres, such as reality programs, telenovelas, and coproduced telefilms and serials, frequently frame their work as extensions of their ethnic and national identities.[87] These identity claims, which fit seamlessly with the identity narratives already associated with television texts and genres, maintain divisions between essential notions of self and others in the texts they work on. They run the risk of simply reframing the story of creative professionals in a narrative in which all differences can be accommodated through the television industries' own meritocratic and multicultural mechanisms.

The cases in this book add to this emerging line of research while extending beyond it to address the theoretical ties that bind identity and labor for people who fall outside the television industries' creative categories or who lack access to their professional hierarchies. Their surplus labor bolsters the symbolic value of television in society, and yet these invisible acts exceed the compensations they receive in market terms. Increasingly, their work defines them, but in return, they lack authorial status, creative credit, or executive authority. This population increasingly encompasses the majority of workers as the new television economy incorporates new sectors and sources for cheap, if not free, labor to create television, sponsor its commodities, and regulate its consumers. The differences in the ways that these diverse groups of people experience work and perform identity illustrates the ways in which labor and identity are mutually constitutive and how they are organized along lines of gender, class, age, nationality, and race. These identities and their performances, fostered by and grounded in political economies past and present, expose the contours for producers' agency, even as this work remains invisible to those who benefit from it.

Case Studies of Television Producers

By looking into an expanded conceptual field for television production, this book attempts to make inroads into questions around how workers identify themselves in the new television economy. I have selected four communities of producers to illustrate the way in which their work has value both to the television industries and to the making of themselves. My use of the term *community* refers more to a social formation unified by joint activities at work, as in "communities of practice,"[88] than to an organic construction based on geography or identity alone. Identity work and goals are embedded in their labors as creators, professionals, sponsors, or regulators in the new economy, even if their job descriptions are not.

The chapters in this book divide into two parts exemplifying the tropes that television production studies have used to identify producers, both through relations of inclusion and exclusion. Part I looks at the tropes of the creative and the professional, which historically have been crucial to identifying producers as a occupational status in U.S. society, while part II looks at sponsors and regulators as tropes that frequently appear to define what the producer is not. The first two chapters deconstruct the assumed symbiosis between identity with the talent and skills that have defined television's creative professionals. By looking at creativity and professionalism as constructions that have appropriated and transformed residual identities associated with other forms of work, it becomes apparent how these constructions function to generate invisible surplus value for industries. The second two chapters then weigh the tensions involved in making identity claims and identifying others in commodity sponsorship and political regulation as two spheres that supplant creative professionals by identifying and embodying television audiences and publics. Though sponsorship and regulation frequently appear to lack human involvement in their operations, these chapters examine the agency of real people who must negotiate their roles in the reproduction of brand fetishes, the applications of liberal identity politics, and the subsumption of their labor to capital.

The communities in chapters 1 and 2 deconstruct assumptions frequently made about creatives and professionals through the work and voices of those never considered creative or professional but whose labors are essential to television production today. Chapter 1 interrogates creativity as the monopoly of the television producer and of above-the-line personnel whose original ideas form the artistic bases of programming contents. To do this, the chapter focuses the communicative acts that articulate identities as creative in what might be considered sites of the most uncreative labor, electronics factory assembly lines in the international industrial zones of Manaus, Brazil. There, workers have experienced radical changes, both in the nature of their work and in the identities that factories find compatible with a new global division of labor. What once might be characterized as the stable employment of passive young females in rote labor roles has become far more competitive, based on the sporadic needs for a flexible workforce that can boost productivity through problem solving and teamwork. No longer just docile bodies with agile hands, assemblers have had to negotiate new identities that explain their own creative acts. To survive this new environment, assemblers talked about the creative ways in which they resolve production problems to serve factory profit margins while striving for autonomy and managing collaborations. By applying creativity as a concept to these assembly-line workers in a Brazilian free trade zone, I argue that producers' monopoly on the label "creative" has more to do with the new division of labor in global economies than with any organic definition of creativity.

Similarly, chapter 2 looks at the ways in which definitions of professionalism have destabilized professional identities today. Whereas creativity has come to refer to an increasingly narrow range of agents involved in television, professionalism has become more expansive, encompassing more job descriptions with fewer material benefits. Chapter 2 explores the work worlds of soft-core videographers who, traveling between shooting locations, sell content that frequently finds its way onto television through its paid programming and infomercials. They increasingly define themselves and their work as professional in the new television economy, despite their marginal status and peripheral positions in relation to Hollywood television hierarchies. Drawing on residual masculinities associated with amateur filmmaking, technological tinkering, and playboy and swinger sensibilities of the past century, these mostly male freelance and contract workers have developed flexible definitions of professionalism that satisfy both themselves and their employers, who see these workers as part of the products. Calling television set assemblers "creatives" and soft-core videographers "professionals" thus deconstructs the identities of television producers as creative professionals through participant observations of the cultural politics and political economic conditions that reinforce old industrial hierarchies despite the changing nature of work in the new economy.

Part II further expands our notions of the television producer with an investigation of the blurring lines between producer and sponsor and producer and regulator that have shifted television labor onto two other communities who conduct identity work for television industries. The men and women in chapter 3 find suitable cast members for the spate of reality programs that now dominate television programming. Although casting personnel have long been members of the above-the-line food chain, reality casters act in broader capacities as sponsors who buy and sell access to the identities that studios desire as talent today and as audiences tomorrow. Chapter 3 thus considers the different ways in which identification contributes to the values of program brands, audiences, and laborers as three types of commodities in television program production. Although the casters are frequently invisible in the reality production process, their public routines reanimate the masculine identities of advertisers, while also performing emotional labor associated with feminine care and friendship maintenance. In their private reflections, these workers, who were most often women or gay men, spoke ambivalently about their identities, taking pride in claiming organic skills and safeguarding identity boundaries while railing against their invisible value to production processes. This chapter explains the cultural factors that both support and erase casting labor, arguing that much of the work of sponsorship and advertising in the new television economy remains invisible, thus unvalued, because it is associated with the supposedly natural skills of its workers.

Chapter 4 turns to the role of everyday citizens in the United States as regulators, a burden that has increasingly shifted onto local municipalities since the 1970s to safeguard public-access television production. In each locale, citizens volunteer to represent television viewing publics to their cable operator. This system asks volunteers to identify themselves as authorities able to speak on behalf of many absent others and thus treats the public as both an agent and an object of its communications policies. Based on my own recollections and on those of key advocates in cable television franchise negotiations, I compare the ways in which supposedly neutral regulatory procedures engage identity politics through the bodies of citizen appointees and the publics that they represent. In recent times of deregulatory flux, these politics have intersected with corporate demands for niche consumers, converging in mutual desires for a multicultural consumer citizenry. The new political economy of cable television creates both opportunities and challenges for citizen regulators, themselves members of identity communities, to articulate demands on behalf of cities stratified by race and class. In the new television economy, this free labor increasingly falls on the shoulders of middle-class experts, many of whom have mixed feelings about their participation when these spheres become biopolitical tools of local governments and cable industries.

Each of the case studies presented in this book results from various ethnographic encounters, contextualized with historical information about changes in the political economy of work and my own working through the cases and their field sites. They aim to examine the ways in which workers identify themselves and understand their practices. What I draw from the cases is that sample sizes, field site boundaries, and length of time in the field are less important than a sustained attention to the ways in which people speak about themselves in the contexts of power relations and what they do in the contexts of material conditions. This research is "ethnographically-inspired," to borrow from Liz Bird, in that the cases contextualize people's social relationships with media, with their content and forms.[89] It is not engaged in "global ethnography" or in the attempt to use grounded human subjects' experiences to explain globalization, neoliberalism, or even all aspects of the new economy.[90] Although people I place in these communities may emphasize changes in the relationships between work and identity in the new economy, they do not explain the latter. While I empathize with my human subjects in these chapters, my voice is ultimately the loudest in accounting for how their voices reference political economic structures, labor histories, and cultural subjectivities. My research goals and methodological approaches produce some unavoidable tensions that arise with the ethnographer's recognition that "she is positioned between two partly incommensurable discourses—the analyst's world as academic and cultural subject, and the understandings, arguments and working presuppositions of the subjects of study—between which no resolution or synthesis is possible," as the anthropologist Mark Hobart has pointed out.[91] The conclusion to this book further reflects on these methodological considerations to formulate agendas for production studies in the new television economy.

The conclusion will also return to the political questions introduced here about the need to highlight invisible labor in the production of television more broadly. The task of deconstructing the producer of television scholarship is more than a simple game of including excluded peoples, their identities, and their labors in the study of production. It is also not based on a desire to erase the term from its common usages or to begin a new producer nomenclature that includes everyone, hence flattening the differences. The exclusion of workers and their subjectivities in the study of what is called labor gets to a philosophical issue around who are legitimate members of the polity and what kinds of recognition they deserve. The absent presence of invisible workers throughout many Western philosophical traditions has been justified through exclusions of work outside the market and property relations, hence beyond state control or remedy.[92] As a result, those with the least power as workers have remained invisible to the state, ostracized from formal rights accorded to legal laborers. For those whose work also includes striving to conform to the normative identities of the worker, labor is doubly invisible; the worker performs activities that are feminized and racialized, for example, but then lacks the formal recognition needed to collectively organize or claim welfare rights.[93] If television indeed involves everyone in its production in some way, then scholars need to ask what the relationship between work and justice is. How can invisible work be recognized and made visible as a formal part of the labor market? What roles might the state play in fostering the visibility of identity work? How can workers identified by their social position in these hierarchies engage in any universalist ethos of justice? Although a full examination of answers to these questions is beyond the scope of this particular book, I hope my intervention at least raises the questions.

PART I

1. Producers as Creatives

CREATIVITY IN TELEVISION SET PRODUCTION

If the study of production as a characteristic of human action has been relatively absent in the study of television production specifically, then the notion of creation and creativity as social manifestations of human action has been similarly unacknowledged by television scholars. The hewing of creativity from a universal social characteristic to a specialized individual trait has a long history. From its Latin root *creare*, meaning simply "to produce," creativity turned into the monopoly, first, of artists who could channel the divine through their metaphysical expressions and, then, of all individuals who could express their inner talents.[1] In the sphere of television production, creativity frequently conflates with the legal authorial rights that certain individuals hold as creators of television programs and series.[2] In the annals of U.S. television history, Norman Lear, Stephen Boccho, Aaron Spelling, and, more recently, David E. Kelley, Joss Whedon, and Mark Burnett are examples of those workers who take credit as content creators. Together with their above-the-line personnel, they form the so-called creative class in the new television economy.[3] To reconstitute the invisible labor of production and the identity work implicated in this limited yet highly visible hierarchy, this chapter both deconstructs the popular associations of creation and creativity and reconstructs the social foundations of these terms by looking at electronics assemblers, a community of practice that has been excluded from scholarly consideration.

A social theory of creation, according to the philosopher Hans Joas, dates to the 1800s, but it has been all but lost in the common associations today between individual genius and creative action.[4] Proposed by Joseph Herder and Karl Marx but developed by American pragmatists in the early twentieth century, social theories of creativity examine how people coordinate their actions using a common language and tools already imbued with social meanings. This dual focus on shared language and tool use connects the creator to a system of symbols and material resources that both contains individual actions and marks them as different, hence as creative. By insisting that creative action has a social context, Joas distinguishes creative actions sanctioned as creative by society from those actions that are not. These conceptions of creation and creativity thus conjoin the interiority of mental labor with the exteriority of a world that enables its articulation. This unison contrasts the presumed division between internal creativity and external constraints in the construction of the paradigmatic producer of film and television studies.

Scholars have long recognized that television program creation is distributed among workers in a large industrial bureaucracy, but they have also maintained creativity as the special reserve of the individually talented producer. As summarized by Michele Hilmes, "Industry study is the translation of authorship into a dispersed site marked by multiple, intersecting agendas and interests, where individual authorship in the traditional sense still most certainly takes place, but within a framework that robs it, to a greater or lesser degree, of its putative autonomy."[5] In its formulation, individual creativity in television production requires but also opposes the social constraints that are effective, practical, conventional, and, hence, uncreative by definition. While some scholars have focused on the limited autonomy that all above-the-line workers hold in a labyrinth of temporal, financial, and stylistic constraints, others have identified a special fraternity of auteur producers who have risen above these constraints to stamp their unique marks on television content.[6] Even those jaded by the industry seem to hail the lone creator who achieves self-expression despite "cronyism, mutual backscratching, behind-the-scenes favors, revolving doors, musical chairs, careers made by falling upward [and] the 'amazing largesse' given to favored members of the 'creative community.'"[7] Indeed, Hortense Powdermaker's early look into Hollywood production summed up the situation neatly by indicating that the industry destroys the creative inspirations of artists, who become mere assembly-line workers.[8]

The limited articulation of creativity within the narrow confines of the creative class has the television producer and (nearly always) his trade oscillating between acting as an artist and acting as an assembly-line worker. Of these two poles, the assembly-line worker is the invisible laborer, the one whose absence of creativity unpins the artist's autonomy. While we may envision the creative producer as a particular type of unique individual, mental images of the assembly line cue up either an anonymous mass or, in the New International Division of Labor (NIDL), images of largely third world young women, docilely moving their agile fingers to the punch clocks of transnational commerce. Uninspired, they threaten the individualism and the creative spirit that above-the-line workers supposedly monopolize. Without them, though, there would be no television creator or a creative community, as the television set is among assembly-line workers' creations. It is this community of electronics line workers and their feminized labors that I turn to in order to deconstruct our received notions of creativity and to reconstruct a notion of creative action that is both social and individual in the practices of assembling.

Based on Joas's exploration of a social theory of creative action, this chapter explores the creative capacities of television set factory laborers in the international industrial zone of Manaus, Brazil. Located at the center of the Brazilian Amazon, Manaus and its inhabitants have had unique symbolic roles to play in national politics and global economies. There, line assemblers are the first laborers to contribute surplus value to television through their underpaid and grueling physical work and their unpaid and unrecognized immaterial work. The former has been the subject of a growing literature on the effects of global commerce and trade liberalization. The latter has appeared in recent ethnographies of factory work, mostly located on the U.S.-Mexican border. In the new television economy, both are equally necessary; the political economy of labor exploitation and the cultural performance of a compliant, feminized workforce reinforce the low status of the assembly-line workers in relation to those content creators who likely never consider them part of the television production process. The segregation of those who are supposedly creative and those supposedly noncreative in the production chain is emblematic of a global strategy for amassing capital by dividing workers and making them compete ultimately in a race to the bottom.

I met television set assemblers in Manaus over the course of five months on two separate visits, first in 2004 and again in 2005. If Hollywood seems geographically remote from Manaus, the social and cultural distances between myself, an Anglo-American media professor, and my subjects, Amazonian electronics assemblers, was probably greater. Initial entry into electronics factories, research facilities, and union headquarters resulted in interviews with executives, scientists, and political organizers, all people whose class and educational status approximated my own. I only spoke with factory workers on my second trip, when I joined two community organizations suggested to me by fellow professors at the local state university.[9] The first, a sewing collective organized through the Catholic Church, recruited unemployed factory workers to generate self-sustaining revenues through contract sewing work (*encomendas*). Thrice a week, I went to chat with the women, help out with a little piecework, and meet with the workers' siblings, children, and neighbors, many of whom worked in the electronics factories. The second group was a class of electronics workers taking a course on social communication and justice as part of a university extension course in a working-class community. There, I participated as a guest speaker and fellow student on weekends, when I could go home with students after class to meet their factory coworkers and families. The contacts I made through these two sites filled my week with twenty-five formal interviews, many more impromptu conversations, explorations of vastly different working-class neighborhoods, and frequent social events, from dinner invitations to street theater performances. Together these form the basis of my (limited) understanding of the tapestry of work practices, routines, and events in the lives of electronics assemblers. For though this fieldwork brought me closer to the realities of television set creation in Manaus, there are still unbridgeable gaps between my recordings in the field and the embodied experience of being on the line.

Life off and on the Line

Terezinha stood almost a full foot shorter than my own five feet, four inches.[10] Her petite hands, however, powerfully pushed fabric bolts through an industrial sewing machine as if they were made of air. Shifting the stitch left, then right, her hands had no visible scars from the years she spent assembling television sets and other electronics for Evadin, a Brazilian company with exclusive technology rights for the Japanese firm Mitsubishi Electric.[11] She was fifteen when she got the job in 1981. Her declarative statements about that time frequently ended with a rhetorical question. "I only did components. Capacitors, resistors, transistors, integrated circuits, you know?" She continued to work in electronics assembly on and off for twelve years, leaving only to raise her family in accordance with her evangelical values. At thirty-nine years of age in 2005, she still remembered the period fondly: "I did everything that goes into the TV and gives it life."

Terezinha was a representative of what could be considered the first generation of television set assemblers. In the weekend classroom, the younger pupils who currently worked in the factories formed part of the second generation. Their divergent experiences and identities mapped the changing political economy of television set manufacturing and assembly in the region, reflecting global trends in the liberalization of trade, the regionalization of production, and the automation of factory work. These were not abstract forces for the residents of Manaus; global trends had transformed the landscape and demographics of the city, its labor economy, and the symbolic meanings of television set assembly from women's work to the jewel for a newly flexible, yet still feminized, workforce. In this section, I present these global shifts and their material effects for the city's working-class majority.

Terezinha began assembling television sets a decade after the first factories began importing electronic parts for television set assembly in the Amazon. Springer da Amazônia and Sharp do Brasil, hired 771 local residents in 1971 and 1972, respectively.[12] By 1974, electronics companies, including Semp Toshiba, CCE, Philips, and Evadin dominated nearly 20 percent of what was then called the Manaus Free Trade Zone (MFTZ).[13] Incentivized with near-total tax exemptions, low-interest loans, and cheap or free access to land, services, and labor, each of these companies complied with the military junta's effort to dominate the Amazon with people and capital. This effort also has a longer history.[14] A century earlier, Manaus had become a synecdoche for the Amazon's domination through its rubber boom. Imperial decree opened the Amazon River to international transport, and the establishment of a national shipping company preceded an international influx of capital dedicated to the extraction and exportation of latex. European and U.S. trading companies directed the boom to steer a new global market, first, for waterproof and elastic goods, and later, for car culture. Brazilian latex monopolized the international import economy from 1887 to 1907, making Manaus the center for its shipping and commerce.[15] The military junta hoped to resurrect this cosmopolitan sentiment of the belle époque in later years, one television set at a time.

Getting a job in an electronics factory in those early decades depended a bit on one's connections and a bit on what Terezinha and others called agility. The immigrants who had occupied extraction jobs during the rubber boom, first from the region, and then from drought-stricken northeastern states, became the first generation of MFTZ workers. They secured jobs early on and indicated their relatives and friends for positions. Assembly lines were segregated by gender. Men worked on the heavy equipment to build set cases and move freight boxes. Women and girls as young as fourteen assembled the small components for the insides of the sets. When Terezinha started working on the line, all the raw materials she worked with came from outside the Amazon. From her chair, she attached the pieces and then manually passed them to the next station. The process of quickly taking various pieces of a component and attaching them to each other was called the "hand game" (*jogo da mão*), referencing the labor power of the manual aspects of the job. "Thank God I was agile," Terezinha reflected on her swift promotions in the factory from one line to another and then to the quality control area. Some of the materials she worked with were toxic. Soldering wires had to be done by hand; the fumes blinded those who stayed too long at the post. The physical repetition required in assembly meant that workers had to be promoted to different stations to keep them from retiring early due to a stress injury or some other hazard. Terezinha said her supervisors let her take breaks to unwind her sore arm muscles at times, but that she was also valued as one of the fastest in her group. The workday was long, from sunrise till sunset, but she, like many workers, stayed even longer to play for company-sponsored sports teams. For her, the districts in the Industrial Pole (which all workers called the "District") became a city within the city, with infrastructure and services better than those in the surrounding worker communities.[16] These jobs attracted new waves of immigration, with up to 93 percent of rural Amazon peoples coming seasonally to Manaus after harvests.[17]

Changes in the global manufacturing economy and in national trade policies sparked dramatic effects in electronics factories and in the labor economy. Responding to international liberalization demands in the 1990s, Brazil legislated an industrialization model based on exportation enclaves to replace the import-substitution model of the previous thirty years.[18] Neither wholly neoliberal nor clearly protectionist, the administration of Fernando Collor de Mello reduced import tariffs and quotas nationally while instituting basic standards for the nationalization of production processes. In other words, television set manufacturers in Manaus no longer paid import duties on many of the raw materials brought into the country, but they also lost their privileged tax-free access to Brazilian markets. The price for television sets fell dramatically as imports entered the national market.[19] Conversely, the export market for the sets grew, particularly to Argentina and other parts of South America, but also to as far away as the United States, whose small televisions were no longer produced in Mexican facilities. At the same time, the Basic Production Program (PPB) ensured that all stages of the television set production process would be located in the city's industrial districts (figure 2), from the making of components to the set's final calibrations. This aimed to prevent a long-standing practice in Latin American free trade zones in which manufacturers simply shipped mostly finished parts to the zone for assembly to avoid import duties. Plants closed and the remaining companies conducted mass layoffs.[20] Television set factories streamlined their operations by contracting with new components companies, many of them simply old enterprises restructured.[21] They began to specialize in fewer core products, while new companies emerged to comply with the PPB. Factories outsourced internal services to a host of new companies maintaining everything from cleaning and the cafeteria to transportation and IT.[22] Human resources companies sprang up throughout the city to provide an imminently flexible workforce that management could hire during periods of high demand and fire without added responsibilities.

All the students who worked in electronics during the week understood this new reality. They worked not only for some of the remaining pioneers of the MFTZ but also for a host of new human resource firms, service providers, and a new series of Korean and Chinese companies that opened satellite factories in anticipation of further trade liberalization policies and despite higher labor costs.[23] The majority of these jobs were not unionized. Collor shut out the Metalworkers' Union, which represented the majority of electronics workers, after the union led the largest local strike in its history in 1990.[24] Involving twenty-eight factories, the strike achieved some concessions, including higher wages, better transportation and meals, and day-care facilities.[25] This meant better

2. One of the primary industrial districts for the production of electronics in Manaus, Amazonas. Photo permission granted by *A Crítica* newspaper, Manaus, Brazil.

overall working conditions than in Terezinha's day, but the lack of union power meant the elimination of its oversight on the line and the no job security for senior factory workers. The number of temporary workers grew from 17 percent of the MFTZ workforce in 1992 to 26 percent in 1995.[26] Strikes were inconceivable for this new generation as they hustled to maintain a job through the regular hiring and firing cycles that accompanied seasonal peaks and lulls in consumer demand. If they left or lost their jobs, they lost the political and social rights guaranteed them as workers in the formal economy, including their state-regulated wages, safety protections, arbitration rights, and both disability and retirement benefits. These rights, even if distributed laxly, made factory jobs overwhelmingly preferable to the alternatives in the informal economy and arguably, more important than being a national citizen.[27]

On the line, the current generation of electronics workers performed many of the same types of physical actions that Terezinha described to me, but with several modifications. First, they worked for a greater variety of companies. In 2005, fifty-four transnational companies operated in a mutually dependent organizational network (table 1). The diversification of companies resulting from the PPB meant that workers assembled

TABLE 1. Companies involved in television production
in Manaus in 2005

Television set assemblers	12
Components manufacturers (transformers, spools, tubes)	10
Circuit board manufacturers (used in digital applications)	10
Video screen manufacturers	2
Cable/satellite receiver manufacturers	9
Television remotes factories	5
Plastics injector factories	6
Total number of producers	*54*

Note: Data for the table gathered from the database of industries registered
by the Superintendent for the Free Trade Zone of Manaus
(SUFRAMA) in October 2005.

a greater variety of television products, from remote controls to satellite
dishes, in a greater number of discrete sites. Samsung, for example, operated different factories, each one specializing in some part of the set, such
as displays or chasses.[28] Second, workers were more likely to labor alongside machines, particularly in hazardous areas, such as those involving
soldering, and in digital technology assembly, which frequently had parts
too minute for human assembly. This situation contributed to the overall
lack of jobs relative to gross outputs of the companies in the industrial
pole. Finally, workers spoke of the changes in occupational culture,
evoked in part by the other two factors. The rise of automation and the
oversupply of labor in Manaus motivated men to seek more assembly
jobs and allowed factory managers to hire more selectively. The students
in the extension class were not exemplary in this regard. Divided equally
by gender, they worked in factories that now required a minimum of a
high-school education. College classes gave the workers points toward
future promotions, along with the hope of opportunities beyond the
line.

These opportunities for factory workers seemed somewhat ambiguous. Since the city's colonization, Manaus has had a reputation for being an El Dorado, a place where newcomers could find their fortune or suffer destruction. This mythical reputation, which attracted immigrant populations from Europe to the Middle East during the rubber boom,[29] now called forth populations throughout Asia and North and South America. The fortunes of these new populations segregated hierarchically by race and nationality, with lighter-skinned European and Asian populations located at the top and darker-skinned migrants from Africa and indigenous areas at the bottom. The two generations of electronics workers also reflected hierarchical stratifications. Although the city's urban infrastructure now enveloped Terezinha's neighborhood, her personal fortunes were limited after leaving the factory. Lacking a high-school diploma, she, like the other women in the sewing collective, found herself in casual feminine jobs, such as sewing piecework, doing hair or nails, domestic work, or selling baked goods on the street.[30] More recent factory workers, meanwhile, could not necessarily rely on city services. Arriving from places as far away as Peru, Venezuela, and the south of Brazil, migrants seeking jobs frequently built or rented one-room houses on burned-out swathes of forest. There, where many lacked paved roads, electricity, sanitation, schools, or health facilities, many residents still caught a 6 a.m. company bus headed to the District. The dream of an El Dorado manifested itself as a living wage and a shot at social mobility.

The disjunction between Manaus as a city of global capital and as a surrogate of massive inequalities fosters an underwhelming ambivalence toward the television set factories as institutions that both exploit and support Manaus, its formal economy, and its people. Since 1985, capital investment in the sector has risen more than 500 percent, giving the state of Amazonas the fastest growing economy in Brazil over the past twenty years.[31] On the ground, however, most people involved in television set production have experienced more stress as higher turnover, increased temporary labor, unstable real benefits, and increased job responsibilities make factory work resemble other jobs in the information economy. The formal number of employees in 2005 finally surpassed the lows of the 1990s, but real wages have not matched inflation.[32] The workers I spoke to, all of them involved in different aspects of television set production and assembly, earned between US$150–250 a month, an amount comparable to the average worker's earnings in the 1980s.[33] Conversely, factories in the Manaus Industrial Pole invoiced nearly US$19 billion in receipts in 2005, more than double the average invoiced receipts in the 1980s.[34] These numbers were not lost on the workers, who saw their energies exploited by managerial elites and their persons ignored by political elites. Factory workers faced a bind to create themselves, given the confines of a political economy with few better alternatives.

Creating Sets, Creative Producers

Ionaia made electronic components for a U.S.-based manufacturer in the District. During her shift, from 6 a.m. to 3 p.m., her line of fifteen people needed to assemble a minimum of thirty-six hundred pieces per day, or about eight pieces per person every minute, one piece every 14 seconds, allowing an hour for lunch and ten minutes each for a break, snack, and exercise. "Even the time to walk to the cafeteria, everything is timed and calculated," she said. These calculations aimed to control the synchronic movements of hundreds of people divided among dozens of lines on the factory floor. Workers on Ionaia's line knew that if they coordinated to work more quickly and exceeded five thousand pieces in fewer hours, their supervisor might let them go home early. Numbers were an incentive for workers to monitor their own time-to-quantity ratios, though material shortages, power outages, or broken machinery could mean that they would fall behind and miss their lunch and breaks. This temporal and spatial management extends to other parts of workers' lives. Ionaia said she lived by the clock. She attended college classes across town each night from 5 p.m. to 10 p.m., returned home to sleep by midnight, and awoke again at 4:30 a.m. to catch the company bus to work. Six days a week on this schedule, she spent most of Sunday sleeping or, ironically, watching television.

The assembly line as an organizational model for set production attempts to control workers to generate capital more efficiently. For Ionaia and other factory workers in Manaus, the factories' control mechanisms extend beyond the workplace, exerting pressures on their actions throughout the entire week. These conditions shape what Joas in "Fundamentals of a Theory of the Creativity of Action" calls a "situation," meaning the ability of the body to move and communicate in an innovative way. For Joas, creativity must be enacted through both the body and the social system of meanings that recognizes the action as different from the norm.[35] Ionaia's highly regulated situation did not prevent her from inventing creative fixes to the physical and emotional problems she faced on the job; rather, she struggled harder to find corporeal solutions that could be enacted given her tightly circumscribed world of social possibilities. From this point of view, television set assemblers needed to be creative to survive the pressures of their workplace. "Some people get very stressed," said Ionaia. "Just try to do my job. [But . . .] if I'm in a place that I know is going to stress me out, I have to find a *means* to talk to my boss, tell him that the post isn't good for me, or it's giving me a headache, or it's hurting my arm or finger." In her situation, creative action was the means for working within organizational models of scientific management that produced her as a working-class woman in Manaus.

Creative action unifies the mind and body in doing something perceived as different, according to Joas. This means that thought must be materialized, but also that the material is cause for later reflection. In contrast to actions that humans do rationally, creative actions encompass a wider spectrum of intentions that are pre-reflective but that the mind registers only after their completion through explanation.[36] For example, whether writing a television script or connecting a television tube, individuals can only say whether the act was creative in hindsight after comparing that individual act to a range of similar moments that provide a standard by which to judge some acts as more unique than others. Further, that determination is filtered through the discursive codes already privileging certain acts as more creative than others. Painting a canvas hence would likely be seen as more creative than painting a fence, even if both moments were comparatively different from other acts in the same day. In some ways, this is what made it difficult for workers to explain the hand games they did on the assembly line. In the factory, the corporeality of the act of assembling the television set could not communicate a creative act in itself simply because of its exclusion from the discourse of creativity. Yet even the artist can distinguish between an act of painting that, in hindsight, was more creative than other painting acts. Similarly, the television assemblers distinguish times at which they feel their hand games lead to unique, original, or even innovative results.

The first time that assemblers said they recognized that they had to coordinate their bodies in a new way was when they were hired. The skills to quickly put components onto circuit boards, wrap and solder wires to spools, and test and calibrate electrical currents and colors are all made up of discrete and unique body movements taught through trainings but that have to be individually embodied on the factory floor. Workers tried to push the automation of their bodies, attempting sometimes to even beat the pace of the machines they worked with. This cycle of creation repeated itself with each new task. A new board, component, or product line could even be fun, as evidenced by calling work the "hand game." Each assembler I spoke with talked with excitement about his or her first months in the District, when conditioning the body to do the physical work signified an important rite of passage in the social world of the factory, admitting the laborer into the city's working class and formal labor market. For women like Ionaia, the corporeal achievement of assembly tasks meant the ability to support themselves, their families, and even have some disposable income for the end of the week. The social recognition of the actions that led to this transformation is important to defining creativity because it reveals the sociality embedded in the concept.

The creative process was also fraught with anxieties. Workers remembered the pressure they felt to make their bodies conform quickly to unfamiliar routines and fit into the factory environment. Take Tânia's story of her first months at a factory specializing in motherboards for digital equipment. Now an experienced assembler, Tânia remembered that in 1996 she was afraid of working at the conveyor belt.

> The belt is rolling and I'm thinking, "I've never done this before!" So I was so nervous. But I picked it up. There was a girl there to orient me. She touched me to show me how to move our hands. Like not this way, but it's better another way. She really exerted herself to help me. People there were really good with each other, not egocentric. I learned how to do the hand games because those are really important. Sometimes you have six different capacitors on a board, and so you need the hand games to get them all in. You grab them and put them in. You have to be all over the board all the time, one hand is grabbing when another one is putting pieces in. Thank God I was good at it. I love to assemble. I would just sit down and play hand games all day. It's so fast. I have no complaints about the work.

Tânia's story reveals both her initial fears and the pride that surrounded her embodiment of assembly work. Tânia repeated this creative cycle with each new variation in her work that demanded her physical and mental coordination.

Constraints for Creative Action The constraints on assembly workers involved two contradictory forms of scientific management that reflected both the variation of organizational cultures in Manaus's factories and the shift in the industrial pole from a free trade zone to an export enclave. Taylorism, which manages workers by parsing complex jobs into tasks, increased workers' efficiency by strictly controlling time and the rigid organization of the production process. Japanization, which refers to a series of social surveillance techniques, increased workers' efficiency by putting a greater range of tasks and their critical evaluation under other workers' control. While Taylorism has been prominent in Manaus since the beginnings of the MFTZ, Japanization became more popular in the 1990s. By 2005, all electronics factories had fostered some mix of these management forms, reflecting different management cultures among the various foreign-owned companies. Taylorism and Japanization constrained creative action in seeming contradiction to each other, with the latter giving workers the latitude that the former removed. This created both stress and potential openings for workers such as Ionaia, who sought creative means to avoid boredom, tedium, or pain.

The excitement that surrounded learning how to assemble and be part of the line culture passed rapidly. Incorporated literally, the manual work became part of workers' psyches. One assembler told me that she dreamed of the hand movements, even after she hurt her hands and could no longer physically do the work. Others frequently joked that they could put together boards with their eyes closed. Like a musician whose instrument becomes an appendage of the body, the laborers incorporated the pieces of the television set as physical extensions of the self. Both socialized and internalized, the hand game was Tânia's favorite part of her job, but it was also the most likely to become tedious as simple assembly became unthinkingly ingrained in her motions: "It gets monotonous, especially with the easy boards. We'll be waiting for harder boards with more capacitors and pieces. Three pieces becomes boring, but five or six pieces that are harder to mount make it a challenge. When a new board comes in, one I've never seen before, I want to do it perfectly without a single defect. So I just focus in and concentrate on that. I don't see anything else." Following the analogy of the musician, Tânia looked forward to new challenges that forced her to move in new ways. She concentrated just on her task, ignoring all other distractions to the creative process. Unlike the musician, however, she had little time or choices in generating a solution to the task.

The scientific management of the line enforced strict temporal controls, limited outside resources, and imposed harsh discipline or dismissal if Tânia failed.

Taylorism maximized profits, not through increased output or product quality, but primarily through the production of a highly controlled workforce. As Frederick Taylor explained, "Perhaps the most prominent single element in modern scientific management is the task idea."[37] This system is not unique to Manaus. Jefferson Cowie's history of RCA shows that Taylorism has been a key technique in managing radio and television set assemblers since the 1920s, even as the company relocated from Camden, New Jersey, to Bloomington, Indiana, to Ciudad Juárez, Mexico, today.[38] The Taylorist organization of the assembly line in Manaus has changed little during the past half century, even with new technologies. Workers in Manaus receive television set kits, or clusters of components, from local, national, and international suppliers. Workers unpack, sort, and stock the components at various posts on the line. At each post, a worker attaches discrete components to a chassis before another worker affixes the component with screws, glue, or solder. Once the innards of the set are complete, workers down the line join the box of boards surrounding a large cone to the image tube or screen. From there, workers sit directly in front of the glowing screens to calibrate the image and test for color and tint.[39] At the end of the line, workers lift the apparatus into a cabinet, packaging and sealing it for stocking and then distribution. By reducing each job to a discrete set of tasks, managers regulate the output of each individual to coordinate and maximize the efficiency of all bodily movements in a confined space.

The repetition and boredom of the job over time made workers prone to injury. The somatic experience of Taylorism was one of enduring physical pains that were hard for other individuals to see and for me to imagine. Assembling a component board entailed the constant back-and-forth movement of the arms, as in climbing a ladder or filling a basket, combined with quick twists of the wrist. Pains regularly affected assemblers' hands, arms, neck, and back, leading to many cases of repetitive stress syndrome. Factories instituted ten-minute exercise periods to prevent injuries, but Ionaia said her line exercised only once every three hours. Ionaia said she never experienced physical pain, though she knew of workers who could no longer sit comfortably, stand straight, or move without some pain. Instead, she attributed her own stress on the job to the management techniques in the factory that demanded that workers control each other.

Referred to in different theoretical literatures as post-Fordism, digital capitalism, and innovation-mediation, Japanization references a cluster of new methods for scientific management in electronics factories.[40] Japanese factories first formalized these surveillance methods in Manaus through what even non-Japanese factories called *kanban* (visible record) and *kaizen* (change for better). These spread throughout factories in the pole as each moved to adopt international "quality management" standards, which certified their products for export markets.[41] *Kanban* organized surveillance through teams of assemblers on the line. Using a system of color cards, teams had more control over the pace of the line, slowing down to pursue resources to improve product quality or speeding up to win incentives for increased output quantities.[42] *Kaizen* boosted efficiency through self-initiated activities.[43] Several factories in Manaus implemented *kaizen* through the so-called five senses, tasks related to the organization, cleanliness, order, standards, and discipline of individual's posts. Multitasking was essential to *kanban* and *kaizen*; line workers did more and different things to discipline both themselves and their team to improve quality and output. Gathering before or after each shift, team leaders implemented *kanban* and *kaizen* by calling on assemblers to make suggestions to improve the production process. These methods, regardless of their proper names, aimed to make scientific management more efficient through increased surveillance and more flexible task work and analysis.

Twenty-year-old Ionaia characterized the system of multitasking and mutual surveillance as "gossip" leading to emotional stress on the job. In her U.S.-owned factory, managers chose team leaders based on workers' performances on tests. They, then, were charged with trying to explain why their line was inefficient. As former line workers, they were prone to repeating the gossip that coworkers spread about each other. Ionaia said, "There's as much gossip there as under the sun. If you come to work with a red face, or you're all made up, you don't even have to speak. Someone will say that you went out drinking, got drunk, and so on. If you have a boyfriend in the factory, which is generally prohibited, people will start saying that he is married, that he's cheating on his wife, and so on." These stories could be grounds for dismissal, putting workers like Ionaia in a difficult situation. "If you tell the leaders that the person working next to you is a liar or making up scandals, they tell you that you have to be a professional." Ionaia said the team organization operated like social cliques, empowering only those who could manipulate the system. Her only strategy in these cases was avoidance: "I just try to do my job and don't look at anyone."

Grounded in the daily experiences of scientific management methods on the line, the physical and emotional stresses of assembly work formed the context for creative action. For as much as Taylorization and social surveillance aimed to control workers' every act, each worker sought ways to evade control and reduce stress. This is a different way of thinking about constraints and creativity. Whereas the history of television production sets these terms in opposition, indicating how constraints limit creativity, assemblers looked creatively for solutions to stressful limits because *they had no other choice*. Assemblers have to be creative in the creation process if they intend to avoid the injuries and damaging gossip that might ruin their future opportunities.

Invisible Creatives While structural conditions may have failed to constrain workers' creative actions, the context of the factory did constrain the ways that assemblers could talk about creativity. None of my interviewees would ever use the word *creative* to describe themselves on the job. That is, even as I marveled at Ionaia's determination to find creative new means to endure the pain and the stress of her job, it was also clear that she was fiercely constrained in applying the term to herself because she was an assembler.

In Manaus, as in many of the manufacturing hubs of the NIDL, assemblers imply a feminine identity and feminized labor. Global electronics factories feminized assembly work throughout the twentieth century through the selection and regulation of women's bodies in accordance with essentialized notions of feminine docility, patience, dexterity, and attention to detail.[44] Interviews conducted with factory managers in two Amazon cities in the 1980s confirmed that they felt females would be best adapted to assembly work because they were more patient with detail-oriented and repetitive tasks, as well as being more submissive and controllable.[45] This led to a gendered workforce in which men operated heavy equipment and performed technical roles while women assembled. Even as men worked alongside women on the assembly line in 2005, the work itself was still feminized in that assemblers were not expected to express the individualism, originality, or artisanship frequently associated with definitions of creativity.

The limits of language in a social system means, following the sociologist Howard Becker, that despite the extensive division of labor and joint coordination needed to produce any object in modern society, only few people can claim the "honorific title of the artist."[46] Further, the social formation of production conventions constrains the artist's definition of the "new."[47] No individual connected to the art world, from the paper printer to the painter to the printmaker, is exempted from the social definition of "what is and isn't art, what is and isn't their kind of art, and who is and isn't an artist."[48] This social constraint reinforces Joas's points that creative action is not necessarily rational because it is not premeditated, but creativity must be rationalized through the language of what is socially possible. Whether or not assemblers understood that they did something new on the job, the social agreement that assemblers were not creative conspired against them recognizing their own actions as such.

The limits of language embedded in the construction of creativity perhaps proved most constraining for my own work, as I tried to understand how assemblers saw themselves in their own words while deconstructing the terms they used. To hear women such as Tânia describe how managers regularly called her "stupid" despite her own initiatives to avoid injuries, to stay awake, and even to train new workers was as much a methodological challenge for me as a theoretical one. Joas is correct to note that humans instinctively know creative action in hindsight. Yet the inability to call these innovations creative, for me meant asking new questions and listening to the answers in a different way. I take this as the challenge posed by Gayatri Chakravorty Spivak in her seminal essay of 1988, "Can the Subaltern Speak?" On one hand, "there is no more dangerous pastime than transposing proper names into common nouns, translating, and using them as sociological evidence."[49] On the other hand, deconstruction demands translation; the researcher must re-present the literal words of her or his informants through analysis. The danger is an imperialist recreation of the subject through the researcher's words. Translation is a "necessary impossibility. . . . It is not a sign but a mark and therefore cannot signify an original."[50] My project involved listening to assemblers in their own words but then translating them to deconstruct a shared supposition that, as a class, assemblers did not engage in creative action.

My conversations with assembly workers began with general narratives of work and the workplace in the contexts of autobiographies. From there, I focused on those moments at which assemblers perceived that they had done something innovative or different from their routines. In this way, I have tried to keep creative actions in their personal and social contexts, even if the terms I use differ and defer from the literal words my subjects used. For as James Maggio points out, it is not Spivak's point that the subaltern cannot speak, but that many researchers have not listened.[51] Translation involves communication, the exchange of meanings between speakers and listeners. Assemblers' oral narratives revealed the value that each individual, on reflection, assigned his or her creative actions. Simply by listening to assemblers, I heard the distinctions they made between everyday experiences, the conditions that sparked their creative actions, and their managers' positive, negative, or ambivalent reception of these actions. These elements are vital if we are to understand how creativity operates socially in the production of televisions but how it is frequently ignored or disciplined. Stories about the reception of assemblers' creativity revealed the ways that the production process produced them as working subjects, even as I may fail to ever grasp, much less translate, the multiple ways in which they saw themselves.

Creativity on the Line

Creativity in television set assembly, expressed individually but reliant on social coordination and recognition, conjoined assemblers' personal experiences with their complex cultural contexts. These contexts were not homogenous. The uneven implementation of managerial strategies across factories of varying national origins in Manaus had generated a diverse array of workplace cultures.[52] Whereas some factories seemed to value essentialist gendered abilities, others seemed to stress education, training, and even the ability to engage in reflective thought, in accordance with the mandates of the International Organization for Standardization (ISO). My interviewees considered Brazilian-owned factories, such as Gradiente, alternatively more or less exploitative compared to Korean-owned factories, such as LG, because of the cultural proximity they felt to management styles and surveillance techniques. Whether or not these perceptions could be grounded empirically, assemblers' knowledge of different factory cultures guided their strategies for working in the District. Whereas some jockeyed for factories in which they might have to work faster but had more bonuses and benefits, other workers preferred factories in which they made less money but had more input into quality improvement, work schedules, or in which they received more training for potential advancement. When I asked assemblers about their experiences on the job, they almost always spoke comparatively, weighing the pros and cons of their shop-floor culture with others they knew either personally or through their friends, family members, and neighbors who also worked in the district.

In the factory, assemblers navigated these diverse cultures strategically but never autonomously. Leslie Salzinger's participant observation in several factories on the U.S.-Mexican border is exemplary in demonstrating this point. Through a comparison of workers in different factory cultures, she argues that work practices reproduced gendered, sexual, and national identities, but also destabilized them, leading to a greater variety of relational positions and identity performances. She states: "Managerial control operates through the constitution of shop-floor subjects. This is a fully relational process. 'Workers' are formed in dialogue with other shop-floor inhabitants. Managers are similarly socially located and formed, nested within their own set of constitutive relations. And depending on the terms of address, the content of workplace subjectivities can refer to many other categories of identity—among them gender and nationality."[53] The dialogic formation of workers implied many potential binds for assemblers who responded to the terms through which they were hailed. Women could lay special claim to assembly jobs but then were expected to perform femininity for their male counterparts, particularly foreign managers, whose expectations around assemblers' identities likely traced to their countries of origin. Men, on the other hand, had difficulty claiming a more powerful position in relation to their fellow female assemblers or male managers. The shifting composition of the labor force and the required competencies of assemblers added to these dynamic interactions. Assemblers of both genders wrestled with contradictory expectations that they be docile but analytically engaged, submissive to superiors yet active team players, controlled and yet also creative.

Assemblers' creative actions could not be extracted from these cultural contexts and identity expectations. Workers' interactions and workplace relationships coproduced working selves that framed the recognition, ignorance, or punishment of creativity. Scientific management tech-niques had made surveillance a public spectacle. Factories displayed workers' names on a wall with colors and symbols that coded their value in terms of daily speed and accuracy. Resistance to company norms be-came public information to all workers, making the stakes for developing creative solutions high. A lack of creativity led to a life of boredom at best. Factory workers whose creative work fit cultural expectations became vested in the factory culture, the national body of workers, and the global division of international labor that marked Manaus's difference from the rest of Brazil. Yet workers' creativity could also overstep expectations, leading to disciplinary actions, dismissal, or even blacklisting.

Sanctioned Creativity Factories both recognized and rewarded creativ-ity when it assisted the production process. Indeed, as part of their Japa-nization over the past decade, electronics factories used creativity as a buzzword for sanctioned worker innovations. Contests, educational pro-grams, and team meetings stressed that workers could harness their creative skills to improve production while boosting workers' motivation in the workplace. Andresa, for example, cited numerous extracurricular activities she did in addition to her regular task of sticking logos on television sets: "This year we started an environmental week. It gives us the chance to participate more. There was a contest to make things out of recycled products, so people made dresses and beach toys. It was really cool. I helped collect the bottles and cans to help the others, and we all won two dinners for our team spirit. There's other days too. I helped coordinate a Bring Your Kids to Work Day. Workers spend all day with the kids in the factory and hiking in the company forest." Andresa found these occasional days the most interesting aspects of a job she otherwise saw as tedious. Rewards reinforced the sense that this was the kind of creativity that could and should be expressed in the factory.

Supervisors frequently talked about their roles in terms of stimulating more worker participation outside of line tasks. Rose and Rosara, best friends inside and outside the factory, became line leaders after the Korean management told them that they were exceptionally motivated workers. Rose used her own experience as the model: "I got promoted because I don't like to stand still. When the line used to stop, I used to look for other things to do. I wanted to learn other posts. When the line stopped, the others would get together and talk, but not me. I looked for other things to do so I wouldn't be in the same place." According to Rose, her flexibility and dedication were precisely the qualities that led to her promotion after only ten months as an assembler. She became a tester, and then a line reserve ten months later. She indicated her friend Rosara to human resources for employment. Rosara also rose quickly through the factory floor hierarchy in the same way. Rose and Rosara together looked for ways to motivate their fellow workers to be active in a way that they felt mutually benefited workers and management.

In their factory, two of the primary forums for creative actions were in-house classes and quality meetings. Classes, with titles like "Worker Innovation," explicitly connected productivity with creativity. Rosara said that the class empowered her, not by telling her how to solve problems but by validating a work process to which she could contribute her ideas. She said she learned this lesson through a thirty-two-kilometer hike in the company forest. The hike, which began before daybreak, featured problem-solving exercises that demanded each worker's input and consensus-building teamwork. She said, "They taught me to overcome my limits. We learn that we are never incapable of doing anything and that we can achieve. This has been excellent motivation for me." Although the class was originally designed for administrators, Rosara convinced her superior to offer the course to all the assemblers so that they, too, could learn that their individual ideas were important to the functioning of the factory as a whole. This concept of worker participation proved particularly important to the implementation of *kanban* and *kaizen* in the company's strategic planning. Rose and Rosara facilitated the team meetings at the beginning and end of each of their work shifts. Rosara explained the aims of the meetings: "Every day the leaders meet with the supervisors to talk about quality and productivity standards. Afterwards, I meet with the thirty-six people on my line and pass along what I learned. Recently, we started an improvement program to reward the best worker on the team each month. But in order to get the reward, you have to make suggestions, to think about what can be done better in terms of health or safety or anything. Everyone has ideas, but they don't always speak up. There are some people who talk and others who don't. Some of their ideas are not that good, but just the fact that they are thinking about them; that's what I think is great. When we talk about it, we always improve."

Classes and quality meetings emphasized the role of the individual in a social process of creative production. The validation of individual expression in a team setting resonated with sociocultural theories of psychology that refuse to separate the individual psyche from group processes.[54] Through working on the line and then talking about it, assemblers learned the rules of the game, both instrumentally and interpersonally, facilitating collaboration when unexpected problems arose. In contrast to the image of a tightly controlled assembly line that erases individualism, Rosara, who had worked previously in a competitor factory, saw her workplace as stimulating independence. "Here, if you show them what you can do, you will be recognized," she stressed repeatedly in our conversation, citing her promotions and showing me the multitude of factory appliances and electronics in her one-room house.

Both Rose and Rosara identified the limits of sanctioned forms of creativity in terms of their own progress in the factory. Rose, the youngest of six sisters, knew that she had to choose between excelling in her job and having a family. Each of her sisters left assembly positions voluntarily in their mid-twenties when they decided to have children. "The company is my boyfriend," Rose joked to her family when they teased her about not being a mother at the age of twenty-seven. This forced choice between factory work and family—itself an effect of gender inequalities in a city in which working-class women are presumed to be primary caretakers and factories have few child-care services after a short maternity leave—demonstrated the gendering of creative actions in production. Whereas men's contributions could lead to upper-management promotions, women expressed their frustration over the glass ceiling they hit when trying to be supervisors. At Rose's and Rosara's factory, only two supervisors were female, creating a sexist climate in which men were presumed to be more capable leaders than women. Rose frequently did the line inventory and closed out the financial ledgers, two tasks she was proud to have taught herself on the company's computers but that she also resented because her supervisor took credit for the work. The gendering of creativity meant that not all creative contributions were recognized equally.

In a different division of the very same factory, Sueli expressed how even sanctioned forms of creativity could be dismissed by feminizing the contribution. In her quality meetings, line leaders asked for suggestions, but these had to be framed uncritically. Sueli reflected on one instance when the line received two hundred defective boards while assembling DVD players. Per the leader's instructions, an assembler called for a meeting with the technician to resolve the problem. A supervisor, witnessing the work stoppage, interrupted the meeting. "The technician was trying to explain, but the super started yelling at the assembler and hitting her in front of the whole world. She started crying. Later, he had to apologize and no one got fired, but people are now afraid to talk." This experience exemplified for Sueli the way in which managers treated creative contributions as personal problems. She continued explaining that the quality meetings were minefields where workers were socialized to only make suggestions that would please the supervisors: "You need to say something that the supervisor already agrees with or thinks needs to be changed. You can't criticize. People come to the meetings thinking they can talk, but afterwards they're afraid to say anything because they don't want to be marked as a troublemaker. Only the veterans will speak up." Although Sueli believed with conviction that women were best suited to be assemblers in the factory, she disabused the notion that sanctioned forms of creativity were ever gender neutral.

Unsanctioned Creativity For all the rhetoric of creativity in Manaus's restructured factories, managers did not sanction other unique innovations in the workplace. These unsanctioned forms of creativity were numerous and primarily aimed at reducing the stress or boredom that the repetitive assembly motions evoked after they became routine. Regardless of the initial challenge that assembly work posed, each interviewee expressed his or her frustration with the tremendous disciplining of their physical movements and time. Workers who never changed their activities had difficulties paying attention and were more likely to suffer repetitive stress injuries. It turned into a vicious cycle, because the more assemblers injured themselves, the more mind-numbing their jobs became, stimulating new injuries. In addition, each factory had its own retinue of rules that scheduled meals, exercise, classes, and even bathroom breaks. Workers responded to these boundaries with an array of tactics, in the language of Michel de Certeau, that channeled production labors in alternative ways.[55]

Killin, twenty-four, and Jamille, twenty-five, were neighbors and friends who talked about the creative ways in which they tried to avoid boredom on the job despite their very different working conditions in the District. Killin, a contracted temp for a components factory, pasted the nucleus for a component with a glue gun from 4 p.m. to 2 a.m. six days a week. Jamille had spent the past two years inspecting LCD parts for another company from 11 p.m. to 7 a.m. five days a week. Together, they shared their difficulties and methods to overcome them.

JAMILLE: Every month a supervisor meets with us to review our absences and behavior. That's a big thing. Lots of people get fired for their behavior.

VICKI: Like what?

J: You can't laugh or talk too loud in the hallway. You can't talk on the line. You have to enter the sector through the right and exit on the left. You can't stand in a group that's bigger than two people. You can't travel to other sectors. If you break any of the rules, there's guards that come and write you up. They then tell the supervisors.

V: So how do you feel at work?

J: I used to feel tired all the time, but now I'm used to it.

V: What do you do to not be tired?

J: I talk with the others, though that's against the rules. We wear masks, so as long as you don't turn your head or smile, you can talk because they can't see your mouth.

V: What do you talk about?

J: Gossip. We talk about how old and ugly the supers are, so we never want to date them! [both women laugh]

KILLIN: We don't have as many rules as that, especially after they get to know our work. Still it gets monotonous.

V: So what do you do?

K: We trade places. I might be on the glue gun and someone else is pasting wires and we say, "Hey, you're sitting in the same seat all day. Let's trade." So I'll paste wires and that makes it less boring and gives my hand time to recover from the gun.

V: Is there anything else you do to make it more interesting?

K: To distract ourselves? Sometimes we'll even sing. The woman next to me will say something like, "Killin, do you remember that song?" She wants me to sing to help pass the time. Singing helps, especially when the line slows down. But you can't look at anyone else or else they'll know. The boss will say, "Hey don't talk with your mouth! Speak with your hands!" So you look down at the belt, but then you'll hear, "Say something," because people are tired and the belt puts you to sleep.

J: We used to be able to bring our cell phones to work. Now we can't do that either.

K: We have to leave them in the locker room.

J: We have that rule too. There's a bag in the locker to leave your radio, CD player, and magazines.

For each rule that prevented communication, Jamille and Killin improvised ways to communicate. Singing, talking, and trading positions passed the time, built relationships across sectors, and helped assemblers avoid injuries. These tactics were both social and corporeal, a process continually subject to small variations, adaptations, and occasional flashes of inspiration. Killin, for example, told me that one day she resolved to learn how to do her coworker's and her own jobs at the same time to maximize the time needed to go to the bathroom and take an occasional break. The benefit of her coworker's appreciation and reciprocity outweighed the challenge she had to coordinate her body to move at twice its normal speed. Soon others began doing the same thing in the factory, generating a creative shared practice to pass time in a way that was both different from the routine and productive, though unsanctioned.

For all the potential benefits of these tactics, unsanctioned creative actions generally stimulated more rules. Jamille and Killin mentioned the increasing prohibition of media technologies on the factory floor, though good workers regularly bought or won their cell phones, MP3 players, and "personal digital assistants" (PDAS) from the companies they worked for. When phone calls became an issue with the management, many workers said they began text messaging, which then too became off limits. Workers talked about the ways in which the rules operated to dehumanize them. Workers lacked all privacy on the line, where their bodies became subject to strict surveillance by supervisors, guards, line leaders, reserve workers, and other assemblers. Rules could even be invasive. One interviewee told me she used to stash hard candies to suck on during work until line leaders submitted each worker to random "mouth checks" to embarrass and punish those eating on the line. Guards in some factories submitted daily conduct reports on each rule breaker. Too many infractions and Rose said she would recommend that the worker be fired, because "it's either her or me."

Tactics that subverted the rules were unsanctioned in that they could lead to disciplining or dismissal, and yet they were necessary for the workers' continued productivity on the line. For example, the desire to communicate about the latest in-house romance motivated them never to miss work, preventing absenteeism, which was the primary reason for dismissal from assembly jobs. Indeed, the interpersonal relationships themselves were not sanctioned, but management frequently looked the other way or developed their own relationships, both platonic and romantic, with workers. As long as *their* superiors did not find unsanctioned actions to be obstructive to productivity, tactics that broke the rules of time and physical movement had the benefit of keeping bored employees interested in their jobs.

Subversive Creativity   When these forms of creativity threatened to reduce productivity, managers considered them subversive, generally leading to dismissal and blacklisting from future factory work. Such was the case with Aline, a line assembler at a television screen factory. Her story, which she relayed to me after a full workday and evening classes, illustrates a mix of creative labors in the context of a complex work environment. This environment became increasingly difficult to navigate. Although her superiors initially praised her ability to make do on the job, managers eventually found her contributions subversive and a threat to a work hierarchy grounded in gender and racial differences.

Aline said she was struggling economically and emotionally when she decided to go to work in the District. She was twenty-one, a single mother of two young children, and eking out a living from cleaning laundry and tutoring grammar to high-school students when a student's mother recommended her to human resources in a Korean screen factory. Aline's monthly salary jumped from US$100 to US$250 when she was contracted; some months she could make US$500 working double shifts. Her sector worked on the innards of the television set, in particular, on the deflection yoke, which controls picture quality and sharpness without distortions. Every day, she connected plastic plugs to the yoke and then attached the yoke to a series of cones and copper wire spools. Although the rolling of the copper coils around spools was mechanized, everything else was "handmade," as she termed it. Like other workers in the district, Aline initially found the work challenging. The adaptation of her fingers to the fine manipulation of wires was an acquired skill, and the busy shop-floor environment was different than anything she had previously experienced. Yet the work quickly became monotonous and tiring. Her division required assemblers to stand throughout their shift, making for about eight hours on one's feet, except for a forty-minute lunch period. There were no permissible breaks in the schedule. Many of Aline's coworkers suffered from sore backs and necks from standing and peering down all day at the rolling line. The rolling machine frequently broke, leaving workers to roll and solder the spools; Aline frequently cut her hands on the wires. Aline did not know any women in the factory older than twenty-eight, a fact that her fellow workers never forgot. She said, "We'd do everything possible to produce quality because that was our jobs. If the factory closed, how would we even get new jobs? Even though [our company], in terms of the District, has a very good reputation; everyone knows how hard we battle. People know we work really hard." After three months, Aline began working even harder, pulling a double shift most days from 7 a.m. until 3 p.m. and then returning at 11 p.m. to work until her 7 a.m. shift began again. With transportation times, she slept four hours a night, six or seven days a week.

To exert more control over and exact more productivity from workers, Aline's employer had several layers of surveillance. Aline's peers and reviewers (fellow workers promoted to oversee their former peers) supervised her work on the line, while the *kanban* system publicly identified high- and low-performing lines. Absences were treated as the worst infractions. A public roll call also served to reprimand and shame errant workers who had been absent the previous day. Quality meetings at the beginning and end of each shift identified high- and low-performing workers. Each month, supervisors awarded high-performing shifts a US$250 bonus to throw a party after work. Low-performing workers received pink slips, generally without benefits if they were let go before the end of a six-month trial period. Together, these strong control mechanisms, hallmarks themselves of Taylorist management and Japanization efforts, were subject to the most intense forms of negotiation on the floor itself.

Although the high employment of women in the District helped destabilize gender roles in Manaus, Aline's factory was strictly gender segregated between female assemblers and male technicians. Perhaps for this reason, much of the social negotiations in the factory were hypersexualized.[56] Women in Aline's section tried to use the surveillance of their actions to their advantage: "We wore these white suits that made us look like astronauts. But, underneath that, you could see everyone wore makeup to attract more attention." In the hallways and during lunch, women flirted and made dates to try to get favors on the shop floor or even promotions. In return, though, the women reinforced their object status in production. Aline said managers openly rated women in front of them or slapped them on the behind in the hallways.

Aline also learned to walk between sexual privilege and discrimination as part of the rules of the game of her job. Aside from her formal qualifications, she knew that her stunning good looks—she was tall, thin, and light skinned—also contributed to her résumé. The human resources manager pursued her even in the initial job interview. With her looks and charm, she curried favors from male technicians and managers to avoid production surveillance. She took bathroom breaks, technical consulting breaks, and even breaks to make Xerox copies for her coworkers. When Aline had a boyfriend in the factory, a mechanical supervisor who was sent to Korea for training, she charmed a man in human resources so she could call Korea directly on one of the company's private phones: "I got a lot of advantages with all the people I knew. I would go to my friend in HR and ask to use the phone there. They call Korea all the time, but I had to be persuasive. I would say, 'Agostiiiinhooo, I want to talk to [my boyfriend] Julio but you know I don't have the money to call from my house. People here call all the time. Can you help me?' He said he wasn't sure but he would see what he could do. So then the next day, he gave me the access code so I could call from wherever I wanted! I called from the cafeteria, the restroom, the lobby."

Aline's effective flirtations made her both a subject of observation ("They all saw me") and exempt from some of the rigid control mechanisms on the job. While sexual banter might have been a way of easing tensions on the job, Aline used it tactically. Managers frequently did not promote women who slept with a supervisor, and they eventually fired the human resources manager that propositioned Aline initially for using his position to secure dates with the assemblers.

Aline developed other methods to creatively achieve more freedom in the workplace. She joined the Samsung sports teams primarily because they gave her a paid excuse to leave the line early for games. Then, she began visiting people in other sectors. She said she did this out of curiosity: "The factory is a place full of every kind of person you can imagine. So I wanted to meet everyone and talk to them." Since she could not leave the line during work hours, Aline skipped lunch to visit different sectors, extending her social network in the factory. Finally, she said she took on the night shift in part because it was the least surveyed of all the shifts: "I liked coming in at night because it was less stressful. We had a radio playing, coffee, and no pressure from the Koreans, because all but one of them went home. We worked the way that was best for us. The Koreans always wanted to know why I was laughing in the daytime." Aline moved more freely at night. She moved in between all the sectors and helped where she could: "I still had my job title, but I ended up helping the feeder, the magnet post, and the technician because they were all alone. Every night I had to devise something new to help them out. I actually liked doing it, and they could take advantage of the fact that I knew a bit of everything." The freedom that the arrangement allowed paid off for both Aline and the company; her shift always won the monthly bonus for the most productivity.

In other words, Aline's strategies inadvertently made her a more productive worker on the line. By visiting other sectors, Aline had to learn their posts as well to seem like she was doing something useful: "When you go to other sectors to talk to people, the Koreans can't see you just standing there talking. So I started doing what they were doing. Of course I wasn't picking up the heavy stuff, but I helped them do light work while I got to know them."

When she was promoted to reviewer then, she used the network she had built to get things done more efficiently. She explained, "You have to be imaginative to get what you want in your job. I never wanted a promotion, just to do my job well; but without any investment in your sector, you have to run after what you need." One primary example she gave was the problem of disassembling faulty television yokes and cones. If the pieces did not test right, her sector had to pry them apart. She said, "This was common, and we often cut ourselves trying to use the spatula to break apart the hot melt on the pieces. So what did I do? I decided to get the acetone from the chemical sector to take off the hot melt. It was located in the chemical sector, and I was the only one that knew that. And we even used it to clean up a few things around there. I got to know the technician and the chemical engineer to get the acetone."

Aline's creative use of the resources in the factory developed her reputation among the reviewers as someone who could get things done. She got small stashes of acetone for all the reviewers and borrowed tools from other sectors that would make the manual work easier. Aline's knowledge and access to people in the maintenance department meant that soon the display department became more modernized, complete with pliers, spatulas, soldering irons, and scissors at every post.

Ironically, though, it was the factory's so-called participatory processes in which Aline's solutions to problems in production could not be validated. At the beginning of each shift, Aline and her coworkers met with a supervisor for a quality meeting. The super would tell them whether they were meeting production goals and ask for worker suggestions to improve the quality and quantity of the output. Aline said that no workers would speak up at the meetings. Whether out of fear or from lack of ideas or even interest, workers stood by while Aline says she tried to make suggestions, based to a large degree on what she saw in other sectors. She suggested that the sector have acetone and its own access to tools. First and foremost, though, Aline thought that the sector would be more productive if women could sit and stand equal amounts of time on the line instead of standing the entire shift. She tried to reason with her supervisor: "For example, in Production 11, all the men worked eight hours, but they alternated one hour standing and one hour sitting. So I got to thinking, if men, who are stronger than us and have more physical resistance, why don't we get to sit ever?" The suggestion, as well as all the others, was always promptly rejected.

Through the quality meetings Aline hit a ceiling in terms of her potential worth in the factory. She said that she developed a reputation as a "revolutionary." "I began to question and put my finger in their wounds," she said. "They began to feel inconvenienced by me. Since I've always been a talker and communicative, I began to access the management. I would see them in the hallway and say, 'Good morning.' That was how I started to get to know them. I knew the director, the manager. The Koreans, being the way they are, had problems with me, because I was speaking to men, to my superiors, and going to other sectors. I was supposed to be quiet in my sector."

Aline's identity, female and Brazilian, prevented her from ultimately fitting into the management culture in her factory. Aline's use of the term *the Koreans* frequently summarized an absolute divide between managers and workers in the factory. Although she said they would talk to her in public outside the factory, inside the factory, "it was like you didn't exist." While supervisors could accept Aline getting to know the technicians or dating an engineer, she crossed the final line when she tried to engage managers with her ideas. "They told me that if the Chinese can work standing up, so can Brazilians," she said, pinpointing a racial hierarchy in which Brazilians and Chinese sat on the bottom of global labor value. In the end, Aline's creative use of her mind and her social network failed to overcome her status in the work hierarchy. After she refused a transfer into a secretarial position, taking her away from the line, Aline was fired after only a year and nine months in the District.

Assemblers' identities are keys to the struggles over creativity in the production process. Assemblers' gender, social class, race, and nationality conspire to negate their innovations as manipulated reactions, negligible infractions, or subversive resistances. These categories, themselves highly contextual, illustrate the importance of reception *within* the production process. Top-down organizational models of production continue to reify creativity in the object of production as an expression of power relations at the top. Yet assemblers remind us that creativity lies in the performances that are subject to interpretation. Sneaking acetone onto the line can be seen as a positive appropriation or as a negative step toward rebellion depending on who witnesses the act and how it is relayed. The continued idealization of Manaus assemblers as docile females and passive Indians serves to continually erase workers' contributions as expressions of the foreign, male management that extracts their labor value.

Assemblers as the Invisible Creative Class of Global Television Production

Integrating social theories of creation, creativity is a feature of all forms of human production, whether it is the development of a program script or the soldering of the wires on a television set. In the words of television set assemblers, their hands are what gives the television set life and what thus sustains all the processes following it in television production. As creators situated in the primary stages of television production, electronics assemblers' ability to create is both individually embodied and socially negotiated. Production involves the mediations between the mind, hands, and the physical objects of the set in the context of institutional rules and interpersonal networks. From this complex interaction of variables, creativity emerges in part from the incentives that the factory provides, but more often from the frustrations caused by rote repetition and dehumanizing work conditions. Indeed, by stimulating mind and body, creative actions reduced the incidence of injuries and absenteeism and thus indirectly fostered productivity. Electronics companies unwittingly benefited from workers' creativity while at the same time repressing it with rigid channels for its expression. This small glimpse into factory work seems to indicate that the creation process demands both physical and mental variations from the routines that scientific management enforces. Creativity, in this formulation, is personal and collaborative, sporadic and local, necessary and yet unruly.

These dynamic contingencies are all but lost in studies of television production that have tended to operationalize creativity as an individual resistance to industrial or organizational constraints. Whether they are framed as triumphant television auteurs or as frustrated producers hamstrung by studio executives, cultural producers, the implication goes, appear to fight economic and social constraints, in the words of the philosopher Heinz Steinert, "all the time . . . carrying the burden of their 'art,' which—in order to maintain some degree of autonomy and self-respect—must be of a significance existing independently of the conditions of production and evaluation."[57] This asocial definition of creativity in production studies further implies a troubling politics based on an atomistic defense of art in the name of personal autonomy and respect. Richard Florida's notion of the "creative class" evokes this politics, conceptualizing television producers as members of a class, in concert with gays, immigrants, and "bohemians," defined as people who work in the arts and entertainment, such as writers, designers, actors, and musicians.[58] Defined purely by geography, education, and cultural capital, Florida's conception of creativity divides workers based on class privilege and professional status rather than on a mutual structure of feeling that might spark a collective agenda for laborers.

Assemblers' narratives and choice of words revealed how easily definitions of creativity could be co-opted into the agendas of others, demonstrating that creative actions cannot be separated from their reception in the contexts of personal reflections and social interpretations. Just as assemblers did not personally create the frameworks through which their labors could be defined as creative, they did not interpret their creative acts outside their managers' regulation, their coworkers' recognition, and their own career trajectories within their community. The incentives to see creativity in line with corporate demands and community expectations were clear. Assemblers had only to perform within the range of acceptable identities to become a vested member of the factory culture, a denizen of the Industrial Pole in Manaus, and a rights-bearing worker-citizen under Brazilian law. In her narrative of her work in the District, Terezinha described her physical labors in terms of a gendered citizenship: "I feel good thinking I've already worked in TV assembly. Nowadays there's people who have never worked in the District. I can always tell that to my husband. He never worked in the District. And he studied to be a technician. He studied to work in the technical area for television sets, but he never worked in assembly. That was my expertise." For the many migrants to Manaus, young people with few opportunities, and often women raising a family, the District has offered dignity and a distinction from others outside the formal economy. These contexts challenge workers not to recognize the vast majority of their creative acts. This lack of recognition supports the invisibility of Manaus's electronics laborers and sustains the existence of the television industry's supposed creative class.

The assemblers, unlike the producers of the creative class, do show the potential for a collective politics. The invisible creatives and above-the-line workers in television alike face the collective threat that their employers move entire production processes to cheaper or more cooperative locales. In a move called "hegemonic despotism" by Michael Burawoy, electronics companies use China as the stick to threaten Manaus's laborers that factories will close and move away.[59] Hollywood's hegemony also depends on the threat of competition elsewhere, from Austin to Australia, giving financial investors and sponsors apt power to chip away at below-the-line union power.[60] These fears can control workers, regardless of geography or identity, provoking fear and, often, submission. The failure of above-the-line guilds to secure a collective solution to the threat signals at best a lack of unity and, at worst, an inability to work outside the narrow privileges secured by their lofty position as the constituents of the creative class.[61] For the other side of the fear of losing electronics companies due to global forces is the feeling that one has nothing left to lose. It is worth noting here that the largest strike in Manaus's history was touched off in 1990 by the public beating of a Brazilian female worker in a Korean-owned television set factory.[62] At that moment, there was no confusing female assemblers with their docile, submissive, or patient stereotypes. Fifteen years later, the continued tensions over class, national, and sexual relations on the shop floor generate a horizon of possibilities for a yet unrealized collective worker identity that supplies its own threat to global capital. This is an abstract nightmare for the multinational corporation and a utopian fantasy that holds hope for the creative class of Manaus.

2. Producers as Professionals

PROFESSIONALISM IN SOFT-CORE PRODUCTION

The notion of a creative professional, as proffered through the descriptions of television producers in the new economy, consolidates a contradiction of endogamous and exogamous terms. Whereas *creative* demarcates the limited labors of those whose work intersect the visual, literary, and performance arts, *professional* covers ever wider spectra of workers and their labors. Doctors and lawyers share the moniker today with actors, scriptwriters, and poker players, but it is unclear what these workers share in terms of their historical formation, their associative access to certain resources or benefits, a predictable trajectory, or even a loose notion of membership in a community of practice. A leading sociologist of professions, Eliot Freidson, claims that his own field lacks a generalizable theory.[1] Unmoored from any objective criteria, the word *professional* —and its related terms *professionalism* and *professionalization*—has rather served as a historical articulation of status and privilege in relation to changing labor markets and their organizing hierarchies.

In television production worlds, the notion of an industry professional, as presented in the introduction, accompanied the modern development of a complex organizational bureaucracy that incorporated various media industries from the 1960s to the 1980s. Studies of professionals' roles and resources, goals and options, stemmed from this relatively stable division of labor emerging in this period. Professionalism among television producers implied routine practices, membership in above-the-line guilds or associations, and predictable goals to the extent that a "hit" program would secure ongoing employment as well as contribute to the industry's bottom lines. From these bases, the image of the creative professional formed around a familiar stable of publicly known television producers whose names appeared at the culmination of the listing of title credits. The credit sequence at once placed this restricted group of almost exclusively white, heterosexual males both synchronically and diachronically in the U.S. star system for creative production and distinguished this figure as the one responsible for controlling the execution of a hit show. In the process, professional television producers earned status, fame, and riches for themselves and the industry as a whole. The explosion of film school students since the late 1970s, enrolling in search of professionalization into film, television, and related media industries, demonstrates the continuing desire to be a member of this club.[2]

By the 1970s, however, the television labor market had changed, its hierarchies having become reconfigured. The casualization of television work, from its outsourcing of tasks to nonguild members who deferred benefits to its reliance on multitasking entrepreneurs to drive down labor costs, had fragmented reliable work routines, rerouted career paths, and divorced professionalism from its assumed material benefits. There were still known professionals. Now touted as celebrities to help brand new programming and to secure the authority of the network in a multichannel environment, producers such as Joss Whedon, David E. Kelley, and Mark Burnett stood in for their largely invisible production staffs of freelancers, part-timers, and interchangeable interns. As Nicholas Garnham explains, television and entertainment industries espouse a division of labor that hires the offspring of the capitalist class while keeping wages low in accordance with a precapitalist notion of craftwork.[3] Studies of the television professional frequently miss this contradiction. Garnham writes, "There is much sophisticated discussion of professionalization, of hierarchies of discourse, of hegemonic and subordinate codes, etc., discussions which often serve to mask a reality which is ever-present to those actually working in the media: losing one's job. This reality is of course often internalized by both the employee and the employer in the form of ideologies of professionalism and managerialism, but it remains no less potent for that, indeed, is the underpinning which professionalism requires."[4] The disconnect between the ideology of professionalism and the real assaults on television labor markets generates considerable anxiety, especially for a younger, film school–educated generation trying to reap the benefits their parents may have benefited from. The other side of professionalism, then, is the instability that marks the realities of labor markets in the new television economy.

Nowhere is this contradiction more apparent than among the workers on the margins of this labor market. There, freelancers, contract workers, and their employers contest the meanings of professionalism from positions only adjacently related to mainstream professionals. This chapter deconstructs the term *professional* through the perspectives of a community of soft-core video practitioners who defined themselves as video and television professionals, despite their utter exclusion from the industry's visible hierarchies or tangible benefits. Instead, this community—itself fractured by competition—revealed other symbolic goods that workers associated with being a professional and an invisible laborer for television industries. These goods had the most value precisely among workers who had little else to lose. What emerges in the case study are not just folk definitions of the professional but also the cultural and economic contingencies involved in workers' self-identification as professionals. Media industries capitalized on the ambiguous meanings of the television professional both to lure workers into casualized production jobs and to discipline their behaviors.

I met some fifty producers in this unlikely community through repeated encounters during the Mardi Gras holiday in New Orleans from 2004 to 2006. All were people who attended and worked during the ten-day season to shoot soft-core video footage explicitly for sale. Of these, I interviewed some twenty producers and became friendly with a handful who let me follow them around. Mardi Gras is, in Nick Couldry's phrasing, a "ritual space of the media" in that social interactions there frequently reveal the power of media industries in everyday life.[5] Since the invention of the portable camcorder, video enthusiasts have come to New Orleans to capture, collect, and sell images of nudity that are generally procured in an exchange ritual for beaded necklaces, T-shirts, or other trinkets. Their efforts have contributed to a soft-core television culture, enacted on the street and distributed through home video, pay-per-view specials, global satellite programming, and a ubiquitous series of infomercials that have been a staple of late-night cable advertising sales. The professionalization of cameramen and the marginalization of camerawomen, together with their layered definitions of professionalism and their assertions that they are professionals, belie the power that they invest in the television labor market. This power, though latently related to producers' desires for financial success and security, were also bound up with definitions of artisanship, teamwork, and masculine identity work. As a result, cameramen forged internal definitions of professionalism that merged postindustrial business logics with precapitalist notions of amateurism and a post-1950s masculine consumerism. The phenomenology of professionalism is thus bound to competing and contradictory notions of identity, even as its political and economic value has declined.

The Emergence of a Soft-Core Professional

Albedo[6] was the nom de plume of the founder of the Mardi Gras soft-core video, according to the few old-timers who remembered the beginnings of soft core as an industrial genre. Starting in the early 1980s, he brought his Sony camcorder to the festivities to "take pictures" of women disrobing in public.[7] Compiling the shots with footage of the local mise-en-scène, Albedo distributed the finished VHS tapes through an area bar, which played them to attract customers and sold them as tourist souvenirs. In 2006, I met Albedo in an apartment suite located on Bourbon Street, where he captured most of his famed footage. There, he reflected on a moment he saw as indicative of the transformation of soft-core video from a cottage industry led by amateurs to a capitalized segment of mass-media industrial networks.

> It was a fairly small community of us back then. It wasn't like today. We didn't do the marketing that *Girls Gone Wild* did. They took it to the next step. I was an aerospace engineer at the time and a retired Air Force guy. They weren't exactly interested in publicizing this other thing I was doing. So I kept a low profile. The interesting thing happened when I was shooting the balcony at Mardi Gras. Renee was a natural J-cup. She was on the balcony and I was shooting her. Well that year, it was 1988, and *COPS* caught the police coming up there to arrest her. That was like the most replayed *COPS* edition ever for two years, and it really launched me as a video cameraman. That was really a seminal moment in the history of the videos.

While Albedo's memory may not have supplied a causal argument about the power of *COPS*—a long-running reality program focused on crime fighting—to incite the commercial market for soft-core video, it did reveal his sensitivities to the mutual imbrications of soft-core and television industries in their pursuit of cheap and marketable content.

The professionalization of soft-core cameramen occurred in tandem with other political and economic changes in media and other commercial industries during the 1980s and 1990s. Legal crackdowns on pornography industries, combined with the liberalization of broadcast advertising and the growth of an entrepreneurial freelance video market, paved the way for an industry based on the distribution and sale of legal nude imagery. These changes cast their net around a greater number of people working at the interstices of the television industry while decreasing their labor value. Meanwhile, the development of spring break and other college-oriented tourism sites as ritual media spaces brought these people together in locations that could foster media consumers' play and media producers' profit. The professional soft-core cameraman emerged in these contradictory tides, resulting in a community of practice at once dependent on and excluded from television's formal labor market.

Albedo's legacy in New Orleans coincided with those of other enterprising cameramen who, focusing on different regions of the United States, began collecting video images of naked people, women and men, in public for commercial distribution. Some of these pioneers began as photographers. Others had dabbled in hard-core filmmaking. Whereas their hard-core films focused on penetration and the so-called money shot, these soft-core productions were distinctly different.[8] While some integrated hard-core scenes, most revealed seminaked bodies performing sexualized acts in public. Frequently set in tourist sites or during holiday events, the videos offered a glimpse into what people do in places that encourage them to lose their inhibitions. College coeds kissed, swingers stripteased, and grandmothers flashed their breasts in public reversals of normalized gender and sex roles.

More important to the producers, these materials were easy and inexpensive to make. Pioneers were self-taught and self-financed. In-camera editing and a bank of VHS recorders kept postproduction and reproduction costs down. The use of unpaid actors or low-paid strippers saved on talent costs. The average hard-core film from 1975 to 1983 cost about $75,000–100,000 to make.[9] By contrast, the most expensive soft-core tape until the early 1990s might have cost $8,000–$10,000 to produce, mostly based on equipment costs and travel expenses. Producers who happened to live in popular shooting locations might spend as little as the cost of the blank tapes. The early videographers of these spectacles distributed their products in the classifieds section of photography enthusiast and music magazines or physically at strategic points of sale. One of the early producers told me that he borrowed his equipment from his local public-access television station and sold the finished tapes from the back of his car in a dance club parking lot.

Producers sometimes referred to their contents as "reality documentary," a distinct generic category with legal implications for their profession. The Reagan administration, operating via the Meese Commission, targeted the porn industry through undercover raids and sting operations, orchestrated to create a moral panic around sex in the United States in the 1980s.[10] Soft core, lacking the emblematic money shot or paid talent, situated itself in a hybrid category of other vérité documentary performance modes, such as celebrity interviews, talk programs, or public media events. As the executive director of the Free Speech Coalition, Jeffrey J. Douglas, explained, the category of reality documentary suggested that video producers had the same rights as journalists and documentarists in getting implicit consent from their public subjects, because "you can't prohibit what one could see naturally." By specializing in narrow confines of soft core, early professionals associated nudity with news over obscenity and with journalistic morays over voyeuristic values.

As the 1990s progressed, neoliberal forces in the political economies of media industries worked their way down to the entrepreneurial soft-core professionals. Guided by faith in free markets, the successive deregulation of media markets allowed for an explosion of the multimedia environment. Broadcast television networks faced competition from cable networks, which in turn also faced challenges from home video rental and sales, followed by downloadable media formats and contents. Facing declining market shares, television networks and studios alike sought cheaper programming strategies and increased opportunities to generate revenues. Of these, the television infomercial accomplished both, raising profit margins with paid programming that financed other contents.[11] For soft-core producers, infomercials opened a commercial space for the exhibition and sale of their videos, giving them access to the national niches that networks also sought. By buying late-night advertising time following programs aimed at lucrative youthful (eighteen to twenty-four), male niche audiences, soft-core companies created synergies with struggling cable networks and local broadcast affiliates trying to create their brand identities through cheaper original programs. Infomercials for the soft-core video series *Girls Gone Wild*, for example, financed original series on the E! Network and Comedy Central that were otherwise hard to sell to traditional television sponsors due to their raunchy content and low production values.

In the meantime, soft-core companies benefited from a booming tourism market, also an aftereffect of neoliberalism. Cities, experiencing cuts in federal funds and a shrinking tax base, turned to tourism during the decade to boost ailing coffers.[12] The City of New Orleans, alongside a growing number of other impoverished local governments, looked to promote events that generated both intense media interest and mass pilgrimages of visitors who would hopefully return annually.[13] Mardi Gras joined the ranks of spring break, Burning Man, Fantasy Fest, Lollapalooza, and other festivals aimed at the same tourist demographics that soft-core videographers were taping and that other media industries were marketing to sponsors. The legal line that soft-core pioneers blurred between their practice, news, and reality documentary were now visibly indistinct as broadcast news crews, cable specials producers, and the soft-core cameramen all worked together in these sites of recurring pilgrimage.

Soft-core cameramen who entered this fray formed part of a new generation of professionals who, unlike Albedo, now worked for soft-core corporations organized like independent television studios. Locating their corporate offices in Hollywood, rather than in the X-rated film capital of Chatsworth, California. executives positioned their companies in the television industry's geographic home base. Following Denise Mann's discussion of the New Hollywood independents in the 1950s, soft-core executives acted entrepreneurially as independent producers, making their own deals and leveraging their company name across several series. They signed talent and developed ancillary products to "tightly diversify" soft-core series as brands.[14] In addition to the market leader Mantra and the *Girls Gone Wild* series, new competitors spun out similarly themed series, such as *Wild Party Girls* or *Extreme Party Girls*, as well as videos aimed at specific market niches, such as "Black Mardi Gras" or "Gay Mardi Gras," each with its own line of branded T-shirts, caps, thongs, and so on. Executives sought synergies with recording companies, retail franchises, and film studio deals.[15] As their celebrities appeared as guest hosts and cameos in soft-core videos, video executives also became members of Hollywood's B-list. In production locales, such as New Orleans, companies rented entire dance clubs and bars for themed events featuring cameramen and celebrities as talent.

Although none of the companies matched Mantra's profitability, the expansive corporate infrastructure of soft-core companies in Hollywood and beyond further integrated soft-core production into mainstream entertainment networks and their star systems.[16]

Reflecting the organization of television production companies, soft-core executives had also adopted the bureaucratic logic of reality-television labor hierarchies by the first few years of the millennium. Companies evaded organized labor, drawing freelancers into short-term contracts for as little as a weekend shoot.[17] Those contract workers could then search out free laborers, namely, the person who stripped in public for the camera. Drawing from a national pool of unemployed, surplus labor, mostly new film school graduates, companies explicitly sought a new breed of soft-core professionals as employees. One Craig's List recruitment advertisement, for example, announced:

> MANTRA FILMS is looking for dedicated, professional cameramen with fun outgoing personalities to travel to several locations around the world to shoot Girls Gone Wild events. Must have at least 1 year DV or BETA experience.
>
> If you are interested, please send photo and resume to: shooters@girlsgone wild.com.[18]

Much like independent television studios two decades earlier, soft-core companies stressed the professionalism of the job's skills and work ethos while evading the image of the "corporation man" as a worker who traded his personality or fun for service to the company.[19] On the contrary, soft-core companies advertised a professionalism that merged corporate television work with the consumer leisure values of tourism events. They promised access to their vast entertainment networks in exchange for flexibility, both in labor contracts and in working conditions.

The soft-core cameraman's work varied by company and contract, with the corporate videographer trading in autonomy for the chance of career stability. The freelancers who signed contracts to sell footage after events subsidized their own travel, lodging, and equipment. Although the freelancers frequently shared expenses to cut costs, they also worked relatively independently on the streets or formed pairs for companionship. Individual payment varied widely. Some received a set fee for the event, but, more often, they were paid only for useable minutes of footage. Freelancers were weekend professionals. That is, each had a day job, mostly in nonmedia careers such as teaching, retail, services, or manual trades like oil exploration or shipyard work. They invested time, energy, and money in covering soft-core events to achieve professional status in the industry, even if status was unmatched with career stability. In contrast, soft-core company employees signed contracts that indentured them to the corporation from three to six months after a brief trial period. Soft-core companies enforced togetherness as part of a team mentality. Their recruits shared transportation and lodging, sometimes piling six or eight into a cheap motel room or tour bus. At night, they coordinated public shooting excursions with branded party event management. During the day, they had crew meetings to review the prior evening's work performances and to suggest improvements, not unlike the assembly workers discussed in the previous chapter. For their commitment, contract workers did not necessarily earn better wages than freelancers. Twenty hours on the job might have earned as little as $200, including a $30 per diem. Months on the road did not include medical insurance or benefits. In compensation, however, the dedicated soft-core employee dreamed of a Hollywood career. As one production crew leader told me before jetting off to a corporate event in Chicago, "This is a great résumé builder and a great prep for reality TV."

During Mardi Gras, these corporate soft-core cameramen and entrepreneurial freelance cameramen co-mingled on Bourbon Street, an eight-block sector of bars and music clubs that has been a hub for New Orleans tourism campaigns since at least the 1980s. Both groups considered themselves professional workers with their various connections to television and entertainment industries. Over time, I could distinguish the workers from various other kinds of video producers on the street (figure 3). The soft-core professionals carried high-end video equipment, frequently adapted to the local climatic conditions, and could be found in standard places for capturing balcony and other distance shots. They carried lighting for night shooting and loads of trinkets to reward the compliant flashers of their choice. Those who worked for a company brand wore either identical garb or logoed T-shirts. I could find them at their sponsored events or traveling in packs on the street, sometimes with a broadcast news or reality television crew in pursuit. At times, it seemed professional cameramen outnumbered actual video subjects in 2004 and 2005. Mardi Gras had become a site of both pilgrimage and "reverse-pilgrimage" in that tourists came to bear witness to media power, just as producers came to exert that power over ordinary citizens.[20]

3. Patiently waiting to capture footage on Bourbon Street,
New Orleans, Louisiana. Photo taken by the author.

Although the brand name Girls Gone Wild had become a popular
slang phrase that intimated public places where women behaved in unexpected, sexualized ways for the mutual pleasure of the performers and
viewers, the videographer was still very conscious of his precarious role as
a worker in the media economy. The political economy of soft-core production operated toward conglomeration, effectively barring aspiring entrepreneurs from entering the market with just a camera and production
skills. New company owners needed vast capital investments and connections to global media networks and their star systems. Large whole-
salers and cable and satellite distributors only signed video series with the
assurance of regular releases at the highest technical standards. Global
retailers, such as Amazon.com, and chain video stores required that producers invest in UPC labeling. Even Internet distribution demanded upfront advertising costs to direct traffic to the site. Legal costs skyrocketed
to protect intellectual property and to safeguard the borders of legitimate
reality documentary. Each of these political and economic forces drove
down the cost of professional videographers and their labor power. Freelancers found fewer buyers for their footage in a saturated market. Albedo retired in 2000, tired of balancing weeks of editing tapes with a
better-paying day job. Contracts favored cheap and disposable workers,
for most did not last longer than their short-term obligations. As one of

the few Mardi Gras video veterans of more than five years explained, "Every year, I see new people thinking they're going to strike it rich in this business, but then I never see them again."

Soft-Core Professionalism

Standing more than six feet tall, with another foot-tall top hat of many colors, Giesel said he had witnessed the soft-core profession develop before his eyes, both literally and figuratively, during the five years he sold footage as a freelance videographer. Like the newcomers, he typically went out on Bourbon Street at noon, knowing he would be outside or in local clubs for the coming twelve to eighteen hours. In a knapsack and fanny pack, he carried with him equipment, tapes, rain gear, and some ten pounds of beaded necklaces and stuffed animals. He was forty-four years old in 2004 when I met him, but he had the stamina of a younger athlete. As dusk came and the streets filled with revelers, he moved lithely between crowds, jumping trash-filled curbs and bounding over beer and vomit puddles to find saleable footage. Flashing in public is a quick motion, taking five to seven seconds per shot. Catching this act spontaneously required identifying a likely target and beating several other people with cameras, both professionals and tourists, to a front-row position. Giesel had mastered the challenging shots through shifting patches of darkness, long-distance balcony shots, and sudden rainstorms. Otherwise, he had to rely on his communication skills, getting a woman to flash for him rather than some other guy. All the while, he shielded his video equipment from jostling during a shot, avoiding cracked lights from flying beads or shorted circuits when a beer fell over the balcony onto his camera. He kept away from confrontations. Given the levels of intoxication on the streets, fights and shouting matches were frequent. Video cameras could attract ire from both men and women, who might throw a punch or publicly try to humiliate the videographers, as in the case of a woman who liked outing men like Giesel by screaming, "Perveeeeerrrtttt!" Police officers then could arrest everyone for disorderly conduct. This routine continued for five days in a row until Mardi Gras Day, when Giesel went home.

When I asked him why he endured these trials, he answered, "You have to love it is the first rule. A guy who comes out here and thinks he's going to make a tape and a lot of money has another thing coming. You have to love it for all the physical abuse you take from it." Indeed, money was not Giesel's main motivation. In recent years, he had ended up spending more money than he earned from his professional grade shots. Rather, the benefits of the profession outweighed material measures.

The expansion and professionalization of a soft-core workforce seemed at odds with the poor conditions for the work and the increasing precariousness of the labor market. After all, these jobs did not guarantee any entry into a stable career or even a reliable trajectory of earnings or benefits. The tourists who berated the videographers and the employers who undercut the value of their work constantly called the status associated with being a soft-core professional into question. The varied usages of the word *professional* spoken by the men I met on the streets during Mardi Gras suggested that professionalism was an elastic discourse. Its mutability covered all workers, despite the generational and educational gaps between freelancers and contract cameramen. Its siren song seemed to lure a racially and socially diverse group of men to the work, even if few stayed beyond a season. Offering soft-core cameramen symbolic goods in lieu of other material benefits, the discourse of professionalism organized and incorporated a wide range of work and leisure activities. The television economy now incorporated these activities, integrating their practitioners as its laborers, even if simultaneously placing them on its margins.

Professionals as Not-Amateurs Over the course of my fieldwork, I heard the term *professional* used in several contexts, but always in contrast to tourists, who were simply "amateurs." In this discourse, professionalism was a marker of pride, emphasizing skills and knowledge in the industry. According to this logic, amateurs may own video cameras, but they did not understand either the production routines or the product norms that defined the professional community. It made for a fine distinction, because these routines and norms formed part of a leisure economy that itself has integrated the traits of an aspired professionalism and disciplined labor in the form of hobbyist societies, fan communities, and lifestyle consumerism. Paid soft-core workers labored to maintain these delicate boundaries, turning to each other for community and support while turning others into saleable footage.

The geography of Mardi Gras shooting incorporated public, semipublic, and private spaces. After the first weekend of Mardi Gras in 2004, I knew where to find people who sold their flashing footage. They frequented the same local bars and hotels near Bourbon Street. Like conventioneers, they reunited every year to reconnect over shared interests: the pace of the flashing, the quality of the women, the attitudes of the police, and other issues relevant to those in the video business. In John T. Caldwell's television production geography, these were "insider spaces" within "contact zones" that permitted media professionals and members of the public to interact.[21] There, they could network and close business deals to increase their efficiency and productivity.[22] More important, they could compare their practices among recognized equals. "You can do this all you want, but you need someone to share it with," explained one cameraman who had invited a hometown buddy to share in his work as his "assistant" by carrying gear and holding his beer. Several cameramen mentored their friends in the business, drawing on their company and the respect they received from their apprenticeship. The cameramen could not necessarily depend on women, tourists, or even their employers to validate their collective identity as workers with professional techniques and standards. By sharing stories, tips, and breaks, however, they could validate each other.

Rick valued company on the street as well as in the clubs. Hailing from Texas, he drove the circuit of spring breaks and New Orleans's events in search of content. In New Orleans, he surveyed the street with Nate, a younger man who shot video for personal use but who had also considered selling his footage. Not in competition with each other, the men selected different women to tape. Rick differentiated his choices from those of Nate in that, as a professional, he had to satisfy his audience first and foremost.

> RICK: I used to shoot everything, but because it's a business, I'm more selective than the other guys out here. [He motions toward one woman.] See, like [the novices], they'll get everything: fat, skinny, old, young. . . . They don't discriminate. We go for just the college coed type.
>
> VICKI: Why is that?
>
> R: Young guys like it. It has a broader appeal. There's a market out there for older women and fatter women, but it's small compared to college stu-

dents. Older guys will look at girls younger than them. But young guys want young women. That's just the way it is. I don't even have to like the girls.

v: What's the cutoff?

r: It just depends. I've seen attractive women into their thirties. It also depends on their bodies. My personal preference is natural tits. But I shoot fake tits too. It's a business. See, that's a good example, I don't even shoot only what I like. But fake tits on an older woman are out of the question. If they've got fake tits, I'm less likely to shoot. See, I can be selective.

Rick was exemplary of a cameraman who presented himself as someone who maintained the boundaries between professionals and amateurs. He prepared for the job by traveling to New York to do market research of the field. "I looked at everything that was out there. Not for myself but to see the market. I knew I could do better," he said. His careful planning relayed a personal investment in internalizing the market standards and the limits of the genre, much as done by other television industry producers.[23] Although Rick tried to distinguish his selections from others, all cameramen competed to select a relatively narrow range of women on the street, producing a divided subjectivity between their personal tastes and idealized profitable standards.

Rick's professional sensibility guided him in his production routines. On the street, he knew who to approach, who to wait for and watch, and who to avoid. Like in other media industries, professionalism implied a shared set of conventions for controlling the complexities of production.[24] He pursued exclusively young and thin women, preferably those without noticeable breast enhancements. He avoided women who looked to him too young, particularly if they seemed to be with a parent; he feared that the girls were legally underage. He also knew who on the street was likely a dancer or strip artist, two other types of workers not likely to flash for free. Subtle clues tipped off who might flash on the street. A woman with a purse hung diagonally across her chest would be less likely to expose her breasts, just as a woman wearing hose would be unlikely to raise her skirt. Tipsy women wearing strands of the biggest or most ornate beads, however, were a dead giveaway for people ready and willing to flash on camera. Rick might wait and watch for those women to affix their gaze, also known as "beads in the eyes," cueing a potential shot. Rick and others took particular pride in their ability to convert their knowledge into free shots, that is, ones in which they did not have to negotiate an exchange rate in return for the footage.

The distinction between who got paid and who did not was vital to videographers' self-definition as professionals. That is, many workers found that even if they earned very little only years later, their personal investments of time, money, and energy were symbolically valuable in distinguishing them from the gullible or naive laborers who were posing for cameras or posting images to their own personal websites. Rick maintained he would eventually make money from royalties, a hope that tied his interests even further to those of his employer. Meanwhile, he had already spent over $5,000 on equipment, travel, lodging, and beads for a Mardi Gras weekend. In the discourse of professionalism, achievement as an unpaid hobbyist had lost value in a society in which almost all cultural practices, such as those surrounding Mardi Gras and other tourist events, have already been sold as a commodity.[25] At the same time, the videographers did not rely on payment alone, preferring to see themselves as craftsmen rather than corporate men.

Professionals as Not-Dependents Whether as freelancers or company employees, soft-core cameramen railed against notions that they served corporations, employers, or really anyone with their craft. The sense of independence from bosses made for an interesting hierarchy when Rick, together with Nate, spoke of his position in relation to other media production professionals. I had asked him if this profession might lead to other careers, a potential marker of occupational mobility:

> RICK: I get approached sometimes to do like a wedding or something, but, frankly, I don't like it. I don't even know what to shoot. This is much more straightforward.
>
> NATE: And you don't have to please anyone. When you shoot a wedding, you have someone always mad at you that you didn't get the right angle or something. You get a lot of complaints.
>
> R: Here, we call the shots.
>
> VICKI: You're more autonomous.
>
> R: Right, no one is telling us what to do.
>
> N: Here, we help other people. Like when *COPS* is here, they follow us around because they know they're going to see something.

V: *COPS* the show?

N: Yeah, they're here every year. Rick and I were in the last year's show. I was helping them set up a shot when the police busted it up. They're cool guys. We talk a lot about equipment.

Together, the men established a hierarchy of video production based on their power to "call the shots" and lead the production. Though it was clear that Rick and Nate placed themselves above wedding photographers, another liminal profession, they saw themselves as relatively equal to the reality television crew they helped by letting them "follow us."

Independence was important to defining a soft-core professional as a craftsman, someone dedicated to the perfection of the art. In this sense, professionalism was a way of identifying one's technique, discipline, and dedication in the face of work that was standardized, subservient, and *only* about wages. In Rick's words, "Video is just another extension of my creative side. That's why I can take my time and be interactive, because I'm not working on the clock. There was a guy last year who was shooting for like an hour and then put his camera in the room so he could go party. I saw him with this woman and said, 'What the heck are you doing?' He said he was paid to just get an hour every day, so that's what he did. Me, I'm going to be out here all the time perfecting my art because I'm serious about it." Rick's separation of slow artistry from quick assembly and creativity from instrumentalism seemed to deny any careerist aspirations. They were tinkerers, hobbyists, artists—all terms for those whose creative labor might be considered leisure. Other cameramen likened their trade to duck hunting and fishing: two sports activities that involve patience and technique to garner the prize, whether a fish, a duck, or a naked woman. "Even the worst day of fishing beats going to work," said Fred, reminding me that even if they were not having the best time of their lives, at least they were not doing their regular day jobs.

The freedom of the profession allowed the cameramen to experiment as well, as evidenced by technology talk. At first, the continuous chatting about technology seemed like a tangential issue in the fieldwork. For months, I paid little attention to the camera model numbers and zoom capacity numbers that cameramen frequently shared with me. Yet this was precisely the kind of talk that helped initiate me into group conversations with them. Rick, for example, was eager to show me a milk carton he had cut up to use as a light diffuser. Attached with a strip of Velcro, the box helped Rick resolve the problematic harsh lighting in evening shots. Other men similarly showed off their reconstructed pieces of equipment: a camera rewired through a metal limb, another with a light made indestructible by encasing it in steel, plastic canopies to protect against flying or falling debris. Many had homemade hairpin triggers for their owners' nimble fingers. By tinkering with technologies, the men positioned themselves as the future innovators in the field of reality shooting.

In these ways, definitions of professionalism integrated the lost values of amateurism that Patricia Zimmerman documented at the turn of the past century, such as the freedom and fluidity among classes, the potential for upward mobility through internal competitions, and the validation and inalienability of creative labor.[26] Formed into almost exclusively male communities of camera enthusiasts, both the amateur cameramen of yesterday and the professional cameramen of today distinguished themselves by dipping into the "cultural reservoir for the liberal pluralist ideals" through social relations "dislodged from the economic by scientism, the division of labor, and the cult of expertise."[27] At the same time, both groups stressed the economic potential of their innovations. Avid hobbyists in the 1890s hoped to develop a new technology that would become the market standard. These amateur entrepreneurs reproduced the "residual ideology of the craftsperson who had sole control over the production and distribution of products, while they simultaneously positioned themselves as beacons of technological and industrial progress."[28] This effort to be both free of the market while controlling its future positioned the men through two contradictory discourses of masculinity, one that eschewed control, the other that embraced it.

Professionals as Not-Feminine In what was a self-conscious performance both for me and for other bystanders, tech talk was a way of performing a heterosexualized masculinity. When they demonstrated their gadgets, the men frequently switched the camera light on and off when it was aimed at my chest. The merging of masteries here, technological and sexual, was a way of putting me in my place. As they looked at the light, I could not help gazing down at my own object status. They never focused their cameras on each other. We are men in control and you are neither male nor in control, they seemed to assert in these moments.

Beyond job skills or career status, the soft-core cameramen phrased their professionalism in gendered and sexualized terms. Rick and others used language that exuded a rugged and tough masculinity, from calling the street a "war zone" to using the term *dog pack* to describe the men who mobbed a woman for a shot. Like sportsmen, cameramen were fishing and shooting prey, in this case, a select group of women revealing themselves in public places. Conversely, they referred to their cameras as sex objects that gave power to the user. In the words of one videographer about his Canon XL-2, "I have my eye on the XL-2. Every time I touch that thing, I fall in love. It's awesome. Very sensitive. . . . I used to get so much less power for the same price." This version of masculinity is not exclusive to soft-core production. Allusions to battles and animalistic behavior already pepper the television industry's trade propaganda, which uses soft-core imagery and action-film narratives to market new film technologies to "what is apparently an ideal camera operator," according to Caldwell.[29] Cameramen frequently aligned themselves with this ideal, striving to show their ability to control lights and ladies equally in the chaotic street settings.

Yet control also had to be fun. The merger of leisure and labor articulated through professionalism constructed a masculine identity within what Bill Osgerby has called the "Playboy philosophy" of the self-made ladies' man.[30] The philosophy, named for Hugh Hefner's persona, constructed a successful man distinguished in his individual prowess in business and his libertine carousing in consumption. Forged in contrast to the homogenized and dependent corporate man of the 1950s and the 1960s, the Playboy man put the values of free enterprise in the service of a youthful "masculinity secure in its consumerism."[31] By the 1970s, images of masculine hedonism spread throughout popular culture, diffusing the Playboy man as an attainable middle-class masculinity for those disciplined enough to achieve their goals. Nearly every time I met a soft-core videographer for the first time, he summoned these images through the story of the "party": the one that drew him to the job, the Mardi Gras, and the babes.

I met Bob and Trick on the street, where they were already legendary among the cameramen for their direct style in getting women to strip. Bob, a middle-aged worker on oil rigs, walked directly up to women, placing himself between them and the path they were walking. Touching the multiple strands of beads around his neck, he asked women if they wanted beads or, if they had some already, "Do you want to add to your collection?" Trick interacted less, but both shot the flash if a woman cooperated. After an hour or so, we retreated to a bar where I asked Trick if the job got boring after a while. He responded: "Look I wouldn't do this if it wasn't fun. Last year, we threw the best party. [The video company owner] gets this house, and we had everyone with us. *Playboy*, *Penthouse*, *Girls Gone Wild*, FHM, they all came to our party. And I didn't even shoot because I was having a good time. Then this gorgeous woman comes running over to me. I don't recognize her. She's the *Penthouse* Playmate of the year. I shot her photo at the past Mardi Gras and she wants to party with *me*." Trick stressed his sexual appeal in the porn community as more central than the work itself. Together Bob and Trick discussed the parties that they had been invited to, which video crews they had had fun with, and the women that threw themselves at their feet. This conversation, which lasted for nearly an hour, bridged the seeming contradiction between leisure and labor by implying that the party was the primary reason to work during Mardi Gras.

It also blurred the line between technical and sexual masteries in meeting their combined goals. Work routines incorporated flattery and humor to woo the women they sought. Rehearsed lines such as, "Your parents won't see you, unless, of course, they buy porn," used a bit of reverse psychology to convince a woman to flash for them on camera. Routines similarly incorporated psychological insights. One kept cameramen from touching their subjects: "Lots of girls will show [themselves] all night, but touch them and that just shuts them down." In this way, men's claims to understand women helped them perfect their techniques on the street. Rick, for example, reflected on why one woman who had resisted flashing that evening finally consented for him: "She won't do it for other guys because she knows she just wants the bunnies. It's that fantasy of theirs that I have to maintain. She's got all the other beads, but she likes pink. I mean everything she was wearing was pink. So she sees the bunnies and has to have them, but she won't show for anything. For a while, she was trying to get them for free, but then she understood I needed the shot. She was just afraid about her parents seeing it, but I convinced her that was unlikely. . . . At that age, it's all about parental approval. I had to know how to close the deal." Rationalizing his female subject's need to collect cute objects while not disappointing dad, Rick attributes his ability to "close the deal" to his knowledge of her desires, needs, and inhibitions. Gender and sexual knowledge thus reinforced action, both motivating routine behaviors and then explaining them in terms of their success or failure.

In another memorable negotiation, a woman who had flashed before would not do it again. One by one, the experienced men tried to bait her with flower beads and teddy bears. When she suddenly flashed for a strand of NASCAR-branded signs, even a veteran videographer was shocked, though pleasantly so. "She knew exactly what she wanted. She went right for #24 Jeff Gordon, just like my dad," he said, now seeing her as an assertive consumer of racing paraphernalia, more like his dad than like a "woman." These shifting narratives of who women were and what they wanted reflected the flexible and unpredictable conditions of the work itself, spurring the men to adapt various masculinities on the street in response. At times, they saw women as consumers par excellence in an open marketplace of options. Accordingly, the professionals willingly embellished themselves with girlie necklaces of assorted pink baubles or toted tens of assorted-color baby T-shirts, tanks, and thongs, embodying the shopping mall that they presumed women sought. At other times, professionals framed women as the weaker sex, in need of protection from the dangers of the street. They acted chivalrously when intervening to prevent aggression or violence toward women, and even paternally when they guided unknowing women away from police officers looking to arrest them for lewd conduct. These performances coexisted with the more predatory male performances, which fancied women as objects or targets of opportunity. The plasticity of their performances as gendered and sexual beings promised to please and satisfy the range of actors in their workplaces: from their female subjects, to their male employers, to themselves.

Together, these masculine performances were both practical and symbolic to definitions of professionalism. They figured male-female interactions in terms that ultimately generated exchange value in the masculine world of media production. Whether through genuine gifting, false flattery, or physical protection, men protected their property, which they could later exploit for their own commercial uses. According to Sam Binkley, sexual relationships after the sexual revolution have premised gendered and sexual identities as both "autonomous object[s] of manipulation and creative play" and as "technique[s] of self-realization and mutual exploration through its perfection as a craft."[32] The soft-core

economy demands that these private modes of relating become public strategies for success. Against the straightness of corporate culture
and the unruliness of amateur culture, "the culture of post-Fordism demanded the insurrectionary body of the swinger, living in the immediacy
of his consumer choices, an endlessly original, personal, and expressive
body of insatiable needs and manifold sensualities."[33] The soft-core cameramen both acted as swingers and served a swinger-consumer base,
represented by their exacting male bosses.

Not everyone could reconcile the swinger persona with the professional ethos of the job. The gendered and sexualized nature of the routines and their product contributed to the difficulties that cameramen
had in mobilizing the symbolic power of professionalism, which generates a sense of awe among ordinary people.[34] To the contrary, the more
assertive cameramen were about their professional knowledge, the more
likely their subjects confounded their assumptions, often with negative
or violent results. One female pedestrian, who happened to be a dancer
on her way to work, publicly outed Bob's precarious claims on professionalism, screaming, "Fuck you; *I'm* a professional!" Performative moments of masculinity insinuated that outsiders, including myself, the
female professor, recognize the mastery of the opposite sex embedded in
their professionalism. Yet women often defied their authority, putting
the men in their place on the periphery of an industrial geography of
media power.

Boundary Work for Playboy Professionals For those on the margins of
fields of cultural production, professionalism has been the discourse of
first resort. Howard Becker, for example, describes how jazz musicians in
the 1940s created their own norms during performances, such as sitting
on a stage, to ensure that others recognized their special status.[35] Norms
coded cultural producers as separate from their consumers. The closer
others perceive the producer to the consumer, the more producer groups
struggle to convince lay people that they are acting professionally.[36] Wedding videographers, as studied by James Moran, are a case in point.
Located at the bottom of industrial hierarchies in media production,
wedding videographers invest in expensive equipment and join trade
associations to distinguish their videos from an imagined "inept Uncle
Charlie," whose amateur video has no saleable worth.[37] Videographers
thus appeal to a "discourse of professionalism to negotiate their amateur

standing in the market at large."[38] Professionalism promises television workers the chance to be professional without a recognized profession. It offers a strategy for the weak to safeguard some symbolic status against amateurs and a material payoff in the form of exchange value.

The distinctions that soft-core videographers drew between themselves and amateurs, other people working with cameras, and corporate media employees highlighted the thin line that barely separated their professional production ideals from those of amateur consumption, and the masculine identity that joined all of them. As Caldwell's work with Hollywood production cultures has demonstrated, professionals' investment in masculinity is ever present through insider narratives that personify technical industry workers as wartime soldiers, daring mavericks, and romantic heroes.[39] What made the soft-core workers unique was the primacy of these masculine identities, whether as a craftsman or a crooner, over other forms of professional capital, such as exclusive access to resources, skill sets, or knowledge. The bifurcation of symbolic and material benefits in soft-core professionals' work indicates the troubled relationship between media work and "the professional project," which historically allowed workers to maximize their value by translating "scarce resources—special knowledge and skills—into another—social and economic rewards," in the words of Magali Sarfatti Larson.[40] The precarity of professionalism has echoed throughout the industry. The fragmentation of above-the-line guilds and below-the-line unions continues to frustrate U.S. labor organizers, while a study of BBC television producers attributed the historic lack of "professional feeling" to the inability to forge a collective identity that would control occupational destiny.[41] The television labor market overall seems to exacerbate workers' status as semiprofessionals, emphasizing professionalism as a means for gatekeeping rather than collectivism.

Like a self-fulfilling prophesy, professionals' solidarities with leisure consumers and their scarce wages proved convenient for the employers or buyers of their video footage. Hobbyists did not deserve professional compensation. Tinkerers did not need to be paid benefits, such as health care or retirement, nor were they claimed on tax returns as working for someone else. Rather, they were self-employed, evidenced by the promise of a check that might never arrive. As avid sportsmen, they could be relied on to ensure their personal safety and guard against workplace hazards. Training was minimal, or unnecessary, as two employers explained:

EMPLOYER 1: I tell them to buy a pair of shoes because by the end, you have to throw them away.

EMPLOYER 2: We want our guys to work. They're not out there to party. They're out there all day and they sleep from 5 a.m. to noon and do it again.

EMPLOYER 1: Friday to Sunday.

EMPLOYER 2: It's total in the trenches.

VICKI: Do you train the guys?

EMPLOYER 1: What's to train?

EMPLOYER 2: It's not rocket science.

From business owners' points of view, the cameramen were neither craftsmen nor career professionals. As indicated by the military metaphor of the trenches, the men who worked for some employers might as well have been soldiers, recruited into a fraternity of shooters whose chance for glory was compensation enough.

The glory, of course, was the party that few had time to enjoy, recreating the producers' paradox. The identity of the Playboy man resurges at a time and among men who lack both Hefner's capital and his career potentials, reinforcing Steven Cohan's argument that masculine performances frequently mask real social differences.[42] Soft-core reality workers, like Trick and Bob, reproduced representations of a masculine hedonism from talking about the party to walking on the street, even though their actual practices more ambiguously served postfeminist and homosocial male consumer desires, such as when they focused on wearing enough toy bunny beads and showing off their cameras. Other masculine identities supplemented the hedonistic one, but no matter how false the fantasy of the party animal was, it returned every time new recruits hit the streets and talked to anyone for the first time. It was this identity performance that was central to the needs of the companies that hired them.

The Wages of Professional Performances

Even as media industries have cheapened their labor, they demand their workers' professionalism. While the cameramen developed their own internal standards of professionalism, the industries that hired them imposed external standards as well. The professionalization of soft core brought the workers for the denigrated genre into line with other corporate media workers.[43] The corporations' impetus to professionalization is clear. Professionals were easier to control from a distance. Companies wanted video professionals who would discipline themselves when they were far away on location shoots. There, company standards or ethics channeled each employee to work independently within the limits of whatever increased the bottom line. Meanwhile, a professional workforce also added value to the product line. By calling their videographers professionals, soft-core companies stressed the respectable quality of their products, as the phrase *professional-grade camera* implies. This new kind of professionally made product through producer performance reversed historical alchemies that detached objective producers from their objects of production, such as in the case of news journalists.[44] These two definitions of professional—as in a professional product and professional self-control—condensed in the bodies of the cameramen they hired. Soft-core reality industries recruited camera operators who could both produce and embody the brand. The struggle for a masculine identity demonstrated so prominently on the street now attached itself to a self-making project that men could market to their employers, and subsequently to their perceived consumer base.

This immaterial labor was not without its own psychic wages, as work figures centrally in masculine identities in the United States. The sociologist Everett Hughes in the middle of the twentieth century described work as a psychoanalytic mirror: "A man's work is one of the things by which he is judged, and certainly one of the more significant things by which he judges himself."[45] Since the nineteenth century, the professional achieved his identity by controlling production. The "organization man," writes David Noble, championed over cycles of capitalist growth: "The bold, confident, and pioneering spirit which moved him and his associates, and his various concerns . . . to counter the forces of instability inherent in the evolving capitalist economy."[46] Loyalty to corporate goals provided men with an environment that fostered each one's talents at relatively little personal economic risk.[47] In return, the professional traded his autonomy for the central pillars of patriarchal authority: power, prestige, and wealth.[48] Under late capitalism, however, the human body has an exchange value no longer bound to identities, according to Donald M. Lowe.[49] He cites consumer markets that tap into sexual fantasies that transgress binaries of female passivity and male activity.[50] Conversely, workers manipulate their gender and sex to produce a simulated self that is more marketable. These transformations could be extended to a wide range of workers in the new television economy, as I will explore in the following chapter, but in the case of soft-core videographers, the new sexual semiotics for consumption meant that men continuously had to negotiate the model of the professional as patriarch with their malleable abilities to satisfy a market for their bodies.

Demands of the Brand Unlike pioneer cameramen in the early to mid-1990s, who stumbled on the industry as visitors or were invited to shoot by a friend, soft-core professionals responded to online advertisements or were recruited through or directly at shooting locations. Corporate executives in the field invested heavily in a standardized workforce contracted exclusively for building the company brand. Management did not want hobbyists or tinkerers on the payroll, but instead recruited laborers who would self-identify as professionals while still earning less than camera operators for television industries. To do this, Mantra, Tahi, and a host of other start-up companies hired full-time but generally short-term camera crews who worked as teams toward the total quality management of college party events that they sponsored. The language of control over technology migrated to cover entire social venues of bar staff, video subjects, and potential video consumers. Corporate managers invested carefully in hiring people who could play management and marketing roles by self-identifying as professionals and as the youthful studs portrayed in the videos. In other words, soft-core reality industries recruited camera operators who could both produce and embody the brand.

Companies defined professionalism visually in the first instance by asking men to submit a photo with their applications. A requirement normally reserved only for people meant to be in front of the camera, the photo helped managers select employees with the right look or style. Attitude also mattered in contracting a video crew. Sunny, a veteran who had become a crew leader for a large soft-core company, said he wanted people who believed in teamwork, shedding the cameraman's more individualist associations with professionalism. He nevertheless noted the importance of dressing fashionably urbane and hip.[51] He described his own interview after sending his photo in: "I just went there in jeans and a T-shirt and all these other guys were in suits. I was sure they wouldn't want me. But the interview process isn't looking for that. Now when I interview people, I know that the first thing we're looking for is like-ability. Do you get along with everyone? Because we travel together ev-erywhere, so it has to be someone we like." Sunny felt his casual dress worked because it displayed something that the company was searching for: a fun-loving and likable dude with a malleable look. Once on board, Sunny began to recruit others using similar criteria. His standpoint changed, as was marked by his speech transition from the position of the "interviewee" to the "we." "Each cameraman and woman we pick for their looks," he said, surveying his current crew. His handpicked crew resem-bled a catalog of multicultural Benetton models, each representing a market segment of youth culture trends. As he described his team, they were an Asian American grommit, a buff African American athlete, a light-skinned African American with Rasta dreads, a clean-cut Latino, and a large Anglo football player. He described himself as playing the role of the blond Anglo "California beach boy," though he was actually from Philadelphia.

The emphases on looks and attitude, characteristics associated with women in front of the camera, now extended to men behind the camera. Both were to perform and to be looked at, though men would still be the professionals controlling the action. This became clear in the various nightclub shoots in which members of the video crew became celebrities. In one college club commandeered by a soft-core reality video company, a disclaimer to shoot in the club mimicked those used on the videos or on Internet sites to sell the videos:

> Disclaimer:
> Videotaping Inside!
> By coming in here,
> you consent to be on tape.
> You must be 18 to enter.

Inside the bar and on the dance floor, the video crew was the center of attention for sales. A disc jockey inside announced, "Let's give it up for *Ladies Gone Loca!*" every so often, while promotional materials for the company littered the club walls.[52] Crew members dressed in tight-fitting and matching outfits, making them highly visible in the crowd.

Soft-core video companies demanded a body already manipulated to have a particular look and then disciplined it through the norms of pro-fessionalism. The masculine performances on the street were counterbalanced by the feminization of the videographers' forms that were to be looked at and to be consumed like the representations of the women in the videos themselves. In a reversal of the striptease scenes in the videos themselves, men were the objects of a female gaze.[53] Male college students strode up to crew members' faces, shouting, "You have the best job man!" or "I fuckin' love you guys!" while females tried to negotiate with the crew for company-logo trucker hats, a reward for compliance to be on camera while interacting with the men behind the camera. In numerous instances, women's five seconds of fame were an attempt to flirt with the celebrity videographer while dozens of men cheered him on. The video crew knew its own allure was part of the product, and nearly none of the public spectacles were actually caught on tape. Sunny never turned his camera on, even as naked and kissing women paraded in front of him. He emphasized, "We do this for them," pointing to a row of the male fans. "Like I said, we're recruiting. Someone here will see us doing this and want to join us."

This candid moment Sunny shared with me both showed off and asserted his unique role in the video market. At the bar, he and the crews working for video companies had celebrity status. Male customers took turns identifying who they saw as hot women for Sunny to catch in the act. Club DJs announced the arrivals and departures of company crews as if they were rock stars, encouraging cheers and jeers. Sometimes they even brought their own media celebrities to raise the hype. Admittedly, it felt more glamorous to be with the company guys than with the free-lancers. As they gave special passes for parties and let me dance with them on their roped-off balcony, I understood the appeal of the image of the labor for our audience. Men approached me as if I was suddenly the life of the party, and a woman offered to buy a free *Ladies Gone Loca* hat off my head. For the crew members, the public attention and brushes with stardom perpetuated the idea that they could work and party, the dream that lured the street cameramen. "We fly in and have a good time. I came in [to New Orleans] once and it was a total party. I didn't shoot anything all weekend," Sunny boasted to me. The line, part real and part marketing, emphasized the seemingly casual control that the camera crews exerted over the crowds, and that their employer exerted over them.

In the meantime, cameramen made everyone's bodies into walking billboards. They distributed their logo shirts to the contestants and logo hats to the audience, clearly marking the territory with their brand. These routines generated marketing buzz, if not content by prepping future video subjects. Women wearing the free hats could be spotted wandering the city all weekend as mobile company ads. Some cameramen spent much of their time convincing women to toss out their competitor's hats, rather than to flash on tape for them.

Teamwork and mutual camaraderie were guises for autopolicing and other-surveillance. "We drink and party together, but on the job you have to be in control and get it done," one crew leader summed it up. The party that drew recruits to the field was now limited to the rewards of not partying on the job, making soft core little different from any other company with an evening happy hour. Fledgling producers who emphasized their ability to control the party found swift in-house promotion. "I could have gone to Dreamworks, but after six months here, I'm a production manager. I could work for two years there and never be more than an assistant," said Marcos, a University of Texas film school grad, who now was pitching his own themed video series. With advancement, his responsibilities on the road expanded, including keeping strict budgets, managing transportation for crew members between locations, and even gathering some audience responses from locals who could tell him how successful the party was compared to that of his competitors and those of past years.

In contrast, professionals who partied on the job received pink slips before Mardi Gras Day even ended. Sunny said the week was "training" after he put one of the new recruits "on probation" for becoming very inebriated. He explained, "That's why we train people here. If they can take all the distractions, they can take anything. We want professionals. We don't care if they drink, as long as they keep in control. When they put on the shirt, they're representing the company. That's the company rules." Although he felt some unease with the reprimand, Sunny was angry that he would have to pick up the slack. He had been doing this job for a little more than a year, and was tired of being the brand.

VICKI: So there's a high turnover rate?

SUNNY: Yeah. Most guys can't take this night after night.

V: Take what?

S: This. [He points to the drunks weaving in the center of the room.] It's crowd control and talking with people all night. I hate that the most. It's the same every night. I can't even stand dealing with the questions: What do I make? Do I party with the girls? Boy, I must be lucky, they say. These guys have no clue. I'm working my ass off. There's two sides to this job. The one they see and the one that only the staff sees.

More than the long hours on their feet, constant travel, and dorm-room-style living in hotels or tour buses, the emotional labor of their jobs exhausted Sunny and his colleagues.[54] Although they always emphasized how well off and lucky they were, the balance between putting up a professional front to pose as amateurs while still getting the job done exacted a toll.

Pricing Professionalism   Caught between the stresses of making fun into a profession and himself into a product, Marcos was the exception to the rule. Most workers stayed in their jobs for limited stints, with a minority staying for five years or more. Three years seemed like eons to younger producers, who seemed insecure about both staying in the job and moving beyond it afterward. Older producers, who now worked exclusively as company freelancers, felt disillusioned that they could ever cash in on the work or leave their day jobs. These problems in exchanging types of capital between industries frequently presented themselves as crises of conscience, illuminating the importance of professionalism to the men's senses of gendered and sexualized selves.

Bob was one of those few producers who had witnessed the industry's transformation in the late 1990s. Away from Trick, Bob did not mention parties or adoring women. In contrast, he talked of the routine nature of the work, one in which men and women were more antagonistic toward each other than enamored. He mulled whether he even liked the work.

BOB: You know, I see all kinds of boobs, but that's all they are to me. I don't care about them. Oh, this one is big, this one is small. What do I care?

VICKI: They probably care about them.

B: You think those girls out there care?

V: Some of them, yeah.

B: Well, I don't fucking care what they think. In all my years, I had one girl who came up to me. She said she had only shown her tits to two guys in the world: her boyfriend and me.

V: So it meant something to her.

B: Yeah, but that was the only one.

v: And you can't imagine her point of view when she flashes?

b: No, I just don't care. I have to pay child support. . . .

In our ensuing exchange, Bob appeared both bored and bitter, which he attributed partially to the women in his private life (his two ex-wives and his mother) and partially to uncooperative women on the street. At the same time, it was clear that the problem with women was money. Bob worked on an oil rig when not shooting, a manual job with little future. In his agreement with his video employer, he received $150 for a full tape or $150 per day, whichever cost the company less. Neither of these jobs would pay his debts, but he could not afford to leave the video gig. "I take what I can get," he said. "This is a part-time job. I have to pay $700 a goddamn month in child support, so I want the money." Still, he seemed stuck, both physically and emotionally. In defiance of his contract employer, who wanted him "out on the street all night," Bob spent three hours with me.

Like many of the cameramen, Bob confided that he felt disrespected by others who did not consider him a professional. The less-experienced and younger recruits, however, viewed these conflicts differently than veterans like Bob. As people still in their twenties, they cared far more than the older producers about what others thought about them, and they wanted to make a good impression. Their concern for what other people thought extended to the ways in which the young cameramen spoke to me as someone clearly older and already in a recognized profession. At first, they identified me in my black leather jacket as an undercover cop or a journalist. They often lied to me, telling me that they were older, more experienced, and more confident in the position than they actually were. When I could convince them I was a professor, some realizing that I knew some of their own professors, they were struck with some awe and embarrassment. Some revealed their true names and ages. Others wanted to pick my brain about their future career perspectives. Though they were quick to name the people in their lives that supported their decision to earn money taping naked college coeds, they also confessed that many of their parents and partners disapproved of their job choice. Even Sunny had difficulty detaching his new work from his sense that it had to be kept a secret from his family: "I told my mom and she was cool with it, but my dad? Not so much. He's a born-again Christian and he doesn't approve of most things that I do. He heard through my step-mom. I told her not to tell, but he called me anyway. He was calm but definitely not cool with it."

Whereas employers talked about weak recruits unable to handle the workload, the crowds, and the easy access to drugs and alcohol, the people behind the cameras spoke of their feelings of inauthenticity in their roles. This was particularly marked for the rare woman who tried to become a soft-core videographer. Kylie, a photography student, came to Mardi Gras to work on a product line dedicated to showing men getting naked in public.[55] She was one of only four women I witnessed collecting commercial footage of soft-core scenes over the course of three Mardi Gras seasons. Despite her training and a positive attitude, she didn't last more than a few days in the job. This meant that she would go back to the West Coast after Mardi Gras instead of on a road tour of college parties. Her eyes welled with tears as she tried to shrug off her disappointment. "I'm glad I got to experience it," she told me.

In these moments, the self-assurance that they were professionals seemed to erode, revealing the insecurity that they were, in fact, amateurs. Elvis started with one of the companies three years before we met, making him a veteran in his crew. He responded to his company's ad specifically, he said, because it was recruiting cameramen for "adult movies, not porn." Six months prior to our conversation, he had begun dating a Hollywood actress, and though she seemed fine with his weekend occupation, he felt miserable.

> ELVIS: When I started, this was a dream job. I mean, I love tits. But I fell in love, I mean, hard. I'm crazy about her and can't stand what I'm doing. You probably want to talk to people who know what they're talking about. Well, I don't anymore. I come here supposed to do a job, and all I can think about is going home. I miss my girlfriend.
>
> VICKI: Is it that the women here don't interest you anymore?
>
> E: No, the opposite. That's the problem. Women throw themselves at me, I get a hard-on, and then I feel guilty. My girlfriend doesn't deserve that. She's completely clean, and this isn't fair to us.
>
> . . .
>
> V: Do you consider yourself a professional out here?
>
> E: With this? Not this year. In my other job [at the cable network], I'm more professional because I'm really good at it. But here now, I'm just an amateur. I mean last year, I was a total pro. Chicks were crawling all over me

and doing everything. This year my heart isn't in it. I can't even fake it, and chicks can sense that.

Elvis's angst prevented him from embracing his professional identity because he could no longer fuse his personas as the videographer and the ladies' man. He left early for the hotel that night, telling his crew leader, "Hey, I don't care. Don't pay me today." Similarly, Kylie spoke of the jarring feeling she had telling strange men to take off their clothes for a camera: "I just told a guy to do cartwheels in thong. I could never tell anyone that back home."

Despite the language of emotional control, the soft-core producers confessed feeling out of control when the ethics of professionalism did not sync perfectly with their personal morals or social values. Being thrown into social situations in which they must be in control and must control others, all the while being on display for others' consumption, proved overwhelming to many of the new recruits. Veterans survived by creating a division of labor between the management of others' emotions and the containment of their own. Eva Illouz explains that this kind of labor is common to all professions, displaying "at once the mark of a *disengaged self* (busy with self-mastery and control) and of a *sociable self*—bracketing emotions for the sake of entering in relations with others."[56] For soft-core workers, the conflicts that arose from this duality seemed to point not to the contradiction between disengagement and sociality, but to the ethics of the performances themselves. To be physically so engaged and emotionally so impassive as a professional might achieve job goals, but it seemed dishonest to the people they were at home. Once again, gender and sexuality mattered to these considerations. If Elvis felt dishonest for losing sexual control while away from his girlfriend, Kylie felt equally so when she exerted sexual control over men. So, even as professional work might have narrowed the gender gap in terms of emotional control expectations, in the words of Illouz, men and women never experienced those expectations in quite the same way.[57]

Elements of Soft Core in the New Economy for Television Professionals and Products

The Orwellian zeitgeist predicted by Henry Braverman in 1974 seems commonplace throughout labor markets today.[58] As occupations become more mechanized, professional labor becomes deskilled and degraded, treated like the vast numbers of proles who can be cheaply bought and easily replaced. While the television professional has encompassed a conflicted notion at best, the promises of the status and privilege have motivated a wide range of workers eager to partake in the maintenance of media power. Meanwhile, the rationalization and outsourcing of television labor "has worked against professionalization and craft strategies," according to Jeremy Tunstall.[59] So, although television jobs were never a stable path to social or class mobility, the centrifugal push to shift production to live soft-core events has widened the geographic scope for producers while breaking their monopoly on media power. Leaner and more mobile independent and international studios have evaded unionized labor, preferring younger and more flexible workers.[60] The shift from permanent labor to freelancers has depressed wages and has eliminated overtime for people expected to do more deskilled tasks, ironically called "multi-skilling."[61] Simpler technologies on the job eliminate the need to provide job training.[62] The erosion of traditional networks of directors, editors, actors, and technicians have further made workers more reliant on personal connections not just to gain entry to professions but also for each freelance project and the now-standard unpaid or low-paid internships that entry requires.[63] These forces have further stressed workers' collective identities, exacerbating the industries' needs for individuals whose leverage is predicated less on skills, knowledge, or talent than on the ability to do more and earn less for their technical and creative services.

Within this political economy, soft-core workers illustrate how professionalism operates as the bait in a deprofessionalized television industry marked by instability and declining material benefits. The flexibility of the term *professionalism* in soft-core cameramen's accounts encompassed a wide range of practices, goals, and beliefs, suggesting a nuanced sense of competing professionalisms in the production process, not just among the producers but also between producers, their subjects, and

their employers. Videomakers looked to alternative pleasures in professionalism when they were not paid or laid, and the party was less than
promised. They were hardly dupes. For some, shooting video offered
a sense of independence and autonomy to develop their skills. Others
earned extra cash, or dreamed of becoming members of the Hollywood
celebrity set. For nearly all, professionalism initiated them into an exclusive collectivity of heterosexual and homosocial men distinguished from
tourists or corporate drones. Soft-core reality video coded masculine
identities that men performed and altered to fit changing contexts and
strategic needs. Video professionalism was not an expression of false
consciousness; or as Moran writes, "an alibi for economic exploitation—
and rarely for artistic expression."[64] Professionalism gave access to identities that they could not otherwise experience in other forms of work or in
their day jobs. Nor was claiming professionalism what Becker called simply a form of self-flattery.[65] Certain professional identities promised the
potential for recognition in highly competitive media and entertainment
production worlds. The more corporate the employer, the more that
professionalism was a prerequisite to entering the field and a perceived
path to future mobility. To be "unprofessional" meant to be unemployed.

In the process, television executives have looked more to soft core to
fill the interstices of their programming schedules and to enhance their
bottom line. The soft-core infomercial introduced a national consumer
market to a product based around video images that previously only
appeared on television as a vice crime. A forerunner of the migratory and
repurposed text, a video clip of a thirty-second flash can exist in profitable perpetuity as it is recombined with other contents and altered to fit
medium and genre specifications. Through professionalized efforts of
soft-core workers in an industry based increasingly on reality video productions, soft core has become part of television culture through home
video, infomercials, pay-per-view, and most recently, global satellite programming. The explosion of what scholars have variously interpreted as
"striptease culture," "pornification," or the "pornography of everyday life"
has put soft-core video at the center of larger media culture trends.[66]
Focusing largely on the women who disrobe and the companies that
profit from this, the merging of soft core into the mainstream tends to
ignore the complex negotiations between the cameramen and the women
as two sets of laborers in the hierarchies of public spaces, tourist events,
and industrial norms. As this chapter has shown, cultural discourses

may prescribe repertoires that favor the cameramen's authority over the women, but they are always unstable and subject to reversals. Only in editing for television norms were those hierarchies reestablished through the careful sifting and omission of the cameramen's immaterial labors and failures.

Although I never knew how many of the aspiring soft-core workers might eventually work in television industries, it was clear that their definitions of professionalism were only as flexible as television markets would allow. It was clear that not every producer could tap into these cultural discourses or perform these professional identities with the same ease. Despite the range of potential laborers in soft-core industries, professionalism had to be embodied through a narrow set of body types and emotional dispositions. Whether due to their own perceptions of the moral universe or the expectations imposed by their employers, women continue to face industrial divisions based on gender and sexuality, despite their increase among the ranks of television professionals.[67] This implies that identity mediates different expectations. In this sense, professional expectations may have allowed workers to appropriate identities and recycle discourses related to sex, leisure, parties, hobbies, craftwork, and consumption, as long as the professional represented the branded laborer, consumer, and product, all rolled into one. The development of the soft-core professional indicates a trajectory for television labor in which the boundaries for work extend beyond production personnel and production practices to the production of the self, a trend that merits further exploration in the next chapter.

PART II

3. Sponsoring Selves

SPONSORSHIP IN PRODUCTION

The return of the television sponsor as an active part of U.S. prime-time content demonstrates the merging roles of the producer, who delights the audience, and of the advertiser, who buys access to them. In terms of content, invented terms such as *advertainment* belie the blurring of generic boundaries between entertainment programming and advertisements.[1] The intense commodification of television sets as travel destinations, wardrobes as fashion lines, and stage props as product plugs has become a visible part of the television landscape. Invisible in this process, however, are the workers who do the integration of sales and story lines, of commodities and characters. The new television economy demands laborers who excel at the art of identifying potential new sources for profits, including human subjectivities and identities. Reality television casters are examples of workers who act as sponsors in the new television economy in how they produce identities as sources of industrial profit.

In most studies of television production, the sponsor remains in the shadows, acting as a foil to producers by constraining their creativity, while playing the necessary role of investing in producers' creations. The negative associations with sponsorship hearken back to widespread and long-standing distrust of advertising, selling more generally seen as fakery at best, dishonest at worst.[2] These practices generate underlying anxieties around occupations that blur the lines between authentic human emotions and instrumental performances of emotion. As noted in the introduction, even the earliest studies of Hollywood film production derided the commodification of celebrity and workers' self-production of their personas, paralleling labor roles with the standardized and inauthentic mass products they produced.[3] The fragmentation of media markets into specialized niches during the past thirty years has done little to allay scholarly concerns about commodification. Nowhere is this more obvious than in the recent explosion of reality programming, which, as June Deery relates, commodifies the most private moments of daily life. The production of reality programming, she writes, "taps into the deep cultural anxieties about the profit motive taking priority over everything."[4] The primacy of profits over artistry and the emotionality of practice over rational skills together push sponsorship to the margins of production studies as a contaminant to creativity and professionalism.

As pivotal players in television sponsorship today, reality television casters exemplify the levels of commodification that saturate production processes. If we revisit the classic role of the sponsor in Dallas Smythe's famed equation, the sponsor produces television content that delivers its target audience for its own advertising needs.[5] Casters take the guesswork out of that delivery by packaging the audience inside the actual television content. Reality programs are thus like game shows, talk shows, or other genres that recruit live studio audiences into production. Yet, much as in the case of diversified programming contents for niche audiences, casters excel at producing highly selective casts to indicate narrowcast audiences. As one longtime caster explained, "We in the industry frown on the job title 'recruiter' because we are looking at something specific for each character." If the audience is the product for sale to the advertiser, then the reality-show participant is the free (or nearly free) sample. Like traditional television sponsors, reality casters develop contests, events, and marketing schemes to *buy access* to those desirable participants who could stand for both the program's talent and its preferred audience. Today, they are both producers and advertisers, creating the program by providing the raw materials for its production and sale.

Beyond this traditional form of commodification, though, casters sell themselves both to their potential casts and to their employers as the authorities over casts as commodities. Much as the soft-core cameramen in the previous chapter, they labor emotionally through listening, relating, bonding, and networking, while still maintaining control in order to harness seemingly genuine feelings to industrial needs. Acting as the mediators between people who are both outside and inside the television industry, casters must embody their employers' brand at times, while disassociating from the program as experts at other times. These interrelated processes of identifying and selling oneself and others join reality casters to other new economy workers for whom communication is the primary goal of professional self-definition, as first identified by Amitai Etzioni in 1969.[6] Casters indicate the importance of identification as an invisible labor practice throughout the new television economy.

That casters' core skills lie in judging and then creatively communicating the commodity value of humans, including themselves, belies the anxiety now spread throughout the television labor market as the divisions between selves and objects disappear. As Eva Illouz writes on emotion work as a coping mechanism: "Communication has . . . become an emotional skill for navigating an environment fraught with uncertainties and conflicting imperatives and collaborating with others."[7] Contracted seasonally and paid less than the key grip on a set, reality casters' anxieties around commodification processes reflected their own low value and status in production chains. Some earned as little as $500 a week, and most earned only up to about one-tenth of the salary of the production directors in the already denigrated genre. "We don't even get invited to the cast party," one reality caster told me with a roll of the eyes. Although a few of the casters have moved within the hierarchy of reality production, the glass ceilings for casters prevented them from moving into more prestigious television or film genres, reinforcing the lines between the professionals who create programs and the semiprofessionals who merely sponsor them. Being both essential and practically invisible marked the central contradiction that framed reality casters as a labor community in the new television economy.

I focus on this contradiction using multiple methods conducted irregularly over three years, from 2004 through 2007. Casters comprise a working population in a field site that is more a network than a neighborhood, to paraphrase Stewart Muir.[8] My research began on the phone, with phone calls placed to reality television casters resulting in twenty interviews over the course of three years.[9] In the meantime, I attended casting calls, bringing me as close to Hollywood as Burbank and as far away as the suburban shopping mall near my home university. There is no center to the caster's trade. Rather, Hollywood travels symbolically with the caster as she or he searches for access to the audience; this cachet can be leveraged as part of the prestige of the program and of the caster's authority. The casters' mobility presented its own challenges to understanding what they actually do. Time spent on the phone, on the computer, and scouting potential cast members does not lend itself to ethnographic study. The diversity of casting practices could not be observed simply because so much of what casters do is private, intimate, and, quite frankly, awkward for an outsider's presence. The narrative that comes across in the interviews and the field notes offers a tapestry of reflections, both casters' and my own, on how casters saw themselves and their work to commodify others given their diverse experiences.

Sponsors of Yesterday and Today

Even as more workers in television production do the work of buying and selling the commodities that give programs economic value, the word *sponsor* continues to be a symbol of debasement and derision, both in the industry and in the academy. The sponsor's role has typically been to sell a product by buying access to audiences through a program. This role generates the financing later invested in the production directly as well as indirectly through spot advertising, product placement, and viral approaches, such as Web site buys and promotional events. These commercial imperatives are now part and parcel of many television genres, especially reality programming, and their production personnel, including casters. The steady merging of sponsorship and production and sponsors' roles with producers' roles indicate the need to explore the labor of commodification in the new television economy.

Negative associations with sponsors as distinct from producers date to the beginnings of broadcasting, when debates around television and commercialism juxtaposed art to advertising and public service to consumer exploitation. As early as the 1930s, advocates for a noncommercial broadcasting system in the United States argued that advertisers "cultivate the lower appeals" and may even "threaten the very life of civilization by subjecting the human mind to all sorts of new pressures and selfish exploitations."[10] These popular sentiments, which peaked in the wake of the 1950s quiz show scandals, were codified, ironically, by the industry itself through self-imposed rules that relegated sponsorship to an indirect investment economy of commercial spots.[11] Subsequent FCC (Federal Communications Commission) rulings reinforced the binary between creative and commercial content, separating sponsors and producers in theory as the "church and state" of broadcasting, in the words of Robin Andersen.[12]

The fragmentation of network dominance and the cross-media merger mania of the late 1980s redefined this division between sponsors and producers. In the wake of cable television, pay-per-view, new digital platforms, and new technologies that allowed viewers to "time-shift" television contents and avoid commercial messages altogether, both advertisers and producers searched for new means to locate and deliver audiences.[13] Driving down the costs of commercial spot buys, advertisers demanded more reassurance that audience measurements reflected the consumers they sought. In turn, producers aimed to protect advertising investments by generating more data evidencing target audiences and by giving their clients more creative control. Producers guaranteed advertisers direct access to target audiences through the direct sponsorship of programming content. Together, producers and sponsors began pursuing audience niches through an array of surveillance technologies and measurement techniques.[14] Nowhere has this convergence of producers and sponsors been more blatant than in reality television. The surge in reality formats to fill television schedules has increasingly relied on sponsors to shoulder preproduction costs and on producers to integrate advertising into much of the programming content. All the while, reality programs have promised to deliver their sponsors niche audiences that seem elusive in the new television economy.

Reality sponsorship has spurred protests, initiated legal battles, and revived outcries reminiscent of those against early broadcasting commercialism. Some critics parallel reality television with mere advertisements, lacking creativity or artistry. Others see the expanded role of sponsors as an ethical threat to the public interest.[15] Product placement disclosure rules recently proposed by Commercial Alert illustrate the salience of this issue in the public sphere.[16] Whereas ethical critiques have centered on the role of the medium in informing the liberal consumer, labor critiques have focused on the importance of television in the liberal work sphere. As sponsored reality programs have displaced other programming formats that rely on studio writers, for example, labor unions have decried their workers as the scabs in the new television economy.[17] At least one strike organized by the Writers Guild of America, West (wgaw) and the Screen Actors Guild targeted reality product placement as the enemy of production personnel. "For actors and writers being forced to shoehorn products into their work—whether they fit or not—there are issues of creative rights, consultation, and fair compensation," the WGAW president Patric Verrone said in a way that linked labor concerns to creative freedoms.[18]

What these critiques sidestep are the ways in which buying and selling —crassly put, the work of the sponsor and of advertising personnel—have become integral to nearly every job in the studio production hierarchy, which focuses on the audience as the primary object of these exchanges. The audience commodity, introduced by Dallas Smythe in 1977, typically referred to the object that advertisers buy access to when purchasing a thirty-second spot on a network.[19] In a contained television economy, Nielsen ratings and shares were the standard means for valuing the commodity audience, promising buyers that attention to program content would ensure attention to ads.[20] This guarantee, though flawed in its own methodological assumptions, was the playing field that industry personnel agreed to, permitting the neat separation of producers and sponsors.[21] It was a way of reducing the anxiety of not knowing and thus ensuring job security, in Ien Ang's analysis.[22] In the multimedia, cross-media environment, guarantees of audience attention have become scarce, and the methods for evidencing the value of the commodity audience have expanded. Creators and marketers have turned their attentions toward audience measurement, not just to what people might consume but also to psychographics, which purport to describe how people consume. To this end, a series of occupations in the new television economy work to create an interactive economy that puts consumers to work in their own commodification.[23] They track Web site traffic, fan blogs, song downloads, call-in voting, and other forms of viewer interactivity as means to haggle over commodity prices, and, hence, the costs of program development, production, distribution, and future sustainability.

With this mission in mind, enter the reality program caster: a member of the production hierarchy who has taken over the role of generating the new cast for each reality program, from their initial development to their last season. Reality casts are commodities in this new interactive economics of television financing. Casts drive interactive content over the phone and on the Web, which evidences the audience commodity. Casting calls generate buzz for a program in the preproduction stages. Cast members themselves can be the objects of product placement, as demonstrated when the Slim Fast company in 2006 paid for a contestant to join *Dancing with the Stars* as part of a reportedly $7–10 million integration deal.[24] As part of their work routines, casters juggle the various ways to profit from casts and cast data. This commodification is an ongoing process, because, like other goods, casts follow basic principles of creative destruction; they must be regenerated with each series and season to maintain value. The dangers are self-evident, as exemplified with the pop-song contest series *American Idol*. The series had both the highest number of product placements and ad rates in 2006, but it nevertheless failed to develop a significantly different cast in 2007, eroding advertiser confidence; the series had reached a "market saturation point," according to the trade journal *Advertising Age*.[25] Maintaining casts as commodities immerses casters in all aspects of salesmanship, such as branding programs to draw new cast applicants, packaging cast members for sale to networks, and selling themselves as the authorities over the product. With their emotional charms and market savvy, casters must convince buyers that the cast will produce in the form of other audience measures. In these senses, reality casters are sponsors in the new television economy. Subject to the generalized critiques of sponsorship and commercialism in general, they nonetheless play crucial roles in the economics of much of their employers' livelihoods.

Reality Casters
NEW JOBS IN AND OUT OF HOLLYWOOD

Although job casting dates to the beginnings of the film studio era, reality casting is a relatively recent segment of the craft. Like that on other Hollywood casters, the literature on the trade is confined to personal recollections of casters or to studies of who is cast, leaving a gap between who casters are and the effects of their labor.[26] Like casters for scripted programs, reality casters occupy numerous roles in their daily work. They seek talent and nurture it, while acting as gatekeepers and communication liaisons for the executive producers. They also search for similar traits in finding a person for a role, looking for the dramatic potential in each actor's skill set. In the reality genre, however, the participant's delivery must seem spontaneous, natural, and exaggerated, providing what Laura Grindstaff aptly referred to as the "money shot" in her likening of talk shows to porn flicks.[27] Casters need nonunion talent to read and respond to the production cues that demand emotion: whether that is a relieved grin or a good cry. One caster made the following comparison:

"For scripted shows, you can have them read the part, do a retake, and see their past work, but for reality, you have to really see what makes people tick." Finally, reality casters' work mirrors that of television sponsors, in that reality casters seek *potential* talent as a commodity. Whereas Hollywood casters seek the perfect match between performer and performance, reality casters work to develop a pool of people who they have little or no intention of casting. They are the commodities for sale to advertisers, so their presence must be both cultivated and managed in addition to the ultimate participants in the programs. Sue Collins calls this the "new disposability of celebrity," whereby television markets require cheap labor that is, at the same time, new.[28] The creative destruction of commodities is a metaphor for the industry's need to dispose of old reality casts and make way for new ones, creating a stream of celebrities for a season, who then animate other branding and merchandising markets.

This commodification is not easy. Contrary to popular perceptions, not everyone wants to be on television. In fact, the prized cast member for producers is someone who is not apt to be on television. The irony captured in the producer's invective, "be yourself, only more so," captures the ways casters need "ordinary" people who can perform "ordinariness."[29] Casters want someone foreign to the industry who also understands implicitly how to talk around a camera, move through a planned space, and interact for the best sound bite.[30] Thus the normally shy person is required to reveal himself or herself to the camera in a way that communicates to the masses. The required skill set eliminates a fair number of eligible people in the world, while also encouraging what talk show producers call the "professional ordinary guest," or the aspiring actor who fakes ordinariness.[31] The limited selection pool means that casters have to be careful not to overuse suitable candidates, lest viewers tire of the program. As with any commodity, creative destruction is a necessary feature to maintain the cast member's value.

The caster engages in buying and selling through three interrelated processes: fetishization, reification, and what Timothy Bewes has called "thingification."[32] Each of these involves the objectification of the living and the animation of the object to make a reality program. The first two processes involve the explicit roles of a caster to represent the brand and sell it to potential participants for the reality program. Thingification involves the selling of the caster herself or himself as the authority over the brand. Like agency advertisers selling themselves to the client, casters sell themselves to the producer. These processes generate considerable anxiety. In the best-case scenario, sales of the program, the cast commodity, and the caster contribute to a long-lasting relationship between caster and producer, thus reducing the anxiety and promising a future relationship after the season ends.

Casters were the first to stress their uniqueness on the job. Depending on the type of reality program and on the caster's position in the internal hierarchy of the casting team, interviewees claimed to have more or less familiarity with different aspects of casting, from scouting participants to pitching them to the producers. Casting, in this sense, was organized much like other above-the-line occupations; there were internal hierarchies of producers or directors, followed by associates, and then assistants in a pyramid of authority and status. Contracts and expectations for these positions varied greatly depending on the run of the program and the network or studio bankrolling the production. In general, the longer the run and the longer the series (for example, a reality soap opera versus an episodic documentary), the more weeks a caster worked on a production. To compare, a casting director for a long-running reality series might put a year into cast selection, sifting through thousands of profiles and staging multiple events, though the casting assistant for this series might only work one event. In contrast, a casting director for a new series based around different characters for each episode might only work three months, without a team, and concentrate solely on effective scouting for the producers. Yet despite these variations according to rank or subgenre, all casters engaged in processes of buying and selling, whether buying access to a cast, selling a show, or selling the cast to producers. The consistency of these techniques suggests that while reality television programs differed considerably in their content, the shared processes involved in casting gave reality television a generic coherency through shared industrial practices.[33]

Fetishization: The Casting Call The casting call animates the reality program in a public space. It is a ritual in which casters can stage anticipation for a program's production but can also gain insights into who anticipates the program. Casters use calls to promote the program, creating a brand fetish that they identify with. Further, the call is where casters aggregate data, both demographic and psychographic, on who potentially will watch the program, because to come to the call itself shows a level of commitment to the program as a brand. This level of commitment is not unlike what product testers look for in forming focus groups; more than who might consume the product, the focus group shows the potentially most loyal consumers and their expectations of the product. Casting calls thus can help a producer adjust the program to expectations before it goes live, reducing network anxieties that no one will watch the show. It is one more place to assure the social relationships between buyers and sellers by demonstrating the relationship between consumers and brands.

Space and timing are key to the success of the call in bringing out the kinds of people that generate the quality data for casters. Festivals or other public events, for example, attract a reliable and captive audience at a particular place and time, though the call then competes for attention with the main event. More typically, casters try to create the call as a free-standing event, choosing a space that will likely attract the desired demographic. Shopping malls are popular locales for family-oriented programs, while nightclubs are more typical for programs that focus on younger viewers. Beyond these decisions, the space of the call must have the proper associations of social class. A mall anchored around a Saks Fifth Avenue could attract a quality consumer to the call, but it is less likely to lure the coveted demographic of consumers who both have high purchasing power and watch a good deal of television. Conversely, people in a low-rent bar might watch a lot of television as their primary form of entertainment, but they cannot demonstrate their purchasing power to advertisers as easily as drinkers who are willing to spend $7–10 more for the same gin tonic at an upscale club. The decisions around where and when to have a call are constantly shaped by other factors, most important, production budgets and the local political economy around public events.

Irrespective of the look of a particular reality program, casting calls are notoriously cheap. Casters have to try to arrange the proper venue using free or nearly free labor and trading favors with people who host and advertise calls. The calls I witnessed frequently involved sparse equipment: some standees or banners, a few folding tables and chairs, a stack of clipboards and pens. Part of the allure of observing a call—there are always people who watch the people queuing, though they have no intention of joining in—might be this no-frills mise-en-scène, giving more authority to the production process. As Nick Couldry points out, the artifice of sets in production-oriented theme parks reaffirms for visitors the power of the producers to make the magic of television.[34] In the eyes of casters, however, the lack of technology or glamour is simply the most cost-effective way to host these mobile spectacles. A season of casting calls can occur in as many as ten cities in two weeks for the cost of a single airfare for the caster and a UPS package of goods. Other costs are absorbed by in-kind trading between the casting director and the property managers, business owners, publicity agents, and media representatives needed for the call. Shopping malls and other property owners seek events that bring in crowds, particularly during times when their space is underutilized, such as during the summer months, when young people spend more time outdoors, or during early morning hours, when food court vendors seek breakfasters. In exchange for event advertising and "foot traffic," as the property owner terms it, the caster frequently receives free space, set-up assistance, signage, security, and cleaning services after the call. Property owners in turn will pay for extra staff or for advertising for these intangible sources of future revenue.

The economics of casting calls make them ripe for several layers of cross-promotion opportunities and synergies. It is said that in the new economy, attention is the scarcest resource.[35] By riding on the coattails of a call for a well-known reality series, local businesses can redouble their efforts to entice the desired demographic to associate the programming brand with a local buy. A store manager might trade radio plugs announcing their sponsorship of a series call. In exchange, store personnel plug the call themselves by placing fliers in the shopping bag of each purchaser. Similarly, the radio station announces the call without charge in exchange for space, time, or publicity in conjunction with the store or, more likely, as part of the corporate synergy with the television station that airs the series. One television station executive explained that the logic of cross-promotion boosts the brands of all event partners:

> There may be a few thousand people that show up for the call, but it's multiplied by all the traffic those people create for the stores with their families and friends. They want to see what's going on [at the call]. That also creates a more intimate relationship with the show and with the station. Anytime you bring people out to meet producers, you create more viewers that are loyal. There's a power with these events . . . even if you're not coming to be cast. Those people will check out the station's newscast later that night to see if

their take on the event was the same as the station's. It's like when you drive by a semi that wrecked on the highway; you check out the news because you want to see if their story is like yours.

Ideally, the casting call creates more buzz than a car wreck. Media stations also publicize casting calls on the chance that a local person becomes part of the cast, or, in the case of a contest program, the winner. "If that happens, there's a ton of promotion potential," said the station executive, who could then integrate a local cast member into soft-news stories, publicity parties, and other events that celebrate the synergy between the reality program and the local television station. He monitored program ratings before and after casting calls to track his own effectiveness in promoting the program. Although he was not a member of the casting staff, his input on and negotiation of casting calls were crucial to the overall orchestration of the events.

In the futures market for reality casts, the caster needs to presell the people who will attend the call. Casters call these activities "outreach," a euphemism for building program sponsorship. Casting-call cosponsors include the local businesses that hang and distribute posters for the event and the vendors that purchase stands at an actual event. A week or more prior to a call, casting producers hire local production assistants (PAs) who know the host city well, can identify these cosponsors, and can hone the sales pitch. Staci,[36] a law school graduate looking to break into Hollywood, volunteered as part of the PA "street team" on several reality casting calls. She told me her pitch was simple: "I'm sure you've heard of [a prime-time network reality program]. You know, it's just like [another comparable program]. Well, we're having a casting call here. If you will allow me, I'd like to leave some fliers with you." Riding on the coattails of other more popular series, Staci said she could entice businesses to distribute fliers and even suggest cast members that might then also promote the local business. After a day of canvassing locations for one such call, she counseled the casting staff from other parts of the country to be more relaxed in approaching business owners in her region. "The culture here is not very formal. We tend to be more familiar with people," she said. She also suggested alternative places to canvass the call; nail salons, it turned out, were receptive places to simultaneously recruit applicants for the casting call and local sites for the publicity. Not everyone she approached was eager to be a free distribution hub for the fliers. YMCAs,

libraries, and other nonprofit organizations or public buildings had codes
against such solicitation, thus stressing the inherently commercial nature
of casting outreach.

Outreach and recruitment occurred in tandem throughout the planning and execution of the casting call. Importantly, they generate the data
that will later reinforce the brand name of the program as product. One
casting call I attended in 2006 offered reams of information on its potential audience through the casting process and its surveillance. As in most
calls, applicants first filled out a survey, which recorded demographic
data. In addition to their names, applicants listed their address, age,
gender, race, and social class through giving their occupation, replicating
the categories of a Nielsen ratings report. Applicants could download an
online survey that was even more extensive, with open-ended questions
and several liability clauses to sign. After the questionnaire, applicants
waited at least an hour to meet a program representative. Whereas some
calls corralled the applicants into focus-group interviews for maximum
efficiency, this particular call took time to interview individuals on camera. In this case, the casting crew was short-handed; only one person from
the actual production staff came to direct the call. At the last minute, he
hired his supervisor's sister, who happened to live locally, to do interviews. His advice to her was clear: talk to them about the show and take
lots of notes. He added in a lower voice, "Find out if there's any abuse we
need to know about." Although the aim of casting calls is to gather data
that correlates positively with the size and scope of the program's desired
demographics, some data will also be excluded from association with the
program. Criminal records, while they might make for good drama on a
program, does not represent the audience that a network, or an advertiser, for that matter, wants to buy.[37]

Videotaped interviews that followed questionnaires (for example, figure 4) generated different data from the surveys. Whereas the surveys focused on demographics, the interviews collected information that would
help the caster form a psychographic profile of the applicant. Casters
have a repertoire of typical questions in each call, nearly all of them
related to why the applicant wants to be on the program and what he or
she can uniquely offer the program producers. Yet the answers to these
questions mattered less than the emotion used in responding. A seasoned
caster wrote only the words *quiet* or *big* on many applications; the latter
of these designations was preferable to the former because it denoted a

4. Casting-call interviews generate video footage of their subjects.
Photo permission from Landov Media.

"big personality." He reinforced the need for psychographic information, saying, "I just want to get a sense of your personality," or, "I'm going to ask you some questions, but I really just want to see your personality." The caster also looked for interesting stories that applicants could tell emotively. An unusual trip to China, a childhood disaster, or a desire to impress an unrequited love all received stars in the casting notes. Local references to culture and history might be interesting to a person's profile, but only if they could be told in visually expressive ways. Once the caster had a psychographic profile, he frequently announced it for confirmation. "So you're a leader," he told an assertive barista. "You like to win," he said to a hairdresser. The summary statements went well beyond the demographic information on each applicant, because while most of the people at the call worked in the service industry, he could now make distinctions between the types of people he felt they were.

Despite the routine nature of each interview, casters labored to establish intimacy within the rationalized time of the call. Candace Vogler in her discussion of sex and talk introduces the phrase "depersonalizing intimacies" to describe the ways in which intimacy can be established without necessarily revealing much of one's self.[38] On the contrary, too much talk seems like labor. Intimacy involves liberation from the self, something Vogler claims many women achieve by talking about their troubles in less personal ways.[39] Through gossip and rehearsing versions of the same story, troubles-talk soothes and creates intimacy by connecting one's depersonalized self with others.[40] Casters worked to elicit troubles-talk and give cues to validate its forthcoming in a public space. They purposely asked questions about troubles, such as, "Why are you unhappy?" The caster I watched took time to compliment applicants, to soothe them by claiming he "knew how tough it is" to talk about troubles, and to comfort them by confiding that he was really just a midwestern boy. Facially, he put in overtime—nodding, empathizing, and making eye contact—all while writing on his clipboard. This work, a "calculated compassion" to generate economic value, took a considerable part of the day.[41] Not everyone excels at this part of the job, veteran casters told me in interviews, indicating the value of historically feminized emotional labor. I, for one, did not give any cues during a poignant story, leading an applicant-observer to say to me, "You must have the most boring job in the world. You hear the same shit all day."

A production assistant videotaped the interviews, and the caster took several photos of each applicant. The images were useful in matching the personality with the demographics of the applicant. In addition, the caster could save these images for later use. It is a growing trend in reality television to have casting calls provide B-roll footage of the diversity of people interested in the program. For this reason, the images had to represent a plurality of ordinary people. The caster noted when applicants seemed to be regulars at casting calls, a flag that an applicant might be just acting, thus giving bad psychological information. Professional audition tapes and head shots in this context dashed an applicant's chances. When taking casting head shots at the end of each interview, comments such as "you know the drill" identified interviewees who would not be called back. The routines of the process served to distinguish those who were the kind of ordinary that casters sought.

As the workday wrapped up ten hours after starting the first interview, the casting staff had succeeded in two separate ways. First, they had promoted the program to a definable demographic of potential viewers. This promotion multiplied through an evening news crew that did a story about the call for the network that would broadcast the program. The soft-news questions, directed at applicants, replicated the casting interview questions, thus spreading this information to a mass audience. At the same time, the casting staff succeeded in ordering each of the roughly fifty applicants that day into definable categories from which to later choose a viable cast commodity. "I don't write much because I've already made some decisions in my head," said the casting director. At the end of each interview, the caster thanked each applicant and asked where he or she had found out about the call. The responses, which included all the promotional vehicles in the casting crew's repertoire, reaffirmed the effective tools for branding the program and reifying the cast.

This particular call did not result in an actual cast member for the program, but it did generate reams of psychographic data that could be used in substituting cast types or even toward talent needs for other programs in the future. Casters stressed the importance of keeping the data they have gathered about each person. When experienced casters teamed up, those alliances implicitly involved sharing this data. Jessie had cast several reality series, from dating and makeover programs to docu-mystery series. He kept "records of everything," using his connections to build a social network that would help him find anyone for any program. "I literally have for every show I've worked on," he said, "I have an Excel spreadsheet with a breakdown of faces and names, contact numbers, descriptions of who they are, and then whatever their status was for that project. I keep those because you never know when that stuff is going to be useful. I've worked on a whole number of shows and this is a record of people I've worked with and the numbers where I can reach them. So it is just like a Rolodex of personalities." Data collection, one of the primary aims of the casting call, would come in handy, if not for the program in the call, then perhaps for the future. Each job is different, but "keep all your paperwork," said one caster. "Who knows? Maybe I'll go somewhere where all those applications are relevant."

Reification: The Role of Scouting "I don't understand what they are looking for" seemed to be the frequent lament of the rejected applicant in a taped casting call. Sobbing or bitter, the outpour of emotions reaffirmed the mystique around what casters are looking for in their search for television talent. Part of the confusion, however, stemmed from the basic contradictions that comprise the imagined ideal cast. On one hand, the cast is made up of unique individuals. Each person contributes his or her personality and inner self. This uniqueness promises to rejuvenate the show daily, weekly, or seasonally with a fresh take on a known narrative. On the other hand, the cast is the only physical representation of the program's imagined audience. Casters spoke frequently of needing to fulfill a particular demographic in making the cast, one that appeals through its ability to communicate with a desired audience. This burden of originality and representativeness together resulted in scouting as the most effective technique for filling particular niches.

Particular programs differed, but casters defined the cast commodity in relation to the target market to sell to advertisers. As one casting director explained, "You have to understand who your market is. Shows are successful because people watch them and believe they could be on that program. So the people on the program have to sort of be like them in order to identify with them. For my show, that's 18−35, heterosexual, college-educated people.... That's why certain shows are so popular. You have a married person and a gay person, but every person on the show is all-American."

This use of the term *all-American* was homologous to the general market, an industrial term for people eighteen to thirty-five, heterosexual, and middle class. For a new series, the target audience could be even broader. Producers hoped to capture enough audience shares to sustain the season's episodes. The more seasons the show ran, however, the more selective casters could be in defining the general market. In the words of another caster, "People have seen the show, so the ante is up, and we can go for more specific demographics, twenty-five- to thirty-eight-year-olds, because that's what the network sees as its viewing audience."

By the same token, the ideal cast member introduced a new facet to the program's narrative. Casters talked about needing a character with a "twist" or a "difference." Said one interviewee, "You work from what the show has already done." This meant identifying people with a unique characteristic within the target market pool. Families with llamas, for example, could be part of the target market of a family audience pool, while introducing a difference that network executives believed would continue their ability to sell the program to advertisers. As another casting director said, "We can't just have white, suburban moms for every episode." This use of difference to both identify and sell the cast commodity integrated its value into the logic of television's creative economy. Scripted programming has typically relied on "hits" to define the creative norms and acceptable variations allowed for new developments.[42] Similarly, reality programs based future episodes on successful ones with limited variations that provided a new product. By varying the type of cast members selected, casters ensured the newness of the product, even if the series theme remained constant. "Now that the show is known, casting is no problem," explained a casting producer. "It's just finding unique versions of the same story." It should be stated that the reality participants had often internalized this knowledge, guiding the kinds of interactions they would have with casters. An applicant might have stressed her differences, for example, while maintaining that she was just a suburban mom in every other respect.

The relationship between the desired cast and racial or ethnic identity deserves special attention. "Ethnic background is always a consideration, because we try to have our shows represent what the U.S. census tells us is the population norm. We're trying to represent the whole country," said a casting producer for a docu-reality series. Casters saw this as a challenge. The producer added, "Some groups are really hard to sell on reality programs. Asian Americans, for example, almost never want to go on shows." All the casters shared the perception that some people would not want to be on reality programs, but most casters were white or African American, making it hard to determine whether Native Americans, for example, really rejected reality programs or whether casting staff had an easier time building casts that looked like themselves. The cast commodity needed to reflect what casters could sell to network executives. The casting process might attract a diverse group of potential talent, but the types had to fit the perceptions that producers thought viewers and advertisers would have. For one caster that meant that "it was very clear we were looking for stereotypes that people could fit into." The difficult dance to fill exactly the right card of characteristics makes scouting a key part of the caster's practice.

If casting calls indexed the potential audience for a reality program, scouting generated the proxies for that audience. Casting calls resulted in a quantity of potential recruits to a program, literally thousands of people with demographic statistics of who might watch the program, but scouting added value to that data by standing in for desired audience groups with more complete data. The well-chosen cast member will make good on the promise of the program by standing in for the audience commodity that a network will try to sell to advertisers. Unlike a talent scout who sought the best baseball pitcher in the universe of all players, the casting scout wanted the best talent to represent an aggregate whole that a network wants to claim as part of its audience. As a caster for a reality contest summarized: "Scouting helps you even out the cast, because, unfortunately, there are stereotypes that you have to fill to reach different demographics. For example, you could say, "OK, this show doesn't reach eighteen- to thirty-four-year-old African-American women," and then go out and find someone who would reach that market. This caster's search for the proxy of the African American, female audience guided her targeted search. Similarly, another veteran caster claimed that while "open calls are really great for some things," if you wanted something in particular, "you're going to have to go find it." In other words, scouting made the production process more efficient in its aims to deliver a particular audience to advertisers.

The well-scouted cast member gave the impression of completeness to the caster, who could then fully articulate the group to the producers and the network. Although the cast member needed to display exaggerated traits within the demographic group, called that "special something" or what makes them "pop," those traits must seem organic to the person. Whereas casting calls or online advertisements succeeded in eliciting a focused response to the producers' needs, casters were wary that these opportunities were too staged. Scouting supplanted the knowledge of each cast member with a snapshot of his or her actual behavior. "Scouting goes beyond the façade of the person," said one caster. The caster Nico further related, "There's no better way to find people out there than just go into their natural habitat and scope it out. That way you can be more selective and scope it out. You can be more selective and just approach whoever seems right. You get to see who people really are because they are in their natural setting." "If I had my way," another caster, Carey, claimed, "that's *all* I would be doing, because that's the best way to get a feel for who people are. You can see how they look, how they act, how they treat their friends. You can really get a feel for what they would be like in front of the camera. I mean I am constantly scouting." The idea that a person has a "natural habitat" in which they can be monitored and tracked for emotion, physicality, and relationships with others facilitated the caster's authority over the cast. As someone who will sell this knowledge to a producer or network, the caster must know as much as possible about his or her product, and the desire to know how a person "really is" cuts to the core of that idea.

For these reasons, scouting happened at all stages of the casting process. Some companies hired scouting crews to publicize a casting call and to gather potential interviewees for later personal visits. A typical call might have more workers out searching for talent than present at the actual tables or in line. After the call, scouting could fill in the gaps needed for a presentation to the producers. Scouting did not require vast experience; anyone could be on the lookout. However, scouting involved work, in particular, getting to know how a person "really" is to sell to the producer, while being able to fit that person into the demographic categories vital to the program's sale to advertisers.

Kate recounted these efforts at making distinctions and classifications in her brief experience as a casting assistant for a self-improvement contest. She applied for the job online, where the company sought "fun, outgoing women who can dance." This final qualification was important because Kate spent the next five weeks dancing and searching for recruits in nightclubs throughout Washington, D.C. As veritable flies-on-the-wall, Kate and a work partner were to observe women who seemed at least eighteen but less than twenty-five years old and invite them to a casting call. Kate explained, "It was a pretty discreet job. No one at the club knew we were there, and we were completely anonymous. We just watched people and if they looked like they were decent dancers, we'd go up to them and hand them a card with the information about the call. Not everyone knew the show, but then we could name-drop that the host of the program was [a celebrity] and they would go crazy." Over the course of the five weeks, Kate estimated she visited some five clubs each night between 8 p.m. and 4 a.m. The production company preselected the clubs to generate a mass of eligible cast members who "could then be screened out later."

Their explicit goal was to find at least ten "hip, young women" to represent the city and the program for a semifinal call in another city. "Both of us looked for physical appearance," Kate said. "Everyone had to be slim and good-looking, someone wearing high heels, hot shorts, and their hair done up. We wanted girls who took the time to look nice. We wanted girls who were going to look good for the call since that was going to be filmed." This search for a mass of young women, however, also needed to be segmented by race and class. Kate, an Anglo-American recently graduated from an elite private college, said she identified different kinds of women to fill different kinds of niches for the final ten than her partner, a woman of color who attended a public university: "We tend to identify with our own. She gave cards to all the girls with the latest jeans, jewelry, and black heels. She also knew a lot of local people. I knew more about dancing and singing because of my own background. I used to go to dance studios, and I'm also from a higher class background. I can tell who had voice lessons to sound better. I was more interested in finding one or two people who I thought would look and sound good on camera." According to Kate, their strategies succeeded in drumming up a diverse group of applicants for the call, while getting the select group of people who could likely be part of the final ten. For her, this select group bore all the traces of an upper-class status, having likely spent time in a dance or music studio. This was important to the company ultimately, which invited her to be a casting associate based on her ability to spot applicants that added value to the mass group. It so happened that what Kate called identifying with "her own" replicated the racial and class dynamics of the desired upscale audience for the program.

Kate left reality casting after this experience, but for full-time casters, scouting potentially never ended, extending the workday indefinitely. Betsy said she scouts whenever and wherever she goes: "I find people everywhere. I mean, I was in the bathroom in a Nordstrom one time, and I said out loud, 'Hey, I'm working on this show. Is anyone interested in being on a reality TV show?' And it was so funny. There was a girl in a stall going to the bathroom that heard me and yelled, 'Oh, my God, don't leave! I need to talk to you!' And I heard the paper rustling and her hurrying up to get to talk to me. But it was so funny." Betsy scouted in queues for Chinese takeout and at the dry cleaners. She continued, "I thought at the cleaners, 'Oh, I really shouldn't be scouting here,' but then I asked a lady if she was interested in being on a reality game show, and she ended up winning $24,000." Betsy took pause at the blurring of boundaries between the workplace and home, between public and private rituals, but only insofar as they would disrupt others' lives, not her own. The fact that so many casters could not draw clear boundaries between their working hours and leisure time merely blurred lines between who they were at work and who at home, evoking the sense that their identity as a caster was always present as a tool to be used in mediating social relations.

Scouting, casting, and selling all speak to the reification process alluded to in Marxist treatments of commodity fetishes and most elaborated on by Georg Lukács in "Reification and the Consciousness of the Proletariat." Inherent to modern capitalist life, reification speaks to the process that transforms subjects into objects and objects into subjects. The leveling of the two is necessary to produce exchange value in commodity markets. For Lukács, the central feature of reification is the transformative process that takes place both at the level of subjectivity and at that of relations between people, which acquire a "phantom objectivity."[43] He insists that commodification is not the hallmark of reification; commodities existed prior to modern capitalism. What indexes reification is the way that commodity relations spread through all parts of life. Workers, no longer in control of their own productive means and rationalized by their employers, become mere objects, or the equivalents to the machines they work with. This objectness seeps into the consciousness of workers who, recognizing their productive capacities in terms of exchange value, use their subjectivity as a productive tool.

Through scouting, casters transformed their social relations with the people they met into a productive means for making cast commodities. Kate, Betsy, and others had to fashion themselves as particular types of people to convince people they scouted to be on the program. As another caster said about his personas, "Sometimes I'm the slick guy from Hollywood, but other times I'm the simple Minnesota boy." These are standard practices in the arts of persuasion. Casters talked about getting together with their teams prior to scouting to make lists of why someone might benefit from being on their program. These reasons became the basis for the sales pitch to scouted individuals. Financial or educational benefits were standard pitches, with the class implications that even if one did not need money or services as a reward, appearance on the program would contribute to society by teaching other (usually lower) classes how to act.[44] As did the casting calls, the pitches involved unthreatening body language and an upbeat or compassionate voice: "You can't just approach someone and say, 'it looks like you could lose some weight,' so you have to be inviting but let them come to you." Often, this meant playing up any similarity between the caster and his or her subject in the hopes of creating an affiliation between the person and the product: "That's a way I can really connect with people; I share my story, how I've faced adversity and am a survivor and yada yada. The bond is critical, however you do it." The crucial aspect of the performance was to create metonymy with the program or network. Walter Friedman relates that since the turn of the past century, salesmen portrayed themselves as the physical visage of the companies that employed them.[45] Casters' personas thus stand in for the entire industrial production apparatus. As one said, "We tell them, you know, we're not going to make you look like an idiot. We're not going to exploit you. We're not FOX."

This process also meant bringing more people into the labor process. Casters frequently used their files to cross-pollinate between programs. Someone who did not work for a dating cast might work for a family cast, and so on. The most useful contacts, many stressed, were the "connector types," that is people in the business of knowing others. Casters especially valued hairdressers, real-estate agents, party planners, and florists as people who could guide them to the next social network, from wealthy debutantes to transgender couples. In this way, data collection continuously brought new people into the circle of casting work. One adage of modern advertising has been to target "influencers and connectors" who can spread word of your product to a vast and far-flung social network.[46] By helping the caster find people, the connector entered into the reification process, working for the program while not receiving wages.

The interaction between casters and their subjects promoted reification, the self-recognition through identity categories that enhances one's exchange value. Identity has been a key component of making a sale since the historical birth of the salesman, mediating the relationships between sellers and clients.[47] This separation of identity into an object completes reification as a process of modern capitalism, per Lukács: "The split between the worker's labour-power and his personality, its metamorphosis into a thing, an object that he sells on the market is repeated here too. But with the difference that not every mental faculty is suppressed by mechanization; only one faculty (or complex of faculties) is detached from the whole personality and placed in opposition to it, becoming a thing, a commodity."[48] The caster's strategic use of some of her or his identity to produce another person as a marketable object reified part of the personality of both the caster and the subject in the first instance. This is not to say that all these social interactions are somehow false, inauthentic, or even distasteful. Instead, most casters seemed to treat reification as a performative game. "I just can't turn it off," enthused a woman about her casting persona. What was unique about this selling proposition is that casters' identities mediated the communication between casters and the people they sought to commodify and then sell to executive program producers. Casters submitted a piece of their own personalities to an objectness that they then exchanged with potential cast members in an effort to get them to recognize themselves as the categorical object that producers desired. The anxiety of reification seemed reserved for a later part of the casting process, when casters had to sell their selected cast members to the production team who would develop the series.

The Caster and Thingification
SELF-EVALUATION AND OCCUPATIONAL ADVANCEMENT

The reification of personality as both an identity category and a productive tool redoubled when casters then had to sell their cast selections to producers. This was the least visible part of the casting process, ensconced in the boardroom of a studio or network. Yet it was the most important. Casters needed to convince their superiors that they controlled deep knowledge of the people that they presented as commodities. It was a tense negotiation relative to casters' seeming lack of anxiety when they talked about simply finding the people who fit their demographic needs. William Mazzarella, writing on the ways advertising agencies work with their clients, calls the negotiation an "irresolvable tension between concretely situated affect-intensive materials and their would-be authoritative discursive elaboration."[49] In other words, the caster as a sponsor needed to develop, indeed, take authorial ownership of, a narrative that helped the network envision the cast commodity as a successful part of the final production. To do so involved as much selling one's self as building a seller-client relationship around a shared story of the product.

In an ideal world, casters and producers would have collaborated in deciding on the people to appear in reality programs. Producers, said one caster for a makeover program, generally communicate the "style and type of psychology" that they would like the cast to have, and casting teams then are to find people with those styles and types. In reality, the process was more often one of building consensus among casters and producers. As another casting director explained, "Executive producers [EPS] don't meet the cast until the shoot, so there can't be anything that they don't like about them. But you can't bullshit either. If you tell the EPS that this person is something or other and then [he or she] is not, it will come out at the taping, and then your ass is on the line. So it's up to you to make everyone happy." The pressure to deliver the product that the client wants, in this case the EP, made selling the cast to the network fundamentally different from selling the program to the person who applies to be in it. If the sale fell through in preproduction, the caster could just go to the files or scout to find a replacement. Once in production, producers could fire a caster if they disliked the cast provided.

As the representatives of the cast as a product, casters essentially had to carve out a zone of expertise around living individuals. No longer ordinary people at the call or on the prowl, casters self-presented as authorities over their subjects. One partner of a casting team said, "People know that we know dwarves, albinos, onion farmers three hours upstate in New York, everything. So when reality hit, that ability was huge." Beyond just finding a match, casters claimed to know "what makes people tick," giving them insights into how a person will act on camera. They developed stories about the participants and pitched them, much like a writer or a developer would.[50] A docu-educational series caster explained, "It used to be just matching demographics, finding what they told you to find, and then they'd take them. Now, it's a lot more involved. You need to argue why this person would be good for the show. You need to type up a pitch, and you are committed to that person because you've spent a few hours on the pitch. Our work is so important because that pitch then becomes their story. If they are approved, the producers go from that document and start building the show around it." Casters wrote pitches that sold the cast member and backstories to fill in the character's history under the assumption that past narration will guide the future story. Some productions made the pitch sessions competitive, where casters were set against each other to see who could get the most pitched participants accepted. In most cases, in the words of one caster, they just hoped "that they [the potential participants] live up to what you wrote."

Nowhere was the power and knowledge over the commodity and the world it represented as concrete as in the demonstration videos that some casters made for their clients. Demo tapes, a relatively new feature of some higher-budget reality programs, show the world envisioned through the casting team's eyes. Casters shot and edited demos much like miniature episodes of the program, giving backstory while bringing the psychological qualities of talent to the forefront. In one series, I watched families misbehave over the course of a caster's afternoon visit. An omniscient narrator told of the families' dysfunctions both in private and in public spaces. Visually, a collage of children crying, screaming, cursing, and acting badly lacked the immediate context that might have allowed the viewer to rationalize why this was happening. Like product advertising, the tapes seemed to "give magical access to a previously closed world of group activities," in the words of Sut Jhally.[51] In demos, cast members demonstrated visibly that they represented the racial, class, and gender demographics that advertisers buy access to through broadcasting markets. For Jhally, advertised commodities appear miraculous because they invite the consumer's membership in the world of the groups represented, while hiding the labor needed for its production. Indeed, the caster was rarely apparent in these tapes; his or her experience was subsumed to the narrative about the characters' private lives.[52] The caster merely revealed what was presumed to have been there.

The pitching process also meant sizing up the psychology of the executive producers. Steve described the law of averages that governed who he presented to his employer at a cable network: "I learned for every three pitches you make, the EP will reject one of them, not because it's necessarily bad, but because they feel they can't accept every one in a group of pitches. So I kept getting discouraged because here I was pitching really solid people, and I kept getting shot down. If I had fifteen really solid people, they will still reject five. And then I have to meet a quota of sixty, so it's a real bitch then to find five more people. It's basically a power trip for the EPs. But once you learn that, then you always throw in a bad one so that one gets rejected and you're not stuck looking for a good one when another good one was rejected." Producers may be collaborators, but they were also clients to casters. Fussy producers seemed capricious —there was no way to corroborate whether they really were—but nevertheless they must be satisfied with the product. The job of the cast-team member in these cases was a war of position. Like an advertising agency, the casting team wanted to position itself to get credit for a successful cast member but also be able to shrug off failures.[53] Future employment depended on a reputation for providing not only a steady stream of quality casts but also "hit" characters, that is, the cast member who attains celebrity status. On this basis, producers have built long-lasting relationships with casting teams that they carry to new projects well after the current series has ended and the cast has been replaced.

Client relations between casters and producers spoke to the cultural nature of the development and sale of cast commodities. As the representatives of "things," casters had to consider their own mediational roles in selling real people to a client they must simultaneously impress and build a relationship with. Bewes uses the term *thingification* to describe how multiple subjects may be used as objects and vice versa. The importance of thingification is not that this mutability occurs, but the anxiety that the process produces.[54] That is, the representation of objects as subjects and of subjects as objects creates anxiety for the representers who must distance themselves from subjects and create affective relations with the objects: "Reification is a self-reflective, neurotic category. . . . [It] both promises and denies the possibility of reconciliation between subject and object. . . . At every moment, the anxiety about reification threatens to flip over into a yearning for the reconciliation of subject and object, which would simultaneously be the *realization* of total reification and its *annihilation*."[55] Bewes turns our focus on reification away from its objects and toward its producers, who have to reflect on these relations to represent them. Casters reflected on thingification as a central part of their daily routines. Constantly in the business of giving a program brand life to produce the cast as a commodity, they had to be able to establish personal relationships with objects as subjects and with subjects as objects.

At times, casters had to objectify the very people they had established a personal relationship with to maintain a relationship with the production team or with network executives. From friendly and chummy to distanced and authoritative, the caster shifted personas to thingify, not just the cast member but also herself or himself as the member's sponsor. Whereas casts were only commodities in their quantitative and psychographic representations, they were humans in the production process. Anxiety manifested publicly when producers expected casters to merge these personas in program production, treating cast members as friends and objects at the same time. Some casters said producers wanted them to stay on the set, or called them in if a problem arose. "If I have a good rapport with the person, it's less obnoxious for me to call the person to tell [him or her] what to do than the director," said a casting director for a reality docu-soap. At other times, the cast members themselves called the caster. In the words of another caster, "Often people won't like the [producers] shooting the show. They'll call me to say they're being jerks. If they didn't have that relationship with me, they wouldn't deliver." Then casters had to convince their cast subjects that they should not be confused with the emotionless business of production, while simultaneously convincing producers that they could control their subjects.

A caster for various reality contests and makeover programs, Lisa, explained how difficult it was to balance the different personas she played to cast members and producers:

> Mostly I like to see myself like the people I cast: outgoing, open, and friendly. But as far as the producers, I think my job is more fast and furious, so career-wise, my job becomes a lot different. I've got to find the people and turn them over for production and it's done.
>
> . . .
>
> For some shows, you really befriend the people, you really get to know them, and you both grow to be able to depend on each other. Some shows, I'll even give them my cell number, which is not something I would do for some other shows, depending. I got a call yesterday from someone I cast two months ago, and now he's having problems with the way the show is being taped or something, and he expects me to take care of the situation. Well, sorry, I finished that show two months ago. They expect you to be their champion and they trust you to communicate their interests. But after you cast the show, it's a crapshoot. Crazy things happen ex post facto. It would be nice if we could stay around for every taping, but in the end, your job is to produce results.

In the end, Lisa had to stick to her role as the distanced authority rather than as the outgoing friend. Her career depended on it. Behind the openness and accessibility in their interactions with applicants, casters expressed that their ultimate goal was to deliver the product and move on. As much as casters wanted to walk away, though, maintaining client relations meant a sustained relation with the product that could be turned on and off at will.

If we take Bewes's cue, the emotional work of casting sponsorship brings us to think more deeply about the need to study the affective aspects of anxiety as a prime feature of reification.[56] For casters, the emotional labor of connecting with their product created anxiety first and foremost because it jeopardized the boundaries between casters and their casts, between subjects and objects. One caster put it most succinctly:

> One of the things that is an easy pitfall for people who work in casting is you fall in love with the talent, you fall in love with the characters. And I don't mean that in a relationship way, but it is hard to separate . . . I mean you had to do so much work to connect with this person to get them to trust you and be a part of the process that it becomes difficult to separate yourself from the process, and you need to be objective. While you are a human being and want to be friends with these people and be a good person, you're also making a TV show, which inherently is not in the interest of everybody; it is in the interest of getting good ratings and making good shows. So sometimes it becomes a conflict of interest when you need a producer or somebody you're working with to come in and get that. You need to step away from the relationships and treat them as story material, and treat them like the content of the show. So sometimes I think casting people get accused of being a little too connected to the talent.

Here, the risks were evident. If casters are just like participants, they cannot be authoritative sponsors or advance in the ranks of other production personnel. The anxiety around someone else's perception, as in the anxiety *to be perceived* as ordinary to the cast but also as an expert to employers, ultimately reflected on the liminal position of the reality caster as someone in between statuses in the new economy.

The Regendering of Selling

Emotional labor and emotion work are common features of most jobs involving sales and clients, referencing, respectively, the public display and private management of emotions needed to generate profits and earn wages in return. In her treatise on emotional labor, Arlie Hochschild argues that emotion work is an ever-growing component of the service economy, but it is also a gendered category. Emotions are historically associated with women, "who are represented as closer to nature, ruled by appetite, and less able to transcend the body through thought, will, and judgment."[57] What this means is that when men do emotional labor, it is likely to be seen as an individual trait, whereas when women do emotional labor, they achieve membership in a group identity.[58] Since at least the Civil War, U.S. corporations have straddled this paradox in attempting to "redefine selling as a masculine profession, dependent on hard work and determination, rather than on the feminized skills of seduction."[59] The construction of the professional identities of salesmen, admen, and later broadcast sponsors relied on the rearticulation of feminized techniques as manly and the development of advertising and marketing as scientific and rational, in short, as unfeminine.[60] In broadcasting, Michele Hilmes writes, advertisers and sponsors traditionally couched their work in sexual terms as one of seducing the feminized masses, who by their definition were "irrational, passive, emotional, and culturally suspect."[61] From the early 1950s, gender did not merely denote who worked in television advertising and sponsorship; it also provided a discursive framework to understand how the business of selling was perceived as masculine and heterosexual.[62] Reality casting, framed by its emotional labor and the blurred lines between workers and audiences, does not fit easily into the symbolic universe of masculinized sales and sponsorship.

Historically, casting has been women's work in Hollywood, largely associated with secretarial duties and done by females hoping to break into the industry. Erin Hill estimates that female casters outnumber male casters by three to one in the otherwise male-dominated world of film and television production.[63] This figure roughly mirrors the gender breakdown in calls I made to sixty casters involved in reality television casting, with much of the male population self-identifying as gay. More important, though, were the ways in which reality casters explained their work in relation to this gender and sexual inequality. Emphasizing feeling over rationality, and intuition over training, reality casters drew on cultural scripts that reinforced the tight correspondence between the feminized discourses of emotional labor and casting, especially when the caster was a female or gay individual who could adopt the discourse as their own. Pride in being a caster accompanied pride in being the kind of woman or gay male *already* expected to excel in the field. At the same time, casters eschewed the relevance of gender or sexual categories when describing their own exchange value or career potential as emotional laborers. Asserting that casting operated as a meritocratic sphere, casters claimed that they were individuals who happened to possess the right stuff, irrespective of their gender or sexual orientation. Forced into emphasizing their identity claims to casting as their turf or justifying why they were uniquely qualified in terms of emotional labor, casters ultimately relied on an essentialism linking emotional labor to gender and sexuality.

Most reality casters recognized the gendering and sexuality of their trade explicitly. Interviewees commented on the gender disparities in casting versus other production roles typically dominated by men:

> I can understand why women dominate here. It's a womanly thing to connect with people. But, boy, there's a lot of women here, and a lot of ass-kissing that goes on. I'm here to get my job done, but there's so many women wrapped up in the gossip, cackling, and everything else. It's really annoying.—TANYA

> Men wouldn't be good at this job, because, unfortunately, they can be pretty sex driven and women would be less comfortable if a man approached them, or less likely to give it a shot. A good-looking woman caster, though, has an easier time with getting the men, because they are more willing to be approached.—KATE

> People are put in a place where they have to be vulnerable and they have an easier time doing that with a woman.—BETSY

Men involved in casting, according to interviewees, would likely be gay:

> The guys who are in casting are all gay, myself included, and gay guys tend to choose more creative careers, and this is more creative than being a producer.—NICO

> Gay guys here are good at it because they can play the Queer-Eye self-deprecating stuff.—JOHN

> Hiring producers didn't think men could cast for this show, but it turns out women love talking to men. You can't make generalizations. We had a woman on the show, and she was terrible.—STEVE

Together, females and gay men were archetypes of the idealized caster. Although alibis as to why gender or sexuality bore on job excellence varied, the need to rationalize what casters perceived as a real disparity in numbers revealed the salience of gender and sexual identity to the labor market.

The gendering of reality casting was also implicit in talking about casting job skills and responsibilities. Casters talked about needing to be naturally communicative, flexible, empathetic, and detailed-oriented multitaskers. Like a secretary, a caster explained, "you have to be great on the phone. You can't stutter or be abrasive. You have to adapt to the person. . . . You have to have great organizational skills in order to keep all the names straight and remember people, what they like and dislike. Photoshop and computer skills are also handy. There's a lot of clerical-level work that really sucks, but you have to do it to keep your records straight." These skills, both emotional and organizational, were in addition to other less service-oriented skills, such as writing and making pitches. These were not feminine characteristics per se, but fit a gendered paradigm for feminine labor. Interviewees said casting was a "people person job" and "all about talking, listening, and being empathetic," qualities associated with other historically female roles that have involved nurturing, such as domestic care. When asked to explain her work, one female interviewee who had cast over fifteen different reality series compared herself to a triad of women famous for their emotional labor: "I've never failed, because it's not an act. It's totally genuine. It's that Mother Teresa nature, where you genuinely care about people. Mother Teresa never made anyone feel bad about who they were or where they were coming from. Do I have the physical problems of the people on [my show]? No. But I can relate to them. Just like Barbara Walters can relate to people. Oprah can do it too." In her exposition, Mother Teresa, Barbara Walters, and Oprah Winfrey were successful as relaters and empathizers, but these traditionally feminized characteristics are valued in a context in which women have demonstrated these abilities in the public sphere.

Casters seemed to internalize a binary logic around gender and sexuality, emphasizing organic or natural bases for their talents. "Either you have it or you don't," said one longtime reality caster. "Training can hone skills already there, but if you aren't born with it, it can't be learned." Other casters spoke of the emotional skills involved in casting's routine decision making as a "knack," "intuition," or "instincts," reifying the notion that casting skills developed from nature rather than training. The logic could generate some tension between what casters saw as naturally feminine traits and what they interpreted as their personal job performance. One experienced female scouter relayed, "I think women have more heart; they get people faster because they can get to their personality faster. They are more nurturing. But I think it's because more women go for these jobs. I don't think men are discriminated against." Using clichés associated with feminine identity, the scouter tried to still disassociate herself from any notion that gender played a role in her position. Casters

explained that good casters were *individuals* who naturally had the required traits. These disclosures were not without tensions. Tanya, the
woman who embraced her "womanly" claims to connectedness, nevertheless rejected other feminized aspects of the work, such as a "gossipy"
work environment. For men, sexuality was a key to claiming a space in the
job market. As one man relayed: "Women are hired by women because
they are perceived as being better at it, I think. That's a myth I don't want
to perpetuate. [My partner] and I had a really hard time, like I said,
convincing them to hire us for [a reality show about babies]. I mean,
really, I have been doubted before because I am a man, but I've found that
once people learn I'm a gay man, that for some reason makes a difference.
It's sad that I think putting 'gay' on my résumé might help me; that's
ridiculous, you know?" Straight men had to work harder to create alternative narratives around casting as an ungendered skill set. A self-identified
heterosexual male told me that sexuality was not so relevant to being a
good caster, but that "alpha males" did not fare well in the industry.
Placing himself in the category of "sensitive males," the caster could nevertheless typecast himself in the role of those with a knack for the job.

This correspondence between types of labor and essentialized views of
gender and sexuality were particularly important given the overall deni-
gration of casting by production teams. Although many casters often said
they worked at being empathetic or displaying the proper emotions on
the job, the desire to suture these to a gender or sexual identity position
may have very well undermined them in seeking higher production positions. By asserting that the caster's skills were organic or intuitive, they
perpetuated the unprofessional stigma surrounding the labor, as well as
undermining its skill set in comparison with jobs that required certifica-
tion or the registration of formal education on a résumé. As one caster
summed it up, "You don't need life experience or an education or anything." In addition, the relative lack of talk about other job skills valued
because they are associated with commerce, such as selling, marketing,
or demographic research, ensured that people outside casting depart-
ments would not be challenged to think of casters outside of their emotional work, which employers likely undervalued. So even as casters'
work may benefit the commercial aims of the producers, adapting the
techniques of advertisers and sponsors, the continued feminization of
reality casting presented a dilemma for how casters could talk to outsiders about their work. While they found it useful, even beneficial, to

stress these feminized skills in their self-presentation, reality casters also had to face the low status that those same feminized skills occupied in relation to more masculinized ones, even if that would mean conceding the field to a larger variety of workers.

Sponsors of the Future

Casters framed their labor in paradoxical terms. On the one hand, they knew they were essential to the future of the new economy for television. Reality programs, whose cheap production values offset the cost of signature shows, could not air if it were not for the efforts of the casters who promoted the programs, developed their talent base, and generated the knowledge about the potential popularity of a new program while it was still in the preproduction stages. Casters universally said they were the key people involved in the success of reality programs because everyone else in the production chain relied on them to find a reliable talent stream from which someone would hopefully become a memorable character, or even a celebrity. On the other hand, casting as an occupation, its emotional labors, and the genre it serves all occupy the lowest positions in their respective hierarchies of wages, labor, and taste. Paid the least among the above-the-line workers and seldom recognized with even an end credit, some casters said they were embarrassed to tell people that they worked in the industry. The low status of reality as a genre, combined with the low status of what they perceived as people work versus technical work, barred their self-presentation as creative professionals in the same ways that other television workers promote themselves.

Who gets credit for selling and buying in the new television economy is still up for grabs. The strike in 2007 by industry writers put product placement revenues on the agenda not only to gain recognition and revenues for their advertising labors but also to redefine the boundaries between sponsors and other above-the-line roles. Reality casters, meanwhile, have had no such standpoint from which to articulate their skills as separate from marketing, or their emotional labor as separate from the commercial project of finding the perfect talent to represent the most desirable demographics. These casters participate in the "total integrated marketing" and "full-service advertising" that agencies have promised their clients since the early 1990s by bringing together advertising, mar-

keting, and public relations functions to animate programming brands
and objectify cast commodities. Writing about the first scouted family for
a reality television program, Jean Baudrillard ruminated on the caster's role in the total commodification of human experience: "This family was . . . already somewhat hyperreal *by its very selection*: a typical,
California-housed, 3-garage, 5-children, well-to-do professional upper
middle class ideal American family with an ornamental housewife. In a
way, it is this statistical perfection which dooms it to death."[64] The transformation of the real into the hyperreal, an object that takes on a life in
the television marketplace, makes the reified objects more significant
than the subjects. Casters, in this articulation, are the foot soldiers of
reification in television. Their roles in finding statistical perfection generate disdain from some in the production hierarchy, high expectations
and hopes from others, and considerable anxiety as everyone involved—
casters, studio and network executives, and advertisers—must have faith
in the value of the object they buy and deliver.

It has yet to be seen how much casting will merge with advertising and
sponsorship. As walking and breathing representatives of audience demographics, psychographic profiles, and consumer tastes, reality program
participants become the ultimate "integrated product," able to demonstrate to advertisers who they are buying access to. Producers can then
rationalize the cast's value much as that of any product. In the next
generation of Nielsen technologies, advertisers and networks can monitor
a product placed in a television program and rate it on scales that correlate
time on the screen, the role of the product in the story, and the audience
rating for that time slice.[65] In what could be eventually an enormous
feedback loop, producers could measure the effectiveness of a character
against audience ratings and assign it value in incremental ratios of dollars
paid per second. In a completely integrated environment, advertiser anxiety could eventually evaporate into Baudrillard's hyperreality. At least for
the present, reification is never complete. Reality casters have unique
challenges associated with their products. Cast members as objects have a
short "shelf life," most of them being unable to reappear in other programs
or to be recycled in syndication. During that short time, the cast member is
often less predictable than his or her casting profile implies. The connections that casters establish with the cast can go awry at any stage of
preproduction, production, or even distribution.

What remains is still the caster's anxiety about reification, the frantic role-switching as casters mediate between objects and subjects to maintain a relationship with studio and network executives. This speaks to the absolute need for casters and, at the same time, to a need to revaluate their worth, both by their fellow workers and in their own self-presentation. The feminized connotations of their labor and the anxiety of reification—the commodification of the self, the positioning of the self in relation to the product, and the inevitable erasure of that labor—may also produce an anxiety about the blurred lines that historically divide professional identities according to gendered bodies and sexualized skill sets. Commodification intensifies social anxieties writ large, according to Luc Boltanski and Eve Chiapello, precisely because human qualities that we judge by their authenticity no longer seem genuine or immutable.[66] For workers, the disillusionment with authenticity cuts to their own core as they must perform their own brand authenticity to guarantee social relationships, while navigating that brand to adapt and change to work conditions. This latter form of anxiety also seems to be the conundrum that a traditional labor movement cannot resolve, demonstrating the resiliency of the new television economy and giving everyone in the industry a little emotional work in the future.

4. Regulating Selves

REGULATION IN PRODUCTION

Any discussion of producers in the new television economy cannot forget the work of the regulator, who provides the framework for the governance and maintenance of television as a communication system. As the commodity function of the new television economy makes increasing numbers of working people into both agents and objects, the regulator does the crucial labor of identifying who are the agents and objects of governance, who may make claims and who must be managed, and who are thus productive and who are their products. Through their own embodied claims in ensconced meeting rooms, regulators must negotiate who are representatives of "the people" within the contradictory identity politics of race and class. Doing this, they execute the state's bio-political functions by articulating who should work and who is worked into a political economy made up of producers, publics, consumers, and citizens. The labor of identifying who should work and who is worked places regulators in the role of defining the people according to their productivity and their commodifiability, thus assisting television industries in recruiting free laborers and targeting new markets. Regulators thus share with sponsors the work of identification that television industries rely on but that becomes utterly invisible to its own production hierarchies.

Invisible labor has been a longtime feature of U.S. communications regulatory culture, but it has increased with each wave of deregulation. Based on a model for radio broadcasting that functioned to distribute military investments through commercial industries, television regulation foregrounds market activities over those of policymakers. Regulators, appointed by governing executives, held the charge of mediating the balance of state and market interests in developing a commercial television system that nonetheless represented the public interest. Proponents for the deregulation of television and communication industries rendered regulators nearly obsolete in these meditative functions. Federal efforts since at least the late 1970s have imagined a self-managed television system, one in which the invisible hands of the market replace the bureaucratic operations of institutions in which real people work. The abstraction of labor from capital as such operates through the deregulatory process, making regulators more invisible as they service the illusion that television production happens solely via the efforts of its own employees.

As this chapter demonstrates, however, regulatory work has not dissipated in a deregulated communications market; far from it. The numbers of people involved in regulatory work have expanded, diffusing among those in the population expected to volunteer on behalf of the polity. Though self-appointed watchdogs of the airwaves have existed since at least the 1920s, the widespread drafting of citizens as official regulators can be traced to the FCC Report and Order on Cable Television (1972).[1] This legislation, which permitted the local negotiation of city revenues in exchange for the construction of a cable communications infrastructure on public rights of way, required a steady stream of volunteers to work on behalf of local municipalities as their intermediaries. Appointed directly by city councils or elected by independent standing committees for public-access centers, the nomination of local volunteer regulators through public utilities committees, cable advisory boards, and public-access oversight were to represent the public physically through a regulatory body. Like federal regulators, the local regulator did not pass television policy but rather worked to safeguard franchise terms and manage access to the local media outlets financed largely through these twenty- to twenty-five-year contracts. Citizen cable regulators became the second line of governance in a longer genealogy through which state functions that used to be monopolized by relatively few elites now rest in the hands of a growing number of people expected to do governmental work without recognition or compensation. In the latest articulation of this trend, recent statewide cable franchises delegate the work of communications management and monitoring to every cable consumer as a citizen duty.

Even as the citizen cable regulator might be an anachronism to emerging modes of communications governance, this chapter looks at people who did this regulatory work on behalf of their municipalities in the late 1990s and early 2000s. From 1998 to 2000, I was an appointee of the Cable Committee of the City of San Antonio, Texas. Soon after, I was elected to the board of Davis Community Television, the public-access station of Davis, California. There, I was a board member until mid-2003. These experiences demonstrate the paradoxical ways in which invisible labor and collective anonymity involve people who are still visible and known to each other, and how this human contact was the basis for constructing cultural identities that gave surplus value to television industries. As Daniel Biltereyst reminds in his history of film censorship, the enforcement of legal obligations and community standards involves the subjective interpretations by "flesh-and-blood people with their own sensitivities, norms and values."[2] This is obvious in the many, often conflicting ways in which policymakers have interpreted the words *citizen* and *consumer* through the past ten years of communications deregulation and marketization.[3] Whether recruiting an appointee or making an argument on behalf of needy consumers, the citizen cable regulators in San Antonio and Davis worked with their own cultural frames to define which members of the people should serve or be served. They did this through their own embodied positions, which then projected onto other imagined citizens and consumers, creating contradictory binds for the regulators to represent themselves and others.[4] In both case studies, the discursive debates between regulators reflected local articulations of liberalism and multiculturalism, but the outcomes of these debates universally helped cities and corporations identify and manage cable and public-access users.

This final case study uses my own experiences as a basis for exploring regulation as an invisible identity work that maintains television's production structures and hierarchies. This choice may seem queer, given the regulator's status as a worker without an identity, but this is precisely the conflict that motivated my work in these spheres and erased my labor. It is also increasingly the position that many academics find themselves in as they are hailed by their institutions to include civic service in their professional duties. Citizens have not disappeared in their regulatory roles over television. Rather, regulation has dispersed further, embedding into the roles of private professionals such as lawyers, consultants, and academics, all of whom work pro bono to maintain the city's cult of expertise over management functions. By inserting my past into the present, I take a cue from Norman Denzin that I may "create the conditions for rewriting and re-experiencing it."[5] Field notes written during the periods I acted as a cable committee volunteer have been dialogic documents with the knowledge I have now. Supplemented with news stories, city records, and interviews, my notes and memories have been reauthored, shaped by official accounts and others' memories. In the summaries of the complex local politics that follow, I am writing myself "into and out of" these historical records in an effort to use my emotions, as Denzin advocates, to foster a new understanding of social cultural politics—one that recognizes the work of television regulation.[6]

The Work of Being Invisible

People undoubtedly become members of television oversight boards in a variety of ways, as demonstrated by the differences in my own experiences. In San Antonio, it was easy for me to join the cable committee. Watching the government access channel, I spotted a nondescript listing of openings for district representation on a series of governing committees, from advocacy to zoning. After pondering the possibilities, I sent in my application and, with a phone call, scheduled a quick trip to the City Hall. There, I met my councilman for a ten-minute interview. He appointed me within a week or so. I figured at the time that no one wanted the unpaid position. In Davis, the tables seemed turned, at least at first. On moving, I approached my councilwoman at a public reception. When I asked if I could serve in a similar capacity, she seemed uninterested. Scanning the government access channel, I did not encounter any calls for public participation, much less a board position related to television. Rebuffed, I told a new colleague at the university where I worked. She was surprised. As a member of the local public-access governing board, she sought qualified candidates to fill openings. I joined the DCTV board soon after she presented me to members for a quick vote of approval. My perceptions of these different processes with similar outcomes, at least for me, would change over the course of my immersion in regulatory culture.

The opaque process of recruiting, selecting, and integrating citizens into cities' governance structures underlines the invisibility of regulatory work, both from public eyes and from scrutiny. Although regulators represent the public's authority, only a few select members of the public join their ranks. Those who do find themselves integrated into a regulatory culture of technocratic imperatives. Based on bureaucratic procedures and a cult of professional expertise, regulatory culture erases individuals' labor into a collective whole, making the public visibility of the handful of individual regulators through U.S. broadcasting history the exceptions that support the rule. Instead, like the FCC as a whole, municipal regulatory boards become metonyms for an authority over television located elsewhere. Their members seem to merely serve the interests of more visible constituencies, such as politicians and broadcasters.[7] Regulators thus exist as a sort of neither-nor, serving as mediators between more powerful representatives of the state and the market that threaten to absorb them. The historical process that renders regulators invisible via co-optation can be heard through generalizing terms such as *the feds*, *the FCC*, or simply *the government*. Local citizens involved in regulatory processes do not even find themselves included in such terms, though the presumption of co-optation seemed apparent. Friends and colleagues would say I was doing something "for the city" or "with the cable company," putting me into two camps I saw myself as independent from. These spoken affiliations frequently accompanied a bit of bemusement, as if my role was so impotent I did not merit a clear sense of the title or charge, if not derision that these activities were a waste of time.[8]

The roots of the liminality of the U.S. communications regulator as between state and market date at least to the rise of the bureaucratic administrative state in the late nineteenth century and have intensified through deregulation. Executive reforms to separate civil service from preferential politics aimed to satisfy Progressive critics of the spoils system associated with public appointment. Yet the professionalization of administration inevitably incorporated citizens whose private activities lent legislators an authoritative legitimacy in their policy agendas.[9] The cult of expertise in communication regulation admitted only a select group in its ranks. Early studies of the biographies of FCC members and its predecessor, the Federal Radio Commission, find that the vast majority of broadcast regulators were occupationally "professional men," homogenous in their geographic and educational training in technical, legal, or academic arenas.[10] Most were over the age of thirty-five and worked as trade or industry lawyers with significant experience in dealing with government officials. The transition to the "informational state," writes Sandra Braman, further incorporated private professionals as the liberalization of public state activities has disseminated more authority to "private decision-makers."[11] This somewhat abstract reference to elites had its class interests firmly aligned with market interests. Between 1970 and 1998, Bruce Owen calculated that the number of Chicago School–trained economists working for the FCC increased several-fold. The call to deregulate communications from public oversight he attributes to an "'invisible college,' or virtual community of communication researchers scattered at different institutions and agencies."[12] The members of the professional class who serve as public consultants, staffers, and appointees thus embody the seemingly tight correspondences between state and market interests in regulation.

This profile largely matched my own in that my education, training, and placement in a university department of communication resonated with the profiles of a long lineage of academic communication advocates. From the intellectuals who volunteered to be President Woodrow Wilson's war propaganda managers during the Second World War to the Chicago School economists in the halls of administrative agencies, the precedent for the university scholar to act as a regulator fit the bill.[13] In fact, the previous holder of my seat in San Antonio was a communication professor too. Greetings such as, "Here comes the professor," preceded me in my initial committee meetings, outing me before business had even begun. In Davis, a university town, my status was perhaps less remarkable. Nearly everyone on the board had some connection to the academy, as an employee, a client, or a partner of the campus institutions. If my role as a researcher resonated with some initially, it was displaced later by my credentials as someone who had experience with cable regulation. In this way, membership in the professional class was a crucial yet repressible feature of my participation. It allowed easy entry into a sphere between state and market that would then operate to normalize my identity and render my labor invisible.

Regulatory labor occurs through a series of rationalizing procedures and a cultural faith in technocracy. We opened and closed meetings according to a tight schedule of routine motions and passive listening to reports. We began and finished on time, with the estimated minutes to elapse often placed on the agenda, as if they were suggestions to ensure orderly conduct. Following Robert's Rules of Order, we operated in sync to receive and approve minutes, lists of programs, budgets, and summaries from staffers representing the city, producers, or the cable company. Reports were mostly routine and technical; they directed discussions within narrow time constraints. We sometimes had visitors, but only those with connections to the city, to corporate, or to public-access staffers received a note in the agenda. Considered experts, they could address various developments in technology, legal matters, and political or economic trends. These acts were to signify that we were enforcing policies inscribed between the city and the cable company in the franchise. In theory, regulators, according to Thomas Streeter, "are expected to use neutral, rational principles to flesh out broad mandates given to them from elsewhere."[14] In practice, the work was often mundane, if not boring, as doodles on the margins of my agendas evidenced.

In this deregulatory period, there were few formal decisions to be made, as legislation curtailed our roles in policymaking and as municipalities lost ground in their abilities to negotiate local franchise provisions. The occasional member of the general public who appeared at a meeting or in an outreach session generally raised his or her cable bill as the foremost issue for redress, but we lost the authority to challenge skyrocketing rates with the Telecommunications Act of 1996.[15] Nor could we determine the organization of television channels according to rate structures. A federal act to ensure localism in cable transmission effectively superseded our authority in San Antonio to prevent a low-power home shopping station from replacing CNN in the basic channel line-up. We deferred to city lawyers to seek legal counsel on recovering franchise fees for digital cable services, such as Internet sales, only to be rebuffed through state and federal legislation. By making municipalities impotent to affect changes over increasingly broad aspects of television policy, the work of regulation at the local level seemed quixotic, though, in another way, it highlighted the more important cultural work of television regulation.

If individual regulators seem to act on behalf of the state or market interests that they rely on, for public appointment, or that identify with, in their private occupations, then regulatory culture as a whole defers individual agency into a collective anonymity. Our organizational operations connected my role to other idealized realms within liberal democratic philosophy that are similarly ordered by the division between private identities and public service, such as court juries, legal proceedings, or other governance boards. In these, citizens leave their private identities to form a judgment that is more important than the sum of its parts.

As a fellow communication scholar and municipal cable activist Lawrence Lichty wrote of the FCC in 1961, "The collective nature of the Commission usually provides each member with a cloak of anonymity."[16] In scholarly accounts of crucial policy debates about broadcast spectrum allocation, technological innovation, and licensing, the subjectivities of federal regulators all but disappear into a Capitol City Beltway culture of government bureaucrats, lawyers, and lobbyists.[17]

In San Antonio and Davis, the sparse public records of our activities reflected this narrative of our collective anonymity and invisibility. Staffers posted the action-free agendas on walls where pedestrians would not see them or buried them in local newspapers with a week's notice. Meeting minutes without editorial comments framed our agency only in terms of motions and votes. Scheduled speakers from the city, public access, or the cable company handed out the research we requested, sometimes without mention in the actual meetings, hence remaining absent from the minutes. These records—the only traces of our textual community— rendered our agency invisible, further highlighting our positions as betwixt and between, as neither state nor market representatives, neither citizens nor consumers, and thus personally unconnected to any social background or experience with the various constituencies in our midst.

Regulatory culture, which evades identification in its collective anonymity, thus generates contradictory perceptions of regulators. They represent, on the one hand, the concentration of elite, masculine authority in the form of "massive hierarchy, institutional conservatism, professed rationality, and entrenched self-interest."[18] They are, on the other hand, utterly feminized as victims to capture by powerful politicians and industrial executives. Capturing this duality, Barry Cole and Mal Oettinger describe the FCC as a "gentlemen's club," in which "troublemakers are politely ignored; their opinions are not sought. They are labeled by the collegiate members of the club as 'radicals' or 'obstructionists.' Unless their presence is necessary to form a quorum or otherwise satisfy the club's ancient by-laws, they are generally excluded from the kaffee klatsches that constitute the club's primary business sessions."[19] Cole and Oettinger describe a culture that indexes masculinity and class privilege at its core. Even if not all regulators are male or collegiate elites, the authors suggest that regulatory culture derives its power from the presumption of a gentlemanly authority that operates to exclude outsiders, crush dissenters, and mollify critique. At the same time, the authors do not characterize this powerful institution as particularly effective. The reference to the institution's primary business as a kaffee klatsch associates the "club" with a feminine gossip culture and an ethnic white identity that is not quite as powerful as whiteness. The authors call FCC regulators "reluctant," as if they were hesitant to act, powerless in the face of politicians or industry lobbyists that are more powerful. Matching the bemusement of my own friends and colleagues in the academy, the invisibility of regulators in their culture seem to create the fantasy that regulators are both dominant and submissive, an agent of power and a subject to capture.

Those few regulators who do escape anonymity seem to have distinct identities that were both visible and transgressed the contradictions of regulatory culture. James Fly, Newton Minow, and Nicholas Johnson, for example, were "Young Turks" among federal regulators, referencing their difference from a presumed "Old Guard."[20] Unlike the latter, the former were men of action. They were characterized as crusaders, and the memorialization of individual regulators lays bare the associations between masculine policymakers and emasculated policy enforcers. Trustbuster Fly, portrayed as someone "arrogant, offensive, hot-tempered, unfair, even ruthless, and to have a Southwesterner's love of a bang-up fight,"[21] was said by the television historian Erik Barnouw to not even "faintly resemble" the preceding chairmen of the FCC.[22] Fly, as well as Minow and Johnson, became news celebrities of their respective eras, and through their own public relations campaigns, writings, and memoirs recast themselves as trailblazers who could wield the authority of the state and elite networks to their own ends. In contrast, the first females of the FCC, as well as the first people of color, did little to trouble the masculine-feminine binary characterizing regulatory culture. Carol Weisenberger depicts the five women FCC appointees from 1930 to 1990 as "mild" activists, relegated to the pyrrhic politics of educational television and antidiscrimination legislation as women's issues.[23] Raul Tovares shows a similar ambivalence toward the work of Benjamin Hooks, the first African American FCC commissioner whose racial visibility supported the enforcement of equal opportunity standards for minority employment in broadcasting but who nonetheless resisted authoring civil rights policies to restrict racist television content.[24] The ambiguous treatment of regulators whose identities were visible, but whose politics stepped outside a routine script only with regards to limited identity issues, reinforces the binary between individual regulators as agents of change and the invisible

5. Television regulation occurs largely in spaces in which the labor is invisible to the general public. Photo taken by Clifford Garibay, courtesy of Davis Media Access.

workers who routinely submit to institutional norms.[25] If anything, these exceptionally visible communications regulators support the invisibility of the majority of regulators' labor as a rule.

This identity trouble accompanied our own visibility and invisibility. For even if our labors were invisible to those outside our small group meetings, we were quite visible to each other. Physically, we represented members of the public body, and, through claims, we articulated memberships, alliances, and allegiances. This work, though still hidden from public view (figure 5), was perhaps the most common way that we performed the real work of regulation, that is, when we made ourselves visible to each other. The small group settings of board meetings made us each into representatives, both of our own subjectivities and of a public that we articulated through the claims we made to each other. Demographically, we seemed to match the dominant racial composition of the cities in which we resided. The San Antonio committee representatives seemed to correspond directly with census counts for each district, with Mexican Americans representing the South Side and West Side districts, Anglo Americans the North Side, and one African American in the East Side. The board members of DCTV were nearly all Anglo-Americans, reflecting the town's demography but not the largely Latino county we also served but did not formally represent in the franchise. A sole Latino representative on the DCTV board never came to a meeting during my two-year tenure there, creating a kind of absent presence that reflected the general desire for multiculturalism in the post–civil rights era. Expressed as a one-to-one correspondence between the bodies of appointees and the electorates of our districts and towns, we were the visible proxies of an invisible public.

In other ways, though, we represented grand disparities in these imaginary publics. We were a group of considerable expertise from a technocratic perspective. We were all middle-class professionals, most of us with backgrounds in communication and media. Besides myself, there was a former telecommunications worker, a newspaper editor, a leader for an international visitors' bureau, and a public radio employee in San Antonio. In Davis, our group membership included nonprofit media producers and staffers, a lawyer, a media consultant, and community activists with political ties to housing and human services. Most were recidivist appointees; that is, they moved between various causes in their respective cities and moved between various civic board appointments. At the same time, we also overrepresented retirees in our ranks, and, including our staffs, women. Whereas the former group often labored as the keepers of public history, the latter group did much of the organizational and secretarial duties by taking the lead on any pet projects that board members suggested. Like in nonprofit work, women are overrepresented in municipal boards and in spheres where their labor is considered voluntary, and thus unpaid, much like in the domestic sphere.[26] As such, any presumed power that we might have had as board regulars and community professionals also seemed undercut by the presumption that we had more leisure time to volunteer for work that had little significance to elites. In the words of one San Antonio committee member, a Latina senior citizen, the lack of power procedurally made her feel like "we're just window dressing."[27]

These ambivalences might seem petty to people outside these representational norms of race, gender, age, and professional status who had difficulty or found it impossible to enter the regulatory cultures that I moved into with relative ease. My blithe assumption, for example, of easy entry into the San Antonio cable committee was disavowed when, years later, at a professional meeting, a former colleague exclaimed jokingly to a mutual friend, "I had been wanting to get on that committee for years, and she just comes on in." The colleague, a self-identified Chicano and a university professor, challenged me to understand the norms of visibility for our exclusive group. For, while he represented demographically and professionally the norms of the committee's composition, he did so from the wrong location. As a resident of an unincorporated part of the city that was predominantly Anglo-American, this individual did not embody a physical proxy for any district as we did. Further, and perhaps more importantly, his long history of public activism for an independent media center in the city made him visible beyond the simple boundaries of the committee meeting room. In this sense, he was marginalized because he was too visible to disappear into the collective anonymity of regulatory culture.

Similarly, the visibility of representatives shifted on the basis of their work in the regulatory sphere and beyond. Although I entered the cable committee as "the professor," at some point, the committee chair began calling me "Legs," as in, "Good evening, Legs, how are you?," or "What's Legs got to say about this?" Spoken playfully, the nickname signified a shift away from my identity based on an unmarked professional expertise to one that marked my gendered and sexualized status in relation to him and his authority. It did not seem coincidental that this shift occurred as I spoke out more critically of the city and the cable company over the period of my appointment. That is, despite the intimate atmosphere of a small community in the regulatory meetings, the culture of professional anonymity and our procedural language still evoked a masculinist authority that rendered subjects with feminine or sexual identities abnormal.[28] As my voice became louder and my labor more visible, the feminization of my identity made it clear that my role was to submit to the universal norms that were implicitly masculine, if not subject to patriarchal disciplining through the chair's authority.

Our labors rendered invisible and our collective identity cloaked in anonymity, the regulatory board's most potent articulation of political power was its membership, not its formal charge. We espoused a liberal multiculturalism based on preserving the differences between racial populations, while avoiding what Davina Cooper calls a "diversity politics" that would make our commitments to social movements or progressive agendas visible in the public sphere.[29] In this way, we could preserve visions of a unified community that supported our legitimacy as television regulators, while enabling ourselves to make claims on behalf of imagined others we were to represent. Framed by the neoliberal politics that gives television industries wide latitude to operate in the public interest, the identification and representation of the public was local television regulators' most important work.

Regulatory Claims on Behalf of the Public

Broadcast regulatory culture conceptualizes "the people" through a similarly abstract notion of "the public," an articulation that joins television to its political functions in serving a citizenry. In the United States, these articulations espouse notions of community, diversity, and commonality in the formation of both a public opinion and, in the post–civil rights era, many public spheres. Frequently juxtaposed against an unruly crowd in need of discipline and uplift, or a mass of atomized individuals in need of coordination and remediation into society, the "public" idealizes the universal citizen who freely associates and acts for the greater good.[30] Historically, regulatory culture ignored cultural differences through transcendence, but its most recent articulation imagines several publics, each unified through a pluralistic civil society that integrates but differentiates cultural forms of allegiance and identification.[31] The tension between the one community and the many communities, meanwhile, is set in a regulatory framework that permits television industries to pursue audiences, an economic formulation that converts political capital into the commodity form. Corporate liberalism, or the faith that the tensions in democracy can be managed in the marketplace, has undergirded regulatory culture since at least the 1920s, deferring the thorniest questions around public representation to private hands. While corporate liberalism does not determine how television industries should operate, it places regulators and industrial executives in a community of like-minded individuals who presume a for-profit media system as common sense.[32] Regulatory culture thus sits at the juncture of a field of contradictory claims about diverse publics and the public interest, while also supporting an industry that elides the difference between citizens and consumers. These differences come into relief in national policymaking spheres, as Sonia Livingstone, Peter Lunt, and Laura Miller have shown in their analysis of the divergent meanings that politicians attached to words such as *public*, *citizen*, and *consumer* through the various drafts of the British Communications Act of 2003.[33] As they show, regulatory culture negotiates these differences through a political process that also frequently obscures their plural meanings in the final policy.

In the local arenas of cable-company monitoring and public-access station management, the citizens who work as the municipal regulators of television must articulate the public and the publics, while presuming corporate liberalism, in the making of claims. Representation claims are central to the technocratic labors of regulation, by legitimating regulators' abilities to balance their roles in speaking for themselves and on behalf of universalized others in shaping policy. Framed as "I" statements on behalf of "the people," claims inferred chains of equivalences between the speaker, the audience, and the imagined public or publics in his or her mandate. Through our claims to representation, the work of media policymaking occurred in the margins of the procedures that circumscribed regulatory culture. The technocratic processes of requesting and receiving collected facts as reports, for example, permitted limited forms of advocacy under the shields of objectivity and legitimacy. In a history of broadcast regulation, Hugh Richard Slotten concurs, "the rule-making process, which involves soliciting responses from industry and government officials as well as citizens groups about proposals, gives legitimacy to decisions and provides for rational and uniform planning."[34] Despite our limited purviews, I found early on that advisory agenda items could provide platforms for action. Definitions of words embedded in the language of regulation like *service* and *diversity* belied differences between speakers, setting the stage for conflicts over the inclusiveness or exclusiveness implied by the claims. Reports that listed static numbers of programs or producers using public access, for example, spurred us to ask follow-up questions, as in: "What were the hours that producers used editing facilities most?" Or, "Do you have a geographic breakdown of access users?" These questions, which implied cultural groups, could instigate new methods of record keeping, leading to motions that supported the franchise by making publicly mandated facilities more accessible, with targeted goals or objectives, that served the people as constructed in the claim.

These claims are always partial and subject to variation. Ernesto Laclau in his thesis on populism argues that "the people" is an empty signifier, torn by the contradiction of being a universal and a totality.[35] Since no one can embody either a universal subject or the totality of subjects, all representational claims are based on a lack, motivated by the desire to represent this impossible whole. Neither inherently progressive nor conservative, Laclau argues that "the people" is a moving target in the politics of representation. Individuals imply chains of cultural equivalences in speaking on behalf of others, but they cannot avoid the antagonistic relationships of universality and the differences that constitute the discursive field. Local regulators needed to refer to others for their claims to be heard, but these popular formations could never encompass either a universal public or the diversity of people they were to represent. As such, regulators may have had good intentions in their claims, but the *desire to represent* is a structural requirement of regulatory politics. It is the basis for administrative legitimacy and the terrain for taking action.

The contexts for the articulation of the people that television served in San Antonio and Davis could not have been more different, resulting in different kinds of representational claims. Davis was a satellite city of the state's capital and a university town. San Antonio featured the largest concentration of Mexican American citizens in the country, with generations of Latinos stretching back to before the state was part of the United States. It was also a largely working-class city, with large agricultural regions to the south, a tourism-oriented downtown economy, and several military bases to the north and west. Davis, on the other hand, was largely Anglo-American, with a small but growing Asian American population. Limited from growing beyond its agricultural surroundings and a benefactor of a state research university that invested in environmental science, Davis promoted itself as a small community that featured ample green space, organic farming, and recycling. Meanwhile the restricted growth policies and university-flanked public schools attracted dot-com families who migrated from the San Francisco Bay Area, resulting in soaring housing prices and the edging out of low-income residents. These differences mattered, both in terms of the composition of regulatory boards dealing with television and in terms of the ways in which people spoke on behalf of the public and the diverse publics in our midst. Claims were always relational and contingent, subject to change with the issue and audience. In general, claims articulated visions of the people based on imagined consumer-citizens, but whereas in San Antonio, committee members also envisioned an injured public, in Davis, board members sought a multicultural public through their claims.

Consumer-Citizens The people who can be mobilized and identified are central to regulatory politics both as the subjects and the objects of making claims. Most of the time, individual board members presented those political issues as highly personal ones, reflected through their own experiences. In San Antonio, I remember spending a quarter of an hour listening to a regulatory representative gripe about finding a parking space at the customer service center, where she would pay her cable bill. Another representative recalled her experience seven months later when she waited in a queue for a half hour to pay her bill at the same center. The issue of parking then reemerged the following month, this time preceded with a complaint that this particular representative did not have a bus line as an alternative to driving.[36] In these ways, mundane irritations associated with individuals' daily encounters with television became local political issues. Each claimant became an allegory for the people, who, aggrieved by poor customer service, geographic inequalities, and a lack of coordination between public transportation and private communications agencies, needed the private cable company to act in the public good. I also used this approach when I complained that my teenage video students could not schedule editing time at the public-access station. Arguing that if my students did not benefit from the access facility paid for by the city's lease of public rights-of-way to the cable company, then the people were not getting their money's worth. All these were consumer issues, involving what services one would expect in exchange for the franchise, framed as citizen rights.

The personalization of the people through individual problems demonstrates the conflation and conjoining of consumerism and citizenship, embedded both in liberal democratic governance and in local regulatory labor. Toby Miller calls consumerism the "logocentric double" of citizenship, legitimating the relationship between government and the market.[37] Since at least the late nineteenth century, the reorganization of government through the permissive expansion of industrial capitalism led to what Alan Trachtenberg has called the "incorporation of America," both literally in terms of the growth of corporations and figuratively, by producing an American "corpus" that engages in governance through the marketplace.[38] Through private stock ownership, citizens charted the transformation of public life, from the growth of transportation and communications infrastructure to the physical, built environment. The liberal democratic state could make good on its promises of equality by extending rights while permitting the concentration of wealth. The expression of citizenship, in other words, presumes private ownership, a fact not lost on theorists of the public sphere, who presume political debate is fostered in commercial locales, that is, the coffeehouse, and mediated by privately owned news outlets.[39] In local regulatory circles, the most powerful claims were also the most personal, representing the individual citizen who seemed to lack equal opportunity in the marketplace. Whether we invoked the public need for better customer services or inveighed against the company's transportation or communications infrastructure, our demands incorporated us into the liberal state as consumer-citizens. Weighing the exchange value of our own television service, we spoke as individuals to be served. Consumer-citizen claims deferred social rights into the privatized realm of customer service while not challenging corporate authority over the public good, making it easy for the company to hear our claims and to respond through market terms accordingly.

Our detachment from the social in consumer-citizen claims fit a neoliberal political economy for television. After the deregulations of the past decade, cable companies have shed the vast majority of their public responsibilities, from minority hiring programs to evaluating fairness in programming. The focus on consumers, however, serves corporate aims to boost their own bottom lines and offset remaining public provisions in the franchise. Through the category of what they considered "corporate social responsibility," Paragon in San Antonio and Comcast in Davis donated services pro bono, sponsored charity events, and supported nonprofit causes. These events simultaneously boost their brand image among consumers while justifying their economic entitlements in the public sphere. Consumption provided companies with the capital to reinvest in local governance functions, releasing further pressure on municipalities to pay for social services. Numbers mattered in this schema. Meeting minutes accounted for every organization involved, the numbers of people in attendance, and money donated resulting from each event. Success, measured quantitatively, could challenge the regulator's assertion that his or her individual claim spoke for a larger constituency. Contrastingly, when only ten people appeared for a public-access training class, we had few figures to marshal support for expanded public-access programming.

Miller writes that citizen claims have been channeled into quantitative metrics for effectiveness rather than into qualitative considerations of diversity or the public interest: "Diversity and debate are measured not by personnel, texts, or interpretations, but by numbers of outlets and varieties of technology."[40] In response to the claims about customer service in San Antonio, the cable company Paragon, a division of the Time Warner Corporation, reported that they fielded 150,000 to 200,000 phone calls per month.[41] To my claims, company personnel responded that they produced about forty to sixty community programs monthly. Countering any inference that my students' negative experience was common, the company registered the number of hours that community members spent in editing bays, studios, and in possession of Paragon equipment. By comparing the individual complaints of regulators to the numbers aggregated from a faceless mass of consumers, Paragon represented its own capacity to serve consumer citizens through a market ethos. Given that corporations could post far higher numbers than individual citizens in terms of their relative public investments, regulatory culture favored corporations' rights over corporeal citizens and exempted them from the responsibility to represent the people in other qualitative ways.

The Injured Public As much as regulatory culture fostered individual claims, it also categorized them. The systems of accountancy that counted and countered personal claims in the name of the people often used the same language of identity and demographics that have conjoined the language of citizenship and consumption.[42] Identity, which guided appointments to the local regulatory boards, also infiltrated the lexicon of claims. Using words like *constituencies* and *communities*, local regulators spoke on behalf of social groups whom they represented both politically through the appointment and culturally through a physical embodiment. In San Antonio, it was implicit that when the African American from the eastern part of the city used the phrase "my community," she referenced the African American population concentrated in her district. Similarly, city council members instructed us to represent our constituents, with whom we presumably shared class objectives. During the period that Roopali Mukherjee calls the "post-soul era," these terms spoke for an ambivalent politics of race, class, and culture that embraces the contradictory notions of a colorblind equality and the historical inequalities that demand remediation and redress.[43] The shifting terrain of identity categories allowed us to participate in the city's governance over its publics

without disrupting the distribution of power over a communications policy that favored the most privileged consumer-citizens.

The allocation of a cable channel for the Catholic Church and scholarships for local college students were two issues that triggered the San
Antonio cable committee to make claims on behalf of an imagined public.
Pat Rodgers, a former committee appointee himself, came to a cable
advisory board meeting in April 1998.[44] His short presentation and complaint set off a series of claims that moved from our chambers to the city
council and into the headlines of the local newspaper. Rodgers claimed
that Paragon was to move Catholic Television of San Antonio (CTSA)
from a channel located on the basic tier to one requiring a higher subscrip-
tion fee. This is a Hispanic city, he argued, one that wanted but could ill
afford the higher cable fees. Though divided in their reasons, board members agreed. Our recommendation to block Paragon's efforts to move the
channel ultimately prevailed. A more ambiguous outcome proceeded
from an ongoing debate about scholarships. Codified in the franchise of
1978 as "minority scholarships for high school students going on to study
communications, engineering, or a related field," Paragon's self-reporting
methods raised the issue of whether scholarships, again, in a predominantly Hispanic city, could be used toward one of the city's five Catholic
colleges.[45] The discussion, held in the wake of anti–affirmative action
rulings, concluded the scholarships could be used in parochial schools,
but not only for minorities. The through line—a chain of signifiers between Hispanic, majority, Catholic, minority, and poor—presented a vision of the public as injured victims both deserving of and suffering from
the cable television corporation.

"We may not be able to take direct action," said the board president Dora
Hauser to Rodgers. "If what CTSA wants is moral support, we can do that
and ask the City Council to revisit this issue with Paragon."[46] This support
included a number of claims about the San Antonio public and audience.
One year earlier, Paragon had suggested that the company was considering dropping the channel altogether, citing low ratings in a corporate-
sponsored survey and the small revenues for a premium placement in the
channel lineup. To this, representatives responded.[47] "CTSA is not the
only religious channel on cable," said one. "So why take away only their
station?" Another asked, "This is a predominantly Catholic community.
So if you have Jewish and Baptist services, why not Catholic?" Said an-

other, "What really bothers me is that most of the people who watch Sunday mass on CTSA cannot get out of their houses." When the issue reemerged a year later, the committee member Frances Cadena invited her councilman to make the case: "Our elderly use this channel as a source of information. . . . We need this channel to communicate with our citizens who can only afford the basic tier."[48] Rocky Aranda complimented a visiting councilman, directing him to address the Paragon officials at our meeting. "CTSA has been part of the community for years," said one, "Why not put it on Channel 15?" Another member agreed, further rejecting the need for Channel 15, the electronic schedule and preview station for the cable operator. "People flip through the stations with their remote anyways," she said. Members doubted the research Paragon conducted over the station, citing friends and family who watched. Noting that the sponsored survey was conducted in English, hence discriminatory toward Spanish-only respondents, one member commented ironically in the sidelines, "What did Paragon expect to find out?," further cementing associations between Hispanics, monolingualism, and Catholicism.

The discussions of scholarships were similarly complex, though representatives used similar claims to characterize the potential scholarship pool. Whereas CTSA viewers were elderly and physically immobile, potential minority students were young and economically immobile. "There are many bright youngsters that would have no options without these scholarships," claimed one committee member. The $7,200 scholarship at the time would completely pay for an associate's degree at the community college and would more than subsidize a four-year college. However, when an audit revealed that Paragon could not account for the names of the scholarship winners, committee members demanded both the names and a reevaluation of the distribution mechanisms. Questions of needy students and student need transformed into ones of choosing students and student choice. I asked, "What are the economic criteria for selecting a minority student?" Another inquired why we used the term *minority* at all if the city was more than half Hispanic. Still others wondered why the students chosen could go only to secular colleges. "Why can't students take their scholarship to [the Catholic college] Our Lady of the Lake?" Although no one claimed to be one of these students, the claims about students, spoken by different representatives of the political body, established the linkages between race, poverty, and religion, which seemingly characterized the populace that we spoke on behalf of and stood for in our own physical embodiments in the room.

Injury is the primary lens for managing populations and their differences in the liberal bureaucratic state, writes the political philosopher Wendy Brown.[49] In a system that assures universal rights, citizens must claim an injury to seek redress for past social injustices. Injury is a moving signifier, though. The civil rights movements of the 1960s and 1970s established identitarian categories of gender and race that anti–affirmative action movements of the 1990s and 2000s sought to replace with categories such as "economic standing, home environment, and neighborhood conditions."[50] Public debates over these categories, as Mukherjee shows in her analysis of educational admission policies, are windows that provide insights into the place of racism within liberalism, as well as "the range of ventriloquisms, adaptations, and containments that liberal discourses enabled."[51] Claims about the loyal CTSA viewers spoke for a racially defined community in which the discussion of race was curiously absent, implicit in the comments about Spanish-language use and "the community." These ways of knowing race without speaking it reemerged in the ways language, class, and faith consciousness replaced racial identity in the scholarship discussions. I found myself stuck between the colorblind language of racial denial and the essentialist associations among race, class, and religion. Identity politics thus imply an ongoing paradox in that in order for some individuals to achieve greater freedoms, structures of oppression must continue. This paradox resonated in San Antonio, a city in which a national minority population has emerged as an urban majority population. By fragmenting the Mexican American population into victimized segments, such as the poor, the elderly, the infirm, and youth, committee members could claim an injury for a part of the community that they established as their own.

Meanwhile, the universal subject of regulation continued to be unmarked subjects, who were at different times implied to be white, middle-class, wage-earning, or mobile consumers with their itchy fingers on the remote. Regulations, following Brown again, assisted in imagining a unified social body otherwise atomized through capitalism: "Indeed, much of the progressive political agenda in the recent years has been concerned not with democratizing power but with distributing goods, and especially with pressuring the state to buttress the rights and increase the entitlements of the socially vulnerable or disadvantaged: people of color, homosexuals, women, endangered animal species, threatened wetlands, ancient forests, the sick, and the homeless."[52]

By outsourcing the distribution of social goods to the cable company, the state extends its power not only via the corporation but also via the citizens then assigned to managing that relationship. Together, committee members, city officials, and cable representatives conspired in enforcing a communications policy that promoted individuals' rights and freedoms while failing to address "the subject constitution that domination effects, that is, the constitution of subject categories 'workers,' 'blacks,' 'women,' or 'teenagers.' "[53] Rather than transforming systems of inequality, our claims for CTSA and college scholarships reaffirmed the parities between political freedom and consumer choice, as well as between empowerment and consumption.

The Multicultural Public   Unlike in San Antonio, where each representative spoke on behalf of a demographic constituency, there was no such burden in Davis. There, DCTV board members spoke for the whole: an idealized hamlet of like-minded progressive, tech-savvy, affluent families in single-family homes. Over the course of a year and a half, few questioned who might not be able to afford cable television, much less the Internet or other more advanced services. Public-access television discussions centered on programming that would address this privileged core, from production summer camps for children, to skills-building internships for students, to digital video training for adults. Our discussions of television seemed to project the reality that the town was a liberal, elite enclave of educated professionals. The homogeneity of the board generated both comfort and anxiety for us, as reflected in claims of a multicultural public that we ourselves never embodied.

By the same token, questions of identity permeated discussions of board membership. As a board without district representation, we could expand. This point reminded the group continually of its homogeneity and whiteness. As staff searched for people they could recruit to the board, they used the term *representative* to imply that members needed to add to the racial diversity of the board. Everyone seemed to have a friend they could invite to join, and we actively sought people we knew, thus preserving other similarities among group members, particularly political orientation and class status. On the surface, these choices would reflect the Davis community that we ourselves claimed as our own. Progressive professionals would support the efforts of a public-access station, while adding to the cult of expertise that was a requisite for board membership. For months, we even met in the conference room of the local food cooperative. There, the affluent and liberal-minded public we represented in the meetings surrounded us, shopping by the door for organic pineapples and fair-trade tote bags. Yet our efforts during this time remained largely unsuccessful. When I joined the group, our chair had invited a "Latino housing activist" to the board, but in my term, that person never came to a meeting. We attracted someone who another member introduced as an "Asian American professional" who worked for PBS. She also lost interest in the board after a few meetings, having been unimpressed with the lack of professional production values in the DCTV television programs. While we envisioned a board that reflected a community, our consideration of racial identity over other forms of diversity, such as sexuality, ability, and particularly, class, reproduced whiteness as the racial norm of the group and rendered our white privilege invisible.

This search was so engrained in the culture of the group that I largely took it for granted that we would continue to search for members from various racial groups. After I had left the group, I talked to jessikah maria ross about this representational paradox as we took nature walks on the town's numerous greenways. Ross was the person who had originally invited me to be on the board and continued to be an informant and ally in thinking about the politics of the group. We talked about this nearly three years after I had moved away from the town.

JESSIKAH: We'll here's the thing. I feel like the leadership at DCTV was always sensitive to ethnic diversity, not necessarily class diversity, but definitely ethnic diversity. But that there is a difference between having an understanding of how useful it is to have representation from different constituencies. There's a difference between understanding it and, how can I put this? There is a difference between recognizing it and understanding it. So, for example, people were very much like, we'll need to look as if we represent the communities, so let's make sure and have an African American, Asian American, Native. It's kind of like check that box. It's something that you should do as an organization and that's really different from saying in the long term we need to make sure that all of these very different constituencies not only understand who we are, value who we are, so they will

advocate for us. So there is a difference between recognizing its importance
and actually doing the work to organize, to build relationships.

VICKI: Right, come out more organically from what the organization is.

J: So, here is a concrete example. Instead of calling the person who started Blacks
for Effective Action, I think that's a group here in town, and this is hypotheti-
cal. Instead of just calling and saying, would you just be on our board because
we need to have an African American that's linked in. . . . And that's not a bad
thing, I am sorry, that is a very important thing to do, but that's very different
than actually going to Blacks for Effective Action meetings, talking about what
you do, spending time to see what their issues are, and then asking them to
come to the station to get involved. I mean really forging the alliance. That's it.
There should be this alliance building or coalition building. There was cherry
picking of people so that they would bring their constituencies to the table if
need be, and that really isn't an effective way to do it.

Whiteness is a source of identity anxiety, writes Kalpana Seshadri-
Crooks, in that it symbolizes both the norm but also relies on a hierarchy
of racial differences that guarantees its position at the top.[54] So whiteness
is both an undifferentiated everything and a master signifier for differences, together forming an impossible wholeness that no individual
could possess. It remains, instead, an impossible desire, motivating social
formations based on racial visibility while disavowing the naturalization
of whiteness as the norm in U.S. culture. Unlike sexual difference, which
Lacanians ground in the realization of the lack of the phallus, racial
difference cannot be simultaneously based on both a desire for whiteness
and a wholeness that obliterates differences. As Seshadri-Crooks puts
it, there is a "lack of a lack," meaning that very desire that promises
unity also guarantees hierarchy and oppression.[55] The search for African
American, Asian American, and Latino/a board members falls into this
pyrrhic desire for a visible difference within a group that might prove our
representativeness of a unified Davis people. It was a desire that could
never be satisfied because no matter who was present, we never represented the totalizing diversity of the real. Having an African American
business leader or a Latina college professor would not compensate for
the lack of a teenager or a worker who cleaned our municipal buildings
each night. These proxies for our differences merely guaranteed the unstable grounds on which we claimed that all Davis residents wanted high-
speed Internet connections and upscale cable and video services.

Cities charge regulatory boards with speaking on behalf of everyone, but board members face an impossible task of being both autonomous bodies and speaking for and on behalf of others. In San Antonio, the racial representativeness of the board offered the fantasy that each member represented a larger group, when, in fact, most of our work took place in isolation and through either personal claims or through essentialist statements. In Davis, the visibility of our own racially unrepresentative bodies enabled and tempered the board's framing of a unified body politic, causing the anxiety of an impossible desire for both total unity and total diversity. By looking at claims making as labor, the work of regulators as workers in the television production process becomes more complicated than simple policy enforcement or identity politics. If it cannot be assumed that a female or black regulator will adopt a particular stand toward particular issues, it can be assumed that identity operates in more complex ways than just a direct correspondence between bodies and politics or even a theory of identity politics. As media historians have dutifully shown, the coalitions in support of nondiscriminatory media policies cannot be reduced to a homogenous identity group. Although popular texts might commemorate the fight to rescind the licenses of racist broadcasters in Jackson, Mississippi, as an African American struggle, the coalition of black and white activists frequently clashed with black leaders who did not wish to destabilize their authority with white elites in local political spheres.[56] Similarly, struggles around children's television, though frequently framed as a women's issue, have drawn from supporters as culturally diverse as religious fundamentalists and anti-sugar hippies.[57] It stands to reason that if the public is formed from complex coalitions of people foregrounding particular aspects of their identities and ignoring others, then regulatory bodies themselves are formed from the same dynamic processes of identification and representation.

In both Davis and San Antonio, the claims we made as regulators ultimately supported a consumer-citizenship in which race could be a mobile signifier while whiteness was always the privileged norm. Through these claims, our efforts to define a community implied a membership based on consumer choice, the distribution of market goods, and the envisioning of high-tech utopias. The needs of capital supplemented our notions of community in the ways that diversity might be expressed in terms of members of the citizen board or the citizenry that those members claim, but always under the aegis of a corporate culture that integrated sameness and differences into consumer markets.[58] Miranda Joseph argues that the corporatization and incorporation of diversity leads to ambivalent results for those who volunteer on behalf of the community. While on the one hand, being citizen regulators identified us as individual members of the body politic, on the other hand, cable operators could exploit those same claims about our uniqueness as market segments.[59] We could debate about identity categories, the formation of our committee, and the articulation of claims about the public, all the while presuming that consumer needs would speak louder, be more persuasive, and be less antagonistic than citizen needs for television. While citizen or consumer identities might have been shifting, unstable, and symbolic—in other words, socially constructed in our activities and interactions—they had real policy effects. The processes of cable franchise renewal in both places reflected the ways in which the regulatory boards mediated cultural identities and made representative claims that ultimately favored elite interests of cable operators and television consumers.

Deregulation and Biopolitical Regulatory Work

The discussion leader called the focus group a "workshop." Hired to help the city achieve the best possible outcomes for negotiating its cable franchise, this leader had called together a group of about twenty Davis residents to City Hall on a Saturday morning. In a cheery but sterile conference room, we sat down facing several pieces of paper taped to the walls. Each piece identified issues we were to talk about: First, the problems in Davis, followed by the problems in communicating for community organizations, the problems with Comcast, and then, finally, solutions. These boundaries in practice were somewhat artificial, because, as we began brainstorming, people blurted out a range of interconnected problems in the city, from the lack of affordable housing, to overcrowding schools, to the costs of the cable bill. The leader paraphrased our issues into broad notions that everyone might be able to relate to, such as unequal technology access, a loss of community identity, and overcrowded studios. When we got to discussing solutions to the problems, we ran out of time. The discussion leader had to rush, filling in the blanks for us, suggesting and trying to explain the possibilities. For example, no one really understood what an "I-Net" was for connecting schools and municipal buildings, but once the leader described it, no one voiced an opinion as to why we would not want it. I piped in a little toward the end of the meeting, using my San Antonio experience to suggest that public-access stations stay on the lowest programming tier in the new franchise. I was certain that many others in the room had no idea what that meant, but it went on the paper. At the end of the meeting, we filled out our questionnaires with some five pages of questions nearly identical to the issues we had raised. They did not ask for our solutions, and open comments were allowed only on the final page.

Beginning in the late 1990s, thousands of municipalities across the United States embarked on a variety of legal processes to renew their cable franchises with the hopes of safeguarding, if not improving, the terms of the agreements. Once encouraged and provided for in the Cable Act of 1972, these franchises—some sixteen thousand of them in 1993— had operated twenty to thirty years through piecemeal addenda as cable companies consolidated, conglomerated, and created digital services and entertainment synergies.[60] The gradual deregulation of ownership laws and cross-market synergies placed cable companies in competition with telecommunications and satellite companies for the most lucrative segments of digital communications markets, but also in an unlikely alliance to divert regulatory power away from municipalities and to statewide institutions, such as utilities boards.[61] The first statewide cable franchise, signed in 2005 by the State of Texas, reduced market barriers to using public rights-of-way for any commercial communications service in exchange for fixed fees for each municipality.[62] The threat of this legislation, which usurped local power over franchise fees, cable services, and local provisions, made it more important than ever to make claims on behalf of citizen and consumer publics. In San Antonio and Davis, where regulatory cultures differed historically, city officials and citizen regulators took divergent paths toward the impending statewide cable franchises, in Texas and California respectively, leading to nearly oppositional outcomes.

In both places, the sphere for regulatory labor increased. As illustrated by the Davis focus group, the technocratic use of citizen groups' voluntarism and activism to gauge and evidence the "public" interest in television and communications marked a new stage with continuities in the regulation of cable companies and municipal television stations.

Whereas selection criteria and gatekeeping processes historically limited who could be members of regulatory boards, from the FCC down to the local cable committee, a variety of civil society groups have also mobilized increasing numbers of citizens to take up the work of monitoring, recommending, and regulating broadcasters. From the tabulation of local contents to the monitoring of production and employment practices, the sphere of regulatory labor has broadened to encompass a host of groups with interests only perpendicularly related to television or broadcasting.[63] In the deregulatory era, these labors have become central pillars of a new regulatory regime, evidencing a public in absentia of regulatory representatives to speak on behalf of the people.

At the same time, the new regime extended the ways that local regulatory cultures already represented citizens. Both in Davis and San Antonio, city staffers were aware of the need for a cable franchise renewal in 1995 and 1998, respectively.[64] In Davis, city and DCTV administrators, in step with our own anxieties around representational governance, created multiple structures to measure and enlist a multicultural public for negotiating a new cable franchise. These methods included surveys, interviews, and focus groups, such as the one that I joined. In San Antonio, where the cable advisory board representatives claimed to represent the diversity of their city, regulatory appointees and their designated staff refused to seek a public outside of their own cable committee, holding no public meetings on the issue of franchise negotiation. The fixed correspondence between the regulators and a constituency identified by race, class, and gender made other outside input unnecessary, if not inconvenient at times. The committee simply resolved that it was in the public interest to dissolve, itself a mandate of deregulation. In its place, civil society groups now bear all responsibility to articulate the public interest in local television programming and broadcasting. The results of these contrasting approaches reveal the continuing need for invisible laborers to work freely in the service of commercial television imperatives, multicultural consumer-citizens, and injured others.

Enlisting and Aggregating the Public   The focus group, one of several conducted for the renegotiation of the city's cable franchise, seemed to mirror many of the dynamics of the citizen boards in which I had participated in the past. Senior citizens, women, and public-access television producers were overrepresented. Some people spoke frequently and some never over the course of two hours, though they politely listened. Most prefaced their answers with personal consumer experiences that were reminiscent of the regulatory meetings in San Antonio and Davis. In comparison, few people spoke for others using the term *we*, and those who did were not referencing those notably absent at the meeting, such as young people, people of color, unemployed or low-income peoples. All these responses, decontextualized from the act of responding to the discussion leader's prompts and the social experiences of the speakers, recombined to demonstrate a multicultural public for the technocratic process of franchise negotiations. The few and select voices heard in the focus group merged into several hundred pages of data aggregated from the contracted consulting firm, the city's three access boards, telecommunications task force meetings, some thousand surveys, consumer service complaints, and nine focus groups to "provide a diversity of perspectives within the identified community sectors."[65] Weighing heavily on the work of volunteers like those who came to the focus groups, these "sectors" overrepresented "leaders in technology, business organizations, educators, and the representatives of major arts organizations."[66] The outcome was called the "Preliminary Report on Community Cable-Related Needs and Interests," and two city staffers used the report in franchise negotiations in 2003 to demonstrate the local need for "the benefits of advances in cable technology in the homes and schools of their communities."[67] As one of the two negotiators, the deputy director of Parks and Community Services, Jerilyn Cochran, explained, the public was both represented and effective: "We laid out that demographic information early for them, saying, 'Look at how much education we have. Look at how much income we have. Look at our property values. Look at our surveys. Get in here and rebuild this system and make this happen.' Dog gone if they didn't do it."[68] In the end, Davis negotiated a contract with the cable company before the passage of statewide franchising legislation in 2006. It maintained DCTV and achieved a faster rebuild of its digital services infrastructure, creating a win for both the city's consumer-citizens and the expanding cable company.

The technocratic needs of regulators to provide expertise and effectiveness in the franchise-renewal process relied on volunteer labor to reaffirm what DCTV board members already claimed to know in our meetings about the affluent, tech-savvy identity of the city's people. In the process, the regulator's burden of representing the public shifted; from the few volunteer DCTV board members, to hundreds of volunteers, back to two municipal employees empowered to negotiate on the people's behalf. At each stage, self-selecting individuals contributed time and effort to making claims on behalf of absent others. Yet on providing their "diversity of perspectives," identifiable individuals became invisible through a report that channeled diverse identities into interest groups and rationalized the products of their labor (from strategic plans and position papers to customer complaints and survey responses) into "public inputs." Those who had volunteered the most time in the negotiation processes felt most uneasy with these biopolitics of regulation.

Kari Peterson and Steve McMahon were two citizens involved in many stages of the negotiations process: first, as the then executive director of DCTV and the director of the Davis Community Network, an organization providing low-cost Internet access for local citizens; second, as two of the seven City Council appointees to the Telecommunications Task Force; and, finally, as organizers of the Friends of Community Media, a civil society group to lobby the city council for community television and communications. I asked both to reflect on the value of volunteer labor.[69]

> VICKI: The whole idea about representative democracy is that it's every citizen's responsibility to take pride in participating in these policy processes, but in a time when so much of regulation is being deregulated and it seems like put on the backs of volunteers, reflect a little bit about was this moment where citizens such as yourselves were called upon to do this. How do you reflect back on that? Is this a measure of cities dumping more on citizens? They could have paid more or they could have had professionals do it. Or is it more like, well, this is the way it should be because you guys as individuals bring things to the table or get the public involved in a way that otherwise it wouldn't have. I haven't decided one way or the other on any of these issues.
>
> STEVE: I think it varies community by community. The idealistic side of myself would like to say it should be more representative democracy. There should be more involvement by the public. Transparent process is the way to go. But the fact of the matter is people's lives are immensely demanding and probably only in extremely affluent, unusually educated communities like Davis that you can get the kind of commitment out of people like we had. The last thing I would do to another community would be to suggest to them, if they aren't like Davis, that this is the way they should do it.

Because if you can't get the people to show up at the meetings and take the time out of their lives, the outcome is going to be bad. And in that sense what government should be doing, that's the business it's in: to deliver a good outcome to the public and act on their behalf. It should be redeemable. We should be able to ask what the government is doing. We are very fortunate to live in the community that is so affluent that the time is available among its citizens. With such a consensus about its identity, and as much as we fight amongst one another, that people do volunteer for community chores is an unusual thing and it's not realistic to think this is possible for many other communities.

KARI: The other thing I was going to say is that this stuff is terribly complicated and there isn't a real clear role for the public. I hate to say that because I am all about citizen participation and processes. It was a frustration that we had throughout. It is just really hard to mobilize citizens around a piece [of the process] where they are going to have an effect. We thought at different points along the way that we could be doing just some community workshops to inform people about issues in general and interest people in broader public policy stuff. We talked about that. That would have felt good. I felt that we had a responsibility. I have colleagues all over the country who are engaged in franchise renewal and, as Steve said, it just varies in different communities. In some communities, there's really an effective mobilization of people around some element of [the process]. We involved citizens in the needs-assessment phase and we trumpeted that a lot. [As in,] "Thank you citizens of Davis for weighing in and helping us shape our needs for the future, and visualize and think about our needs. Tell your story so we can serve your needs." It's just hard. It's hard to find a way . . . a realistic, a practical and useful way to involve people in the process.

Even if the expansion of regulatory work has become more effective, it is not altogether more satisfying. The anxieties around multicultural representation that I heard in the DCTV board meetings remained in this new regulatory scenario, now tempered by the pressure to exercise a biopolitical governance that channels free labor into the competitive advantage of municipalities. The continuing desire to represent the people in regulating television could not be reconciled with the need to preserve a community identity that had value, both to the commercial interests of the cable company and, more importantly, to legitimizing interests of the city. Volunteers gave negotiators the representational authority that the DCTV board lacked on its own.

Dodging and Dispersing the Public   In San Antonio, where city council appointees served as proxies for the absent public, the process of franchise negotiation moved the burden of representation almost immediately to disparate individuals who then mobilized. Begun only two years before its expiration, the negotiation process remained ensconced in City Hall between two rate analysts, one with an engineering background and the other with a legal background, and the supervisor for the Public Utilities Department.[70] As this technocratic triad worked with the cable provider, the advisory committee that I had served on disbanded. Despite its demographic representativeness of the people, the lack of the governing authority over consumer issues, such as cable rates, station placement, and service equipment, sapped interest from the committee. "We were left reviewing the basic-tier calculations. The Cable Advisory Committee seemed to have problems getting members to show up. Meetings were cancelled more often because there was no quorum," said the Public Utilities rate analyst Ben Cadena III.[71] With no one left to make claims on behalf of the public, Senate Bill 5 passed the Texas Legislature, and days after the cable company received its statewide franchise, the city lost its television studios, equipment, and personnel. The public-access station went black.

The labor of making claims about television on behalf of the public fell to citizens who mobilized into the Texas Media Empowerment Project, an organization that combined representatives of nonprofit groups around the region. Representing the African American, Mexican American, and Anglo American communities that once had representatives sitting on the cable advisory board, citizens had to work across scales as city officials scrambled for emergency funding and the new official cable regulators sat in the state's Public Utility Commission.[72] "The public was never really involved in the initial negotiations," said Patsy Robles, a public-access producer and one of the group's leaders.[73] "So really the only way we found out about this and got involved was because of news leaks to us by reporters who let us know what was coming down the pike. We were the ones who found out from the outside and then ended up going down to talk to city staff." Seven months and several meetings later, the cable company began distributing public-access television programs again; a former Time Warner representative to the cable advisory committee opened a simple retransmission studio on the ground floor of the city's municipal building. Having lost the battle to keep a public-access television studio in San Antonio, citizens continue to work as the monitorial watchdogs that preserve regulators' roles in producing television, while the state renders them invisible. As the assistant city attorney, Gabriel Garcia, phrased it, the regulation of television had changed: "You lose that interpersonal relationship. . . . So that means now you're dealing with lawyers, and it becomes much more confrontational. In the past, these negotiations could have happened in face-to-face meetings, but now that doesn't happen anymore. If there's any issue that the city wants to address, the only way is to change the law at this point."

I was present at the beginning of the cable-franchise-renewal processes in San Antonio and Davis, but not at their ends. It seemed, though, that even from a distance, the cultural politics of regulation in each city continued to utilize citizen labor in the commercial interests of television and communications companies. In San Antonio, with no one left to speak for the injured public, state regulators severed the practices of media policymaking from those of media regulating, leaving citizens with the work of monitoring television production on the margins. In Davis, municipal regulators preserved their policymaking roles by assimilating those commercial interests as citizen interests. Despite these oppositional outcomes, the deregulation of municipal franchising authority led to the effective shift of regulatory work onto the shoulders of some citizens who must speak for a people that they can neither wholly represent nor make television industries respond to.

Regulators in Television Production Processes

Regulators have always performed largely invisible labor in the service of television production processes in the United States. Existing as neither agents of the state nor of the market, their practices result in serving both entities through the technocratic bureaucracy of media governance. Deregulation was to eliminate the labor of governance, making television's structures seamless with the public interest and its management effortless. Instead, the shrinking purview of regulators' policymaking authority has done the opposite, pushing the work of representing "the people" onto a greater number of volunteer citizens, themselves the embodiments of interests in overlapping social and cultural hierarchies at local, regional, and national scales. As their numbers have waxed, any correlative dignity associated with regulatory work has waned, motivating some citizens to abdicate volunteering for regulatory roles altogether. More commonly, though, regulatory work has become regularized as part of everyday middle-class life. Cities hail the citizens presumed to have the time, energy, and information for focus-group or survey participation. Media industries desire those same people as part of their consumer base. As a result, the local cable regulator's roles of monitoring and making claims have spread to a public of unpaid and unrecognized consumer-citizens. Rent-seeking states and markets require these inequities in labor power and shared logics of cultural identification for the mutual enrichment of municipalities looking to cut costs and industries looking to expand.

In the meantime, these new everyday regulators have little power over actual communications policy. As Des Freedman writes, "Being a 'stakeholder,' identifying yourself as someone who has interest in the outcome of a decision, is in no way a statement about your power."[74] Stakeholders in television and communications policy have grown in a global sense, evidenced by transnational social movements for media reform and justice, but the numbers of people empowered to make policy and regulatory decisions seems to have contracted, limited to elites speaking to other elites in increasingly private social networks.[75] In the United States, visions of localism in regulation have empowered political and economic elites since at least the 1920s, when civic boosters and radio station owners allied to preserve their status and competitive advantage, both with businesses in adjacent polities and with national broadcasting affiliates.[76] Regulators' definitions of the public interest privileged those at the top of local class and cultural hierarchies, while classifying everyone else in categories to be sold to advertisers. Localism provisions in municipal cable television policy in the late 1960s incorporated these privileged citizens directly into the regulation process. Hailed as "a window . . . in American media for ordinary citizens to take control of both content and policy for the first time [in broadcast history] in decades," local regulatory boards included a larger constituency of citizens selected for their abilities to mediate between their private identities and the public interest.[77] Yet as illustrated in this chapter, local board appointees have hardly been ordinary citizens. Chosen from the pool of citizens who have the professional status and political networks to be considered qualified for civic service, localism in practice has preserved the local hierarchies of race and class through board membership. Even as regulators multiply and seem increasingly diverse, standing as proxies for local publics, their authority has dissipated over the past four decades. This leaves well-meaning citizens to represent the people with little correlative authority.

Emerging forms of regulatory culture emphasize the continuing importance of regulators in the new television economy as their labor enables new production realities. The explosion of reality television that models self-management mirrors the deregulated state that disregards its diffused power by disavowing its potency and repudiating public responsibility.[78] As Laurie Ouellette and James Hay point out, vast segments of the television landscape today—from lifestyle TV and court programming to financial-advice shows and self-help talk shows—both advocate for and make use of consumers who recognize themselves as civic service providers.[79] Conversely, the programs insist that these citizens see themselves as members of consumer lifestyles, assisting in their delivery to sponsors, as described in the previous chapter. The work of making claims, providing expertise, and offering personal testimonies fits neatly with what Joseph Turow describes as the ongoing technologies of customer-relations management that relies on both data collection and customization.[80] The erasure of public and private boundaries places these citizens in the often awkward position of representing the public and identifying new customer niches. The widespread production of these programs emerges from the historical conjuncture in which the state's efforts to resolve how to manage a private broadcasting system as a public service merge with the corporate demands for deregulation.[81] Regulators who recognize themselves as independently responsible for monitoring and managing broadcasting systems through everyday acts and volunteer labor thus become both the means and ends of a self-perpetuating governance system ruled primarily by television industries.

As described in this chapter, regulators are not dupes in serving these state and market imperatives. The call to be hypervigilant in monitoring television industries in the name of the multitude of stakeholders not present is not an easy task. The local citizen regulators I encountered in my own experiences knew instinctively that to empower constituencies, enable communications access, or free citizens from discriminatory conditions, they had to present the people either as demanding consumers or as injured victims. They relied on what Brown calls the "rationalized procedural unfreedom" of the state to reference and evidence the differential values between normative television consumers and those injured as a result of historical and ongoing exclusions based on class, race, age, and abilities.[82] On these bases, regulators' work paradoxically promoted a colorblind consumer-citizenship and a liberal multicultural public of injured others to be remediated through television markets and corporate-responsibility programs. Instead of stimulating civic pride, these outcomes frequently alienated the regulators, who wondered what their institutional function was or why they continued doing this work. Through the negotiation of their claims, they had to struggle with their own senses of invisibility and impotence in contexts of winnowing windows for public access, rising rates for communications services, and shrinking spheres within which people beyond the chosen few could speak to power. I know these complaints all too well myself, which is perhaps why academics should be sensitive to the double binds of regulatory work, particularly when they are the ones called to do this work in the future.

Conclusion

RETHINKING PRODUCTION STUDIES IN

THE NEW TELEVISION ECONOMY

Television set assemblers, soft-core videographers, reality casters, and civic cable volunteers speak to transformations in production in the new television economy. In one sense, the very definitions of creative and professional seem increasingly indistinguishable from other forms of mass production and casual labor. In another sense, the dispersal of television work across the market and political boundaries has involved increasing numbers of everyday people in the work of television sponsorship and regulation. Those doing this labor would be apt not to see themselves as television producers, while they nevertheless recognize their contributions to the television's production operations and personnel hierarchies. Television industries, as well as the industrial and governmental organizations that support them, need a self-controlled workforce to be creative, professional, commodifiable, and regulated in supporting their profit motives. The routine enlistment of workers who do not recognize their own labor value and who yet provide forms of low-cost and no-cost services to the industry, demonstrates how the cultural processes of identity and identification are integral to the formation of television's invisible labor force.

These elisions and slippages between those identified as producers and those who work without labor value or symbolic status indicate the need to broaden the scope of television production studies to account for these changes in production work, while also interrogating the dominant paradigms by which we have defined television producers for at least the past half-century. This book has attempted to understand who television producers are by looking at how the processes involved in making television

—from set to program to policy—then make producers, thereby excluding the vast majority of those whose invisible and immaterial work might be considered below the lines that separate producers from all other forms of television labors. My hope in doing this work is that future scholars of television production may become more aware of the ways in which people work to produce television and in which these activities are vital to the reproduction of producers' authority and the maintenance of powerful centers for television production.

Much has already been made of the changing role of creatives and professionals since the mid-1990s, when scholars began taking note of the unusual nexus of policymakers, entrepreneurs, and university-educated workers who coalesced in branding television production work as a driving force in urban cultural economies. Using a new Darwinian logic organized by identity and geography, studies correlate economic growth with the presence of workers already known to be creative and professional by virtue of class position, social bonds, and location, location, location. By these indices, Hollywood is the analogy for a population of creative professionals in television simply because, in the words of Richard Florida, "Business gets done there . . . creative people congregate there, network with each other and are readily available."[1] The new television economy cashes in on an exclusivity of identity and place, distinguishing cities and their populations based on their presumed production niches and labor power. At the same time, the new television economy exports the semiotics of identity and place, challenging cities to develop their own competitive advantages to develop professionalized workforces with the lure of cheap and abundant resources, whether it is the supposedly docile workforce of Manaus or the ongoing street party in New Orleans. It is precisely this expedient use of culture as the reified product of multicultural labor and industrial capital that exemplifies what politicians since the 1990s call the "creative economy."[2]

Deconstructing the rhetoric of the creative economy and its implicit material inequalities in the first instance means breaking down artificial distinctions between the mental and the manual, between skilled labor and organic labor, between above the line and below the line. These dichotomies continue to justify the perception, especially in the middle class, that some types of work are categorically better than others, that their workers should be better compensated and more entitled to societal rewards. The aura of the creative professional in television operates to efface the ways in which capital captures all workers in a universal logic of accumulation while dividing them into categories based on conflict and contradiction. From the factory to the music club to city hall, each field site presented in this book generates surplus value for television industries through technologies, both legal mechanisms and physical tools, which control labor costs and demote labor power by replacing living laborers with objects. As Laikwan Pang has shown in his critique of the creative economy, both mental and manual laborers generate value through their ability to take raw materials, whether aluminum for a television tube or an idea for a sitcom, and bring them into a profitable form through technologies and other living laborers.[3] Whether making a television set or an intellectual property, workers need to coordinate with each other to navigate the technologies that seek to discipline and devalue their labors. The case studies show that workers across fields and occupations use their bodies and minds to coordinate, adapting creatively to new conditions while striving for an individual autonomy that cannot be reduced to an exchange value.

At the same time, the case studies in this book reflect the structural forces that have created creative professionals as a privileged sector of the new television economy. *Dynamic, global, networked,* and *flexible* are among the buzzwords of the new economy transferred onto the television producer.[4] The plasticity of boundaries between job roles, which demand more skills for less pay, and the time crunch that then expands the workday over the course of the whole week—these seem as common now to television production as they have been to computer programming, speechwriting, art curating, academic researching, or any other series of labors that have monetized ideas in so-called "creative industries."[5] Clusters of temporary work communities collaborate more sporadically for shorter-term contracts and then must migrate and remobilize in search of sellable content, whether tangible products or intangible data. Production processes rely on sanctioned forms of creative innovation to boost profit margins, which lead producers to ignore or repress other creative actions that may interrupt team-based work flows or dynamics. Employers seek to promote and distribute a professionalism that promises fun or autonomy but delivers self-control and other-surveillance in lieu of material benefits or job security.

In the process, the work of creative professionals presumes that they also do the work of television's sponsors and regulators. Capital subsumes labor in that producers have become adept managers of their emotional resources and personal relations. The awareness of identities —their own and that of others—creates their own representational politics that help dictate how to satisfy personal interests in social interactions. In the struggles for legitimacy and recognition, workers commodify their social bonds as television's sponsors and represent their consumer demands as television's regulators. Political power and economic survival alike thus rely on the ability to defend television's commercial aims, even to embody them. Angela McRobbie identifies the new economy's labor force as cultural entrepreneurs of the self: branding themselves to emphasize marketable traits while disciplining away their eccentricities to fit the temporal demands of an employer.[6] Meanwhile, those same people absorb the political work of regulation into semiprivate spheres as forms of volunteer activism, homework, or as just a personal responsibility associated with one's civic persona. These rhetorical and performative labors come to stand for the "ordinary," as Laura Grindstaff argues, not only because it is the U.S. middle-class subject who works as the representative ordinary person but also because these presumed labors, largely immaterial and invisible, are the normative bases for the new television economy.[7]

Work has colonized the social, McRobbie claims; and while I agree, I also see this as part of a longer historical trajectory in which the political economy has produced workers based on an oversupply or the scarcity of identities. Since the latter half of the nineteenth century, women's exchange of "free" work for their survival was the crucial element to the reproduction of an abundance of wage workers idealized as the working-class family across Europe and the United States.[8] The invisibility of the women's labor doubled through subcontracting practices of sweatshop employers, named so because the contractors could "sweat" off their workers in the absence of regulatory oversight and an oversupply in the labor market.[9] At the same time, the valuation of mass commodities increasingly relied less on their scarcity and more on the uncompensated work of exclusive niches of consumers, who in their gendered and class-based communities have acted as amateurs, hobbyists, and artisans. These practices did not so much disappear as transform through social spheres, reemerging in diverse employment markets such as the burgeoning informal economies of the developing world after the 1970s and the service sectors of postindustrial urbanities after the 1980s. The shifting value of work performed outside the formal workplace sought to exploit the value generated by those most peripheral to the labor force: young people, freelance and precarious workers, and the unemployed.[10] Today, the presence of these practices as part of producing television suggests less a fundamentally new economy than one in which, as Andrew Ross puts it, labor that used to be on the margins of capital accumulation is now part of the core.[11] The market determines the value of one's creativity and professionalism based on the artificial scarcity of workers able to buy, sell, and stand for the commodity audience.

What is perhaps new in the new television economy is the ways in which it produces value for television beyond its programming content and audience commodities. Though television has always expressed excess as a mass industry or as a tool of modernity, the seeming democratization of the work associated with television production places these symbolic meanings in the hands of everyday people. Personal subjectivities and social identities in this economy have use value as tools and exchange value as commodities. Whether connecting the tubes or creating the content, to be a television producer—or, someone whose labor, however small, contributes to its production—is a powerful piece of symbolic capital for workers. In turn, the shared recognition of media power makes workers more vulnerable to respond affirmatively to industrial needs for cheaper labor and to serve the political utility of being consumer-citizens.

In addition, the cases show that this capital—and the individual ability to claim it, tout it, or mobilize it to other ends—is contingent on a marketplace of values attached to gender, race, class, sexuality, age, and nationality. From factory line operators in Brazil to civic appointees in the United States, individuals involved in production chose to stress the saliency of one identity, thus repressing or denying the value of others. New management techniques wanted active workers on assembly lines, but only women assemblers could cash in on their ability to flirt with the male management. The male cameramen who shot soft core on the weekends reaffirmed masculinities not associated with the feminized service sector. Conversely, casters claimed competitive advantage by naturalizing their feminine emotion work as women and gay men, but they still claimed racial and class alliances when it added value to their identities as audience authorities. As in any marketplace, the unstable value of identities correlates with the invisible labor in the product. In accordance with Lisa Adkins's observations, straight men can more easily reap the advantages of feminine modes of work simply because their employers consider them skills and not natural features of their identities.[12] Local volunteers for public-access television boards stressed identities that emphasized their claims about the public because industry and politicians could recognize the value of the identity to the construction of the people and the market, and not necessarily of the claim. These complicated negotiations over identities should be considered part of television production both enabling and in limiting which media technologies are made, what programs are pitched, and how communication policies are enforced.

My provocation in studying production is to connect these practices, values, and subjectivities through what Sherry Ortner has called an "ethnographic stance" that contextualizes places, spaces, participants, and their observers.[13] If the lived realities of cultural workers, according to McRobbie, include "non-groups, non-labour markets, non-institutions, as well as non-places," then production studies need to expand beyond the studio workers and unionized trades, or even beyond television networks and Hollywood.[14] The hidden transcripts for articulating power relations between workers in the production of television can be found in the rituals of work performances, the syntax of insider languages, and the layers of what John Caldwell calls the deep texts of production, from technical manuals to trade-show propaganda.[15] The convergence of work and play, home and office, private and public illustrate, as Mark Deuze argues, that media workers exemplify and accelerate convergence themselves through their own hypermediated "liquid lives."[16] Whether or not this particular personification is tautological, the apparent multiplication of merging sites for understanding production justifies why studies of television production need to look as intently at work on the street as at that in the studio, and as deeply into the nature of freelancing and contract work as into emotional and surveillance work.

Production researchers frequently frame the spatial and temporal dimensions of the new television economy largely in terms of access to human subjects. Overworked and mobile, the new television economy worker is difficult to find at a single field site, within temporal rituals, or even among a stable community of peers. Ethnographers focusing on the top of media production hierarchies have long noted the unavailability of field subjects, from Hortense Powdermaker's ruminations on the difficulty of walking onto film studio sets in the 1950s to Georgina Born's frustration with unreturned phone calls and snarky comments by BBC executives at the end of the century.[17] As Ortner herself has found, even "studying sideways" by tapping into work communities with relatively parallel levels of cultural and economic capital has not yielded easy entry into the field of power relations governing production sites and their personnel.[18] Access to all labor processes relies on traversing contractual laws, legal gag orders, and bureaucratic barriers that have drawn all aspects of workers' lives into corporate property relations. Meanwhile, workers have their own imperatives for controlling their own narratives about their working selves, whether they are aspiring to advance their careers or are fearful not to end them. As Caldwell suggests, it is hard for researchers to distinguish between the producer and the performance of the producer.[19] This accounts for why critiques of television work remain so hidden. When being a worker means being a certain kind of embodied subject, the most oppressive masters over workers were they themselves. This does not mean that their voices are fake, disingenuous, or not worth listening to, but that excavating the layers of meaning in their discourses of personal success and competency takes time and patience—resources that seem in short supply for researchers too.

Indeed, I have found that doing ethnographic work on different sites of production has required me to perform a variety of my own identities in the shuffle to juggle the needs of each case study and my nonresearch life. Whether based in Manaus or in New Orleans, I always was coming from the academy, which could signal a validating authority to some, but also a threatening intrusion to others. The disappearing boundaries between corporatizing universities and corporate industries in terms of shared employees, financial interests, and cultural milieus created opportunities for me in terms of shared connections and knowledges, but also limitations to who I could study, observe, or speak with, and on what terms.[20] Managers for soft-core companies talked to me only off the record; their employers directed me to their legal staff. Access to casting directors did not lead to interviews with the network producers who accepted or rejected their casting choices. My own paths in getting to know workers in Manaus or fellow regulators in San Antonio or Davis embedded into the daily rhythms of my own life, from joining a sewing collective each afternoon to attending focus-group meetings to support fellow board members, blurred lines for me between work and leisure, observation and advocacy. Here, the advantages of the ethnographic stance are clear, for it enabled me to move between these spaces and times in which contexts varied radically, thus situating identities, including my own, in communicative relations.

These shared material realities between my subjects and me leave me less concerned with the canonization of particular methods that will generate reproducible outcomes than with expanding the ways we think about television production in self-reflexive ways. My experiences lent themselves to what Liz Bird calls "ethnographically-inspired" methods that contextualized people's relationships with media, contents, and forms, but without the expectation that a particular path would lead to a universal generalization.[21] This suggests that while participant observation or autoethnographic techniques have no more epistemic authority than the trade story or the practitioner interview taken at face value, they are important additions to the tool kit for studying television production precisely, because they open up the potential to examine our academic assumptions and biases as we participate in the work worlds we observe.[22] Production studies should embrace a discussion of these exchanges, which recognize researchers' own complicities with the characteristics and mechanisms in the new television economy. From the disappearance of temporal and spatial boundaries, to the commodification of the self through branding, to the seemingly mandatory participation in a host of regulatory spheres, researchers' lived realities may parallel trends they critique across other work worlds, even as they sit in positions of more or less privilege. These insights, based on points of commonalities and differences, may be building blocks on which to build future alliances, while avoiding production studies from becoming a series of relativistic points of view in the landscape for studying television.

Instead, the case studies offer ways to see how shifting identity claims across a variety of contexts most often reproduce social definitions of who can be creative or professional, while subsuming the work of sponsorship and regulation as features of creativity and professionalism in the new television economy. Though the people in my case studies frequently framed their identities to me as natural, organic, and, thus, intrinsically authoritative and valuable, it was also clear that identities shifted in response to employers, clients, and coworkers, not to mention intimate friends and relatives. Factory workers were sisters, aunts, and moms at home. Being a man on Bourbon Street could encompass more

6. Workers to include in studies of television producers. Photo permission granted by *A Crítica* newspaper, Manaus, Brazil.

than one kind of masculine performance, from the skilled technician to the playboy at the party, or even the bouncer. These masculinities could even decline in saliency, if not disappear, in their interactions with me, when I became the proxy for an older, and disapproving, media professor. The shifts in the ways in which subjects talked about themselves and their work provide insights into historical and contemporary points of solidarity, empathy, tension, and conflict with other workers, including those writing about television in the academy. In other words, the people presented in this book, including myself, may all be considered producers in the new television economy (see, for example, figure 6), but it is through a careful consideration of our diverse interactions around television production in ordinary life that scholars might better comprehend the origins and reproduction of our popular and academic assumptions about producers.

At a more pragmatic level, the inclusion of more people and their roles in relation to television industries in production studies reveals that not everyone experiences media work as liquidly as others do. The fact that converging boundaries brought hierarchies based on gender and sexuality or class and educational status from one sphere into another reveals the contradictory ways in which liquidity for some has meant restrictions, rejections, or marginality. To be part of a work community means participating in the biopolitics of identifying bodies and then disciplining them to safeguard those boundaries, but workers do not participate in these processes unconsciously or without moral reservations. My field subjects' anxieties around the identification of people with marketable emotions, brand-ready bodies, politically viable claims, or remediable injuries showed the unease people have in categorizing and objectifying others. Identity work was implicitly the subtext when subjects had these crises of conscience, as well as when they themselves felt objectified, sexually humiliated, racially or ethnically pigeonholed, or simply too embarrassed to tell friends and parents about what they really did for a living. Employers can also use their employees' identity work against them to justify low pay scales when the presumed tasks come more naturally to some of their employees. Many workers cope with their invisibility, misrecognition, impotence, and marginality thinking that, in exchange, they achieve more independence, more mobility, and more status. Disjunctions between their expectations and the realities of their work contribute to feelings of alienation when they realize that they not only lost control of the final product of the labor, but that, in many cases, they also lost control over their own persona, which needed to fit frameworks for economic profit. At those points, the pride in working for or with the television industry reveals the larger social conditions of work itself as subjects can take solace in the fact that at least they, unlike others, had a job or were part of a formal economy. These fault lines should be considered ample terrain for future research questions into the ways workers affected by the political economy of liberalization and globalization not only produce television but also produce themselves in relation to standpoints for understanding television labor.

Production studies informed by an ethnographic stance can reengage through these fault lines with the real dynamics of class struggle. Vincent Mosco heralds the need for a "labor standpoint theory," one that blends a critique of political economy with workers' points of view.[23] Derived largely from feminist critiques of epistemic claims to neutrality and objectivity in social scientific research, a labor standpoint theory would reveal the ideological bias that continues to marginalize groups of workers in production processes and research alike. Importantly, standpoints are not neutral, articulating a political project for researchers, but they can be strongly objective; standpoints should frame knowledge both historically, in terms of social relations of disfranchisement, and contemporarily, through the voices of those disfranchised in the new economy.[24] The question of voice is particularly important today because so many of workers' experiences seem purely personal, individualized, and depoliticized from any form of class struggle. The neoliberal impetus in the United States, grounded in the discourse of economic theory and enacted through sweeping policy changes over the past thirty years, attempted to sever the market from the state, making the market independent of politics. In this schema, individuals would be reduced to desires that could only be resolved through market exchange and competition; the psychological becomes subordinate to internalized economic rationales and calculi. What is missing, as Nick Couldry has aptly pointed out, is attention to the importance of voice in a democratic society. By this, he means that people do not just need the opportunity to reflect and account for their own activities in the world but that institutions also need to foster and promote voice as a value toward developing collective solutions.[25] In a market-first society, voices exist as individuated opinions expressing wants, and their reducibility makes it easy for governments to resolve dissatisfaction through injury remediation or consumer-based services. These actions may be efficient, but they do not eliminate workers' own recognition of their conditions, or the varying ways in which they understand these conditions, which, depending on the context, may range from complete nihilism to incisive critiques of the political economic order. The job of the critical researcher is to listen to the range of responses that indicate an individual's resources, but also to excavate the voices of those whose dissatisfactions, or even latent anger, might one day challenge media power. Their expressions as standpoints of communities of practice one day might bear out new social critiques and solutions.

For through collective standpoints and toward articulating political voice this book demonstrates the universal logic of capitalism toward all laborers in the new television economy, as well as the processes of identification through which workers can either comply with these impositions or struggle back. The universal logic of capitalism does not mean the erasure of differences between the people called to produce themselves in the service of television industries in local and specific ways. To the contrary, the fact that new television economy demands authentic identity differences to standardize for ever-expanding markets ensures contradictions that threaten its own survival.[26] Following Dipesh Chakrabarty, the ways in which people feel as though they belong in capitalist economies subverts capitalism's imposition of a universal logic on the ground; shared life experiences challenge the othering tendencies that serve profit motives.[27] For though workers above and below the line may not recognize each other as collaborators in a global labor movement, they can identify those in their own communities that share life experiences because of their gender, race, or generation. Already these fissures in the new television economy have begun to open. In the United Kingdom, Mark Banks has already identified unique coalitions between white cultural workers across media industries and sectors in lobbying for environmental and social renewal in their shared residential neighborhoods.[28] Even more dramatically, general strikes in Latin American, African, and Asian communities have drawn workers from very different labor sectors to protest the unequal effects of neoliberal transformations on women, indigenous peoples, or the HIV-positive poor.[29] These identifications can be points for identity-based forms of solidarity and alternative notions of justice that critique the legitimacy of the new television economy and the politics that support it. By illuminating conversations across identity lines of class and nation, sexuality and gender, production studies may actually stimulate new ways to think through the ways in which markets, both labor and consumer markets, not only reinforce individualization, social hierarchies, and depoliticization but also, contradictorily, may help workers imagine collective bonds, mutual benefits, or revolutionary politics. Undoubtedly, television industries could also identify these places as centers for future extraction, but insomuch as they may help people articulate a political voice, they may be able to push a critique that would force capitalism to change. With this goal in mind, production studies should look to a horizon of possibilities that connects research with political realities that struggle over definitions of professionalism and creativity, theorize alternatives to the commodification of working selves, and take a stand in the efforts to repoliticize the ordinary.

Notes

Introduction

1 Williams, "Industry," in *Keywords*, 137.
2 This standard definition can be found, among other places, in Horace New-comb, ed., *Encyclopedia of Television*, 2nd ed., 4 vols. (New York: Fitzroy Dearborn, 2004).
3 Marx and Engels, *The German Ideology*.
4 It is unclear to me when these costs came to connote the differences between human beings and their presumed capabilities.
5 For these histories in relation to capitalism, see Zunz, *Making America Corporate, 1870–1920*, for a review of the "corporate professional"; and Hartley, "Creative Industries," for a review of the "creative arts."
6 Foucault, *The Birth of Biopolitics*, 147. Foucault actually traces the begin-nings of an enterprise society to thinkers in the Weimar Republic of the 1930s who took Walter Lippmann's call for a new liberalism to mean one in which market mechanisms could work with no state interference. After the Second World War, these thoughts traveled across the Atlantic to form a new "art of government" in which states managed populations to encourage individual-ization and the capitalization of all human traits that could be set into com-petition in a marketplace.
7 Crawford, *Shop Class as Soulcraft*; Sennett, *The Craftsman*; de Botton, *The Pleasures and Sorrows of Work*; Ho, *Liquidated*; Sennett, *The Culture of the New Capitalism*.
8 Pollin, *Contours of Descent*.
9 Rosten, "A 'Middletown' Study of Hollywood."
10 Powdermaker, *Hollywood, the Dream Factory*.
11 Rosten, *Hollywood*. Powdermaker later reflects on her human subject selec-tion as a problem of access rather than a decision to exclude others. See Powdermaker, *Stranger and Friend*.
12 Rosten, *Hollywood*, 19.
13 While Tyler's argument centered on Jewish and light-skinned blacks who would attempt to pass for white to gain on-screen roles, Powdermaker and

Rosten seem to show the boundaries that prevented identity passing. Tyler, "Hollywood as a Universal Church."

14 Gledhill, "The Motion Picture Academy, a Cooperative in Hollywood," 268; see also Dawson, "Hollywood's Labor Troubles"; Ross, "Labor Relations in Hollywood"; Tyler, "Hollywood as a Universal Church."

15 Schiller, *Theorizing Communication*.

16 Clark, *Negotiating Hollywood*, 5.

17 Wheeler, *Hollywood Politics and Society*, 73, 97.

18 Rosten, *Hollywood*, 360.

19 A developed critique of Dewey regarding labor can be found in Schiller, *Theorizing Communication*, 25–35.

20 "When men give up an exaggerated emphasis on breaks as inherent in movie production and a magical form of thinking, and face the world of realities, which encompass logical thinking, hard work, knowledge and talent; when they cease being primarily gamblers reveling in crises and become good businessmen with a capacity to plan in advance; when they have the courage to try out new ideas as well as new processes in color tinting; when the power for the sake of dominating other human beings as if they were property ceases to be a major goal and is supplanted by a human form of collaboration in which the interests of the movies and the movie public are important—only then will the real gold in Hollywood replace the glamorized tinsel." Powdermaker, *Hollywood, the Dream Factory*, 303.

21 Hirsch, "Cultural Industries Revisited," 359.

22 See, for example, Martindale, *Functionalism in the Social Sciences*.

23 Elliott and Chaney, "A Sociological Framework for the Study of Television Production," 361.

24 Peterson, "The Production of Culture."

25 See, for example, Lerner, *The Passing of Traditional Society*; Lerner and Schramm, *Communication and Change in Developing Countries*; Schramm, *Mass Media and National Development*; and Rogers, *Modernization among Peasants*.

26 Schiller, *Mass Communications and American Empire*. See also, Mattelart and Mattelart, *Theories of Communication*.

27 Mattelart and Mattelart, *Theories of Communication*, 36.

28 Cantor, *The Hollywood TV Producer*, 206.

29 Alvarado and Buscombe, *Hazell*, 4.

30 Ibid.

31 Gans, *Deciding What's News*; Tuchman, *Making News*; Ettema, "The Role of Educators and Researchers in the Production of Educational Television"; Turow, *Entertainment, Education, and the Hard Sell*. One useful overview of these studies of production processes can be found in Grindstaff and Turow, "Video Cultures."

32 Lotz, *The Television Will Be Revolutionized*.

33 The explicit use of the phrase *television professional* postdates the implicit articulation of the producer as a professional. See evolving iterations of the phrase in overviews by Ettema and Whitney "Introduction"; Ettema, Whitney, and Wackman, "Professional Mass Communicators"; Cantor and Zollars, *Current Research on Occupations and Professions*; Whitney and Ettema, "Media Production."

34 Schiller, *Theorizing Communication*, 80.

35 See note 33 for some of these citations.

36 Turow, "Learning to Portray Institutional Power," 211.

37 Cantor, *The Hollywood TV Producer*, 3.

38 Although community complaints about unfair representations can be traced back as far as the nineteenth century, the national orientation of social groups dedicated to changing broadcasting representation via hiring practices is most closely tied to social movement activism of the 1960s.

39 See, for example, Richard Iton's citation of the civil rights strategist Bayard Rustin in *In Search of the Black Fantastic*, 4–5.

40 My characterization of this period is largely drawn from a collection of resources on political activism and media reform, especially Classen, *Watching Jim Crow*; Hendershot, *Saturday Morning Censors*; Noriega, *Shot in America*; Perlman, "Feminists in the Wasteland."

41 Noriega, *Shot in America*, 29.

42 Institutions as varied as the National Commission on the Causes and Prevention of Violence, the Annenberg School for Communication, the Screen Actors Guild, the National Cable Television Association, and the Turner Broadcasting System sponsored these studies. All are cited in Shanahan and Morgan, *Television and Its Viewers*.

43 Perlman, "Feminists in the Wasteland," 415.

44 These groups were the Association for Motion Picture and Television Producers and the International Alliance of Theatrical and Stage Employees. Shanahan and Morgan, *Television and Its Viewers*, 60.

45 Ibid., 101.

46 Turow, "Casting for TV Parts," 18.

47 Gitlin, *Inside Prime Time*, 11.

48 Newcomb and Alley, *The Producer's Medium*, xiii (emphasis in the original).

49 Gitlin, *Inside Prime Time*, 165.

50 "Bochco and Kozoll, like their creature Furillo, supervised an unruly organization that had its own obstinate structure, its own powers, desires, and limits. Up against relentless time, restricted by budgets too small for their hopes, beholden to bureaucracies, obligated to their publics, producers and police captains all had to produce results today.... And then, too, the politics of a police station are not altogether alien to the politics of a television producer, with its collectivity, its squabbles, its array of off-center personalities, its moods and morale problems and delicate balances of ego and responsibility." Ibid., 310.

51 See, for example, Meehan, "Ancillary Markets—Television."

52 Wheeler, *Hollywood Politics and Society*, 124–25.

53 Newcomb and Alley, *The Producer's Medium*, xiii.

54 Sylvia Lawson, "General Editor's Preface," in Moran, *Making a TV Series*, 5–6. Interestingly, Moran's actual study does include the presence of many studio workers in the trades, but Moran's analysis of these workers in terms of their roles and functions reproduces the scholarly paradigm associated earlier with the work of Philip Elliott and David Chaney.

55 Consider, for example, two recent examples: Mann, "It's Not TV, It's Brand Management TV"; and Landman, "Not in Kansas Anymore."

56 Newcomb and Alley's *The Producer's Medium* may have been the first in a long line of such studies in the United States, including Broughton, *Producers on Producing*; and Thompson and Burns, *Making Television*. British and Australian television scholars, such as Albert Moran, Jeremy Tunstall, and Edward Buscombe, have also explored the use of above-the-line practitioner interviews to understand the production of popular genres and hit programs, though according to Christine Cornea, the growing popularity of interviews can be attributed to the global convergence of film and television studies. See Cornea, "Introduction."

57 Quote from Andrew Beck, "Introduction: Cultural Work, Cultural Workplace—Looking at the Cultural Industries," in Beck, *Cultural Work*, 3. An extended critique of above-the-line reflexivity as publicity can be found in Caldwell's *Production Culture*.

58 Florida, *The Rise of the Creative Class*.

59 Hesmondhalgh and Baker, "Creative Work and Emotional Labour in TV," 101; Florida, *The Rise of the Creative Class*. See also the critique of the creative class as defined by identities in Miller, "From Creative to Cultural Industries," 88–89.

60 Schiller, *Digital Capitalism*; Mosco and McKercher, *The Laboring of Communication*.

61 Ross, *Nice Work If You Can Get It*; Yúdice, *The Expediency of Culture*.

62 These critiques are vast, but to give a few good collections of articles, see du Gay and Pryke, *Cultural Economy*; Beck, *Cultural Work*; and McKercher and Mosco, *Knowledge Workers in the Information Society*.

63 Poovey, "Feminism and Deconstruction."

64 Dalla Costa, *The Work of Love*; Fortunati, *The Arcane of Reproduction*; Oppenheimer, "Voluntary Work and Labour History"; Kessler-Harris, "Voluntary Work and Labour History."

65 Fortunati, *The Arcane of Reproduction*, 8.

66 Nakano Glenn, *Unequal Freedom*.

67 Immanuel Wallerstein, "Marx and History: Fruitful and Unfruitful Emphases," in Balibar and Wallerstein, *Race, Class, Nation*, 133.

68 Mario Tronti, quoted in Wright, *Storming Heaven*, 38 (emphasis in the original).

69 Maurizio Lazzarato, "Immaterial Labour," 2004, trans. Paul Colilli and Ed Emery (http://www.generation-online.org).

70 Morley, "For a Materialist, Non–Media-Centric Media Studies," 114.

71 These examples are drawn from Salzinger, *Genders in Production*; Pringle, *Secretaries Talk*; and Chopra, "Invisible Men."

72 Two sources for this multiplicity of appropriations are Ross, *No Collar*; and Boltanski and Chiapello, *The New Spirit of Capitalism*.

73 Hesmondhalgh and Baker, "Creative Work and Emotional Labour in TV."

74 Connell and Wood, "Globalization and Business Masculinities."

75 Wichroski, "The Secretary"; Pringle, *Secretaries Talk*, 171.

76 Lowe, *Immigrant Acts*, 5–25.

77 These are the subjects of chapters 1 and 2 in Banks, *Bodies of Work*.

78 Gray, *Cultural Moves*, 77–88.

79 Brophy and de Peuter, "Immaterial Labor, Precarity, and Recomposition," 181; emphasis mine.

80 Augustín, *Sex at the Margins*, 8.

81 There are too many of these studies to name. Forerunners in the field included Janice Radway, David Morley, James Lull, and Ellen Seiter.

82 Peterson, *Anthropology and Mass Communication*, 162.

83 Dornfeld, *Producing Public Television, Producing Public Culture*, 16. Work by these new researchers in production can be found in Mayer, Banks, and Caldwell, *Production Studies*.

84 Dornfeld, *Producing Public Television, Producing Public Culture*, 186.

85 Grindstaff, *The Money Shot*.

86 Caldwell, *Production Culture*.

87 Examples of these studies can be found in Levine, "Toward a Paradigm for Media Production Research"; Seiter and Mayer, "Diversifying Representation in Children's TV"; Moran and Keane, *Television across Asia*; Ginsberg, Abu-Lughod, and Larkin, *Media Worlds*; Acosta-Alzuru, " 'I'm Not a Feminist' "; Acosta-Alzuru, "Tackling the Issues"; Barkin, "The Foreignizing Gaze"; Painter, "The Telerepresentation of Gender in Japan"; Tinic, *On Location*; Ashuri, "Television Tension."

88 Husband, "Minority Ethnic Media as Communities of Practice."

89 Bird, *The Audience in Everyday Life*, 6.

90 Burawoy et al., *Global Ethnography*.

91 Hobart, "Just Talk?," 497.

92 Falguni, *Labor, Work, and Citizenship*. Falguni writes that this is even a contradiction for Marxists, who despite the insisting that to be human is to produce, exclude housework, cooking, child care, and all unwaged work from the category of labor. "That for these philosophers labor masquerades as a descriptive category is not an incidental charge," she writes. "The insistence upon the 'descriptive' rather than the 'prescriptive' or 'normative' character of labor enhances certain political ends." Ibid., 11.

93 Such is the case described in Chopra, "Invisible Men," 164–65.

1. Producers as Creatives

1 Williams, *Keywords*, 83.
2 Stahl, "Privilege and Distinction in Production Worlds."
3 Florida, *The Rise of the Creative Class.*
4 Joas, *The Creativity of Action.*
5 Hilmes, "Nailing Mercury," 22.
6 In the former category, see Reeves, "Rewriting Television"; and Sandeen and Compesi, "Television Production as Collective Action." Several books in the latter category can be found in the introduction, as cited in note 56.
7 Gitlin, *Inside Prime Time*, 156.
8 See the final chapter in Powdermaker, *Hollywood, the Dream Factory.*
9 I am very grateful for the assistance of several professors at the Federal University of Amazonas, in particular Dr. Elenise Scherer and Ivânia Vieira.
10 Each of the interview subjects is referred to in this book by a first name that is a pseudonym in order to protect anonymity as required by the Tulane University Institutional Review Board.
11 Electronics factories tend to make several different objects, including television sets. In recent years, factories have begun to specialize in particular parts of TV sets, rather than assembling the entire set, multiplying the number of factories involved in set production.
12 Garcia, *Modelo de desenvolvimento Zona Franca de Manaus*, 62.
13 Ibid., 66.
14 Two excellent histories of the political economy of the Amazon can be found in Souza, *Breve história da Amazônia*; and Ferreira, *O desenvolvimento do capitalismo em Manaus.*
15 Ferreira, *O desenvolvimento do capitalismo em Manaus*, 19. The boom ended in 1910 with the opening of competing rubber plantations in Asia, particularly in Malaysia. After the boom, Brazil's position in the world rubber trade continued to decline throughout the following two decades.
16 The Manaus Industrial Pole (o Pólo Indústrial de Manaus) today is made up of several industrial districts, most dominated by electronics and motorcycle factories. Manauras, however, usually use the phrase "the District" (o Distrito), which references the historical development of the pole from a single industrial district.
17 Ferreira de Melo and Freitas Pinto, "O migrante rural e a reconstrução da identidade e do imaginário na cidade," 15.
18 Valle, "Globalização e reestruturação produtiva."
19 The price for a twenty-inch television fell from US$500 in 1990 to US$300 in 1995 to US$150 in 2002. Salazar, *Amazônia*, 261.
20 Scherer, *Baixas nas carteiras*; and Vieira, *O discurso operário e o espaço da fala da mulher.*

21 Samsung, for example, broke the monopoly of Philips over the fabrication of cinescopes with the launch of a new Samsung display factory. Valle, "Globalização e reestruturação produtiva," 145.

22 Nogueira, "Um olhar sobre a Zona Franca de Manaus"; Scherer, *Baixas nas carteiras.*

23 The multilateral discussion of a Free Trade Agreement for the Americas (FTAA) was a primary reason that foreign national companies based in Asia relocated resources to Manaus according to plant managers I interviewed.

24 Vieira, *O discurso operário e o espaço da fala da mulher,* 34.

25 Emilia Santana Valente, director of the Manaus Metalworkers' Union, interview with the author, Manaus, 19 July 2004.

26 Baçal de Oliveira, *Reestruturação produtiva e qualificação profissional na Zona Franca de Manaus,* 65.

27 This argument can be found, for example, in French, *Drowning in Laws.*

28 The transnational companies associated with television assembly in Manaus included Philips, LG, Sony, Samsung, Semp Toshiba, Philco Iautec, Panasonic, CCE, Evadin, Cineral, and Gradiente.

29 British, French, German, and Portuguese settlers occupied elite positions in the local government, economy, and cultural life, building Manaus's infrastructure while turning it into a Europeanized colony of the belle epoque. Spanish and Italian immigrants opened import shops and markets in the urbanized downtown neighborhoods of the city; Syrian and Lebanese immigrants additionally offered workers credit.

30 Scherer, *Baixas nas carteiras,* 81.

31 José Alberto da Costa Machado, "A atuação da superintendência da Zona Franca de Manaus" (report prepared for SUFRAMA, Manaus, Amazonas, 2005, 27).

32 The total number of MFTZ workers in 2005 was 89,758 (ibid., 17). According to Valle, the total number of workers in the MFTZ fell from 76,798 in 1990 to 45,283 in 2000 ("Globalização e reestruturação produtiva," 119).

33 Nilson Tavares Pimentel, "Emprego industrial no pólo industrial de Manaus, na década de 90" (master's thesis, Universidade Federal da Amazonas, 2001).

34 Ralphe Manzoni Jr., "Pólo industrial de Manaus vive novo ciclo de expansão," *PC World Brasil,* 19 June 2006 (http://pcworld.uol.com.br).

35 This is a summary from the chapter "Situation—Corporeality—Sociality: The Fundamentals of a Theory of the Creativity of Action," in Joas, *The Creativity of Action,* 145–95.

36 Ibid., 162.

37 Taylor, *The Principles of Scientific Management,* 39.

38 Cowie, *Capital Moves.*

39 This step was unnecessary for the production of digital television sets.

40 For more information and a theorization of these shifts in factory work, see,

for example, Harvey, *The Condition of Postmodernity*; Schiller, *Digital Capitalism*; Elger and Smith, *Global Japanization?*; and Kenney and Florida, *Beyond Mass Production*.

41 The shift in Manaus to an export enclave meant that each factory had to attain the International Organization for Standardization's (ISO) 9000-level standards. Promulgated in 1947, the ISO importantly evaluates quality through the management of the labor market in the industrial district by defining categories of workers and documenting their interpersonal work relations. The achievement of ISO-9000, for example, required that factories engage in a new "quality politics" at all stages of the production process. This meant tighter documentation of workers and production, so that all workers could "critically analyze" their role in production and "make recommendations for improvement." Quoted from *NBR ISO 9001: Sistemas de gestão da qualidade —Requisitos* (Rio de Janeiro: Associação Brasileira de Normas Técnicas, 2000).

42 Kenney and Florida, *Beyond Mass Production*, 39.

43 Ibid., 106.

44 Salzinger, *Genders in Production*.

45 Ferreira Moura et al., *A utilização do trabalho feminino nas indústrias de Belém e Manaus*, 20.

46 Becker, *Art Worlds*, 14.

47 Ibid., 30.

48 Ibid., 36.

49 Spivak, "Can the Subaltern Speak?," 66.

50 Ibid., 69.

51 James Maggio, "Can the Subaltern Be Heard?: A (Re)Examination of Spivak," paper presented for the Southern Political Science Association, New Orleans, 3 January 2007 (available at www.allacademic.com).

52 Humphrey, "'Japanese' Methods and the Changing Position of Direct Production Workers."

53 Ibid., 20.

54 A review of these theories can be found in Sawyer, *Group Creativity*.

55 Certeau, *The Practice of Everyday Life*.

56 This point has also been made in Salzinger, *Genders in Production*, regarding her work in an electronics maquiladora on the Mexican-U.S. border.

57 Steinert, *Culture Industry*, 65.

58 Florida, *The Rise of the Creative Class*, 41.

59 Burawoy, "Between the Labor Process and the State," 587.

60 Christopherson, "The Transformation of Industrial Relations in the Motion Picture and Television Industries."

61 Mosco and McKercher, *The Laboring of Communication*.

62 Emilia Santana Valente, director of the Manaus Metalworkers' Union, interview with the author, Manaus, 19 July 2004.

2. Producers as Professionals

1 Freidson, "The Theory of Professions."
2 From 1975 to 1995, film degrees increased over 300 percent, with film student graduates accounting for 72 percent of first-time directors. Anita Gates, "Lights, Camera, Action, and Tuition Bills," *New York Times*, 21 November 1995.
3 Garnham, *Capitalism and Communication*, 33.
4 Ibid.
5 Couldry, *Media Rituals*, 12–15.
6 I've used psuedonyms for all interviewees in this chapter.
7 At the dawn of the portable camcorder, Albedo said many of his subjects did not understand that the camera shot moving images. They stood still, exposing themselves, while demanding that he "hurry up and take the picture!"
8 On hard core see Williams, *Hard Core*.
9 Holliday, "A History of Modern Pornographic Film and Video," 344.
10 In addition to the testimonies of the producers, there has been much written about Ronald Reagan and sex panics in the 1980s, for example, Nathan and Snedeker, *Satan's Silence*; and Berlant, *The Queen of America Goes to Washington City.*
11 A more detailed narrative of this legal history and its economic impacts can be found in Mayer, "Soft-Core in TV Time."
12 This is documented throughout critical studies of tourism. A theoretical summary of the impacts of neoliberalism on cities' construction of places can be found in Harvey, "From Space to Place and Back Again."
13 Gotham, *Authentic New Orleans.*
14 Mann, *Hollywood Independents*, 8.
15 Mayer, "Soft-Core in TV Time," 315.
16 Mantra officials claimed profits of over $100 million in 2004, a figure that even other industry executives admit dwarfs their own. This figure is impossible to verify and may well be inflated like other financial figures in porn and other private media industries. See Mireya Navarro, "The Very Long Legs of 'Girls Gone Wild,'" *New York Times*, 4 April 2004.
17 On the lack of union labor in reality, see Hendershot, "Belabored Reality."
18 Posted on the Craig's List Los Angeles Web site (http://losangeles.craigslist .org/).
19 Mann, *Hollywood Independents*, 65.
20 Couldry, *Media Rituals*, 93.
21 Caldwell, "Industrial Geography Lessons," 185–86.
22 Through their network of sex workers and media contacts, cameramen shared the names of willing participants for hard-core backroom scenes, many of which would be shot in area hotel rooms. Although some companies avoided

all hard-core content, most mixed the two types of content in the 2000s, using a hard-core scene as a climatic finale to the soft-core footage.

23 Gitlin, *Inside Prime Time*; Whitney and Ettema, "Media Production," 166.

24 Whitney and Ettema, "Media Production," 163–66.

25 This claim, which hails from a Frankfurt School perspective, has been further developed in relation to cultural production in Garnham, *Capitalism and Communication*.

26 Zimmerman, *Reel Families*.

27 Ibid., 5.

28 Ibid., 18–19.

29 Caldwell, *Production Culture*, 175.

30 Osgerby, *Playboys in Paradise*, 135.

31 Ibid., 139.

32 Binkley, *Getting Loose*, 171.

33 Ibid., 208.

34 Couldry, "Media Organisations and Non-Media People," 278–80.

35 Becker, "The Professional Dance Musician and His Audience."

36 Hughes, *Men and Their Work*.

37 Moran, *There's No Place Like Home Video*, 65.

38 Ibid.

39 Caldwell, *Production Culture*.

40 Larson, *The Rise of Professionalism*, xvii.

41 Tunstall, *Television Producers*, 204.

42 Cohan, *Masked Men*.

43 Journalists, for example, have been a prime example of an occupation wrestled into a professionalizing mentality despite the old vestiges of individualist and anticorporate attitudes that still attract people to the field. See Aldridge and Evetts, "Rethinking the Concept of Professionalism."

44 Ibid., 559.

45 Hughes, *Men and Their Work*, 338.

46 Noble, *America by Design*, 52.

47 Zunz, *Making America Corporate, 1870–1920*, 65.

48 The sociologist Keith MacDonald summarizes that being a professional has been a way to assert patriarchy through socially accepted masculine norms *and* male identities. See MacDonald, *The Sociology of Professions*.

49 Lowe, *The Body in Late-Capitalist U.S.A.*

50 Ibid., 132.

51 This is described in more detail in Mayer, "Fieldnote," 58–59.

52 The brand name has been changed so as not to implicate any particular company in this series of standard production practices.

53 Discussions of the gaze in film studies have a long history. Most germane to this discussion is the interpretation of the female gaze, as found in Miriam Hansen, *Babel and Babylon: Spectatorship in American Silent Film* (Cambridge: Harvard University Press, 1991).

54 Hochschild, *The Managed Heart.*
55 Although there are many public-nudity series made by and with gay men, this is the only series I know of that recruited women to entice heterosexual men to strip on camera.
56 Illouz, *Saving the Modern Soul*, 104 (emphasis in the original).
57 Ibid., 77.
58 Braverman, *Labor and Monopoly Capital.*
59 Tunstall, introduction, 15.
60 Ibid.; and Murdock, "Back to Work."
61 Thynne, "Women in Television in the Multi-channel Age," 79; Ursell, "Labour Flexibility in the UK Commercial Television Sector," 136.
62 Thynne, "Women in Television in the Multi-channel Age," 80.
63 Tunstall, introduction, 22; Ursell, "Labour Flexibility in the UK Commercial Television Sector," 813.
64 Moran, *There's No Place Like Home Video*, 81–82.
65 Becker, *Sociological Work.*
66 For these references, see McNair, *Striptease Culture*; Paasonen, Nikunen, and Saarenmaa, *Pornification*; and Caputi, "The Pornography of Everyday Life."
67 This is the subject of a conference poster presented by Miranda Banks, "The xx Factor: A Critical Reappraisal of the Gender Gap in Film/tv Production Labor" (poster presented at the annual meeting of the International Communication Association, San Francisco, 24 May 2007).

3. Sponsoring Selves

1 Deery, "Reality tv as Advertisement."
2 Perhaps the best historical account of the popular distrust of early admen and their products is Marchand, *Advertising the American Dream.*
3 See the discussion of Hortense Powdermaker and Leo Rosten in the introduction.
4 Deery, "Reality tv as Advertisement," 2.
5 Smythe, "Communications."
6 Etzioni, preface, xii.
7 Illouz, *Saving the Modern Soul*, 88.
8 Muir, "Not Quite at Home."
9 These interviews were a group effort. Special thanks to Denise Gass for making casting contacts and conducting phone interviews.
10 Joy Elmer Morgan quoted in McChesney, *Telecommunications, Mass Media, and Democracy*, 95.
11 Of course, the industry had its own economic imperatives for this change; specifically, networks could better control their schedules, contents, and profit margins if they eliminated direct sponsorship of television programs. As such, networks began a protracted process in the 1950s that moved their

investment economy from direct to indirect forms of sponsorship through commercial spot buys, producing a magazine format in the schedule. See Boddy, *Fifties Television.*

12   Andersen, introduction, 10.

13   Turow, *Breaking up America.*

14   Amanda D. Lotz, "Recounting the Audience: Integrating New Measurement Techniques and Technologies," in Lotz, *The Television Will Be Revolutionized,* 193–214.

15   One example of the former is Jennifer Pozner, "Triumph of the Shill, Part Two: Reality TV Lets Marketers Write Scripts," *Bitch: A Feminist Response to Popular Culture* (spring 2004), 55–61. An example of the latter is Schiller, *How to Think about Information.*

16   The nonprofit organization claimed that product placement is an unfair and deceptive business practice in violation of Section V of the Federal Trade Commission Act (FTC). The FTC denied hearing the request in September 2005 according to the group's Web site (www.commericalalert.org).

17   Meg James, "TV Trend Triggers Concerns," *Los Angeles Times,* 18 May 2006.

18   Jesse Hiestand, "Guilds Picket over Placement," Hollywood Reporter.com, 9 February 2006.

19   Smythe, "Communications," 286.

20   "Advertisers are consumers of audience attention, not content," Oscar Gandy sums up. "Advertisers think of their audiences as markets, but they purchase access to them as commodities." Gandy, "Audiences on Demand," 329.

21   On the shortcomings of audience measurement, see Meehan, *Why TV Is Not Our Fault.*

22   Ang, *Desperately Seeking the Audience,* 49.

23   Andrejevic, *Reality TV.*

24   Claire Atkinson, "Slim-Fast Thanks Its Lucky 'Stars' That TV Partnership Pays Off," *Advertising Age,* 13 November 2006, 12.

25   Phyllis Furman, " 'Idol' Is the Big Star with Advertisers," *New York Daily News,* 23 September 2006, 27; Cecily Hall, "Well-Positioned: The Top-10 Network Television Shows Ranked by the Number of Product Placements in 2006," *Women's Wear Daily,* 11 January 2007, 12; Meredith Deliso, "If 'Idol' Keeps It Real, There's More Potential for Promotions," *Advertising Age,* 15 January 2007, 4.

26   I am indebted for this insight into scripted casting to Erin Hill at the University of California, Los Angeles, who has collected this historical work and has conducted interviews with casters currently in the profession.

27   Grindstaff, *The Money Shot.*

28   Collins, "Making the Most out of Fifteen Minutes."

29   Grindstaff, *The Money Shot,* 70–74.

30   See this point also in Ytreberg, "Formatting Participation within Broadcast Media Production."

31   Grindstaff, *The Money Shot,* 97.

32 Although "thingification" derives from the German *verdinglichung*, Bewes uses the word to speak about the subjective dimensions of reification, or becoming an object. See Bewes, *Reification*.

33 In his discussion of the constitution of cartoons as a television genre, Jason Mittell in *Genre and Television* argues against textualist conceptions of the genre, citing industrial practices as a prime reason behind the cohesion of the genre. I am suggesting that reality as a genre might be considered by a similar logic.

34 Couldry, *The Place of Media Power*, 112–16.

35 See, for example, Lanham, *The Economics of Attention*.

36 I used pseudonyms for all the interviewees in this chapter.

37 Although there might be legal reasons why a former felon cannot be on television, the primary reason casters cited was ideological. "People won't believe in the redemption theme for a mother who does drugs," said one casting director. From this, it is easy to extrapolate that television networks and their advertisers would not want such associations with "unredeemable" characters.

38 Vogler, "Sex and Talk," 49.

39 Ibid., 79.

40 Ibid., 81.

41 "Calculated compassion" is defined in detail in Woodward, "Calculating Compassion."

42 Meehan, "Conceptualizing Culture as a Commodity."

43 Lukács, *History and Class Consciousness*, 83.

44 This is discussed in far more detail and with greater analysis in Grindstaff, *The Money Shot*.

45 Friedman, *Birth of a Salesman*, 42.

46 This is common knowledge in advertising, from the research of Paul Lazarsfeld to recent articulations, such as David Schwab, "Need a Celeb? Be Sure to Choose an Influencer," *Advertising Age*, 2 October 2006, 22.

47 See, for example, the importance of identity in Friedman, *Birth of a Salesman*.

48 Lukács, *History and Class Consciousness*, 99.

49 Mazzarella, " 'Very Bombay,' " 45.

50 For members of the Writers Guild of America, this is a very touchy subject, because if reality programs have "writers," producers should pay union wages and royalties to them as such.

51 Jhally, "Advertising as Religion," 92.

52 In one of the tapes I witnessed, one of the potential cast members lashed out at the cameraman, jarring the viewer from any illusion that the caster is just a fly on the wall in these cast worlds.

53 Mazzarella, " 'Very Bombay,' " 56.

54 Bewes, *Reification*.

55 Ibid., 96–97 (emphasis in the original).

56 Ibid., 110.

57 Ahmed, *The Cultural Politics of Emotion*, 3.
58 Hochschild, *The Managed Heart*, 20.
59 Friedman, *Birth of a Salesman*, 13.
60 See, for example, Lears, "The Rise of American Advertising."
61 Hilmes, "Desired and Feared," 19.
62 Wang, "'The Case of the Radio-Active Housewife.'"
63 Erin Hill, "Women's Work: Femininity in Film and Television Casting," paper presented at "Console-ing Passions: International Conference on Feminism, Television, and Video," Milwaukee, 27 May 2006.
64 Baudrillard, *Simulations*, 51 (emphasis in the original).
65 Michael Learnmouth, "Smaller Deals, Bigger Bucks in Product Placement," *Variety*, 15–21 January 2007, 16.
66 Boltanski and Chiapello, *The New Spirit of Capitalism*, 447–62.

4. Regulating Selves

1 Mullen, *Television in the Multichannel Age*, 100.
2 Biltereyst, "Productive Censorship."
3 Sonia Livingstone, Peter Lunt, and Laura Miller, for example, chart the slipperiness of these terms in "Citizens and Consumers."
4 This is the double bind of representation as described in the classic work Spivak, "Can the Subaltern Speak?"
5 Denzin, "Analytic Autoethnography," 423.
6 Ibid., 426.
7 Braman, "Policy as a Research Context," 44–46.
8 Interestingly, this same tone of dismissal permeates analyses of the FCC on both the political left and the right, which call the institution inefficient, slow, and ineffective, and its regulators unknowledgeable and incapable. These works would include Cole and Oettinger, *Reluctant Regulators*; Havick, *Communications Policy and the Political Process*; Horwitz, *The Irony of Regulatory Reform*; Krasnow, Longley, and Terry, *The Politics of Broadcast Regulation*; Robinson, "The Federal Communications Commission"; and Symons, "The Communications Policy Process."
9 Braman, "Policy as a Research Context," 36–37.
10 Lichty, "The Impact of FRC and FCC Commissioners' Backgrounds on the Regulation of Broadcasting," 27. Lichty's work was followed by Williams, "Impact of Commissioner Background on FCC Decisions."
11 Braman, "Policy as a Research Context," 42.
12 Owen, "A Novel Conference," 354.
13 To this club I would also add the critical scholars Dallas Smythe and Lawrence Lichty, who were involved with the FCC and municipal television regulation, respectively. Thanks to Bill Kirkpatrick for alerting me to Lichty's activist past in "Bringing Blue Skies Down to Earth."

14 Streeter, *Selling the Air*, 134.

15 Furchtgott-Roth, *A Tough Act to Follow?*

16 Lichty, "Members of the Federal Radio Commission and the Federal Communications Commission, 1927–1961," 23.

17 Streeter, *Selling the Air*, 125. Among those arguing that the FCC is captured by industrial interests or that there has been a collusive culture of regulators and broadcasters are Horwitz, *The Irony of Regulatory Reform*; and McChesney, *Telecommunications, Mass Media, and Democracy*. A critique of these characterizations can be found in Napoli, "The Federal Communications Commission and the Communications Policymaking Process"; and Slotten, " 'Rainbow in the Sky.' "

18 Krasnow and Longley, *The Politics of Broadcast Regulation*, 24.

19 Cole and Oettinger, *Reluctant Regulators*, 11.

20 Streeter, *Selling the Air*, 125.

21 DeLaun and Flannery, "Fly, James L., 1939–1944," 60.

22 Barnouw, *The Golden Web*, 173.

23 Weisenberger, "Women of the FCC," 197. Consider, as well, Laurie Ouellette's comparison of the FCC commissioner Freida Hennock with Minow. Whereas he and others wanted educational television to reflect "urban, upper-middle-class, white, Eurocentric, university-bound, and, very often, masculine experiences," she fought, and lost, a bid to frame educational television as a more practical ticket for working-class social mobility. "Remembered by her colleagues for her unpolished Brooklyn accent, non–Ivy League credentials, and gaudy clothing," Hennock's vision of educational television, according to Ouellette, would have to be negotiated with those who framed public television as a salve for low and unsophisticated masses needing to be guided by "men of culture and ability." See Ouellette, *Viewers Like You?*, 30, 60, 73.

24 Tovares, "Hooks, Benjamin Lawson."

25 The long-standing binary between active policymakers and passive policy enforcers is detailed in LeDuc, "Transforming Principles into Policy."

26 Odendahl and O'Neill, *Women and Power in the Non-profit Sector*.

27 Irma Reyes, phone interview with the author, San Antonio, Texas, 8 May 2008.

28 This is a common feminist critique of the state's masculinist power, as summarized by Brown, *States of Injury*, 167.

29 Cooper, *Challenging Diversity*.

30 Butsch, *The Citizen Audience*.

31 Somers, *Genealogies of Citizenship*, 16–17.

32 Streeter, *Selling the Air*, 114–18.

33 Livingstone, Lunt, and Miller, "Citizens and Consumers."

34 Slotten, *Radio and Television Regulation*, 69.

35 Laclau, *On Populist Reason*.

36 City of San Antonio Cable Television Advisory Committee, minutes of 12 January 1998, 13 July 1998, and 10 August 1998.

37 Miller, *Cultural Citizenship*, 29–30.

38 Trachtenberg, *The Incorporation of America*.

39 Somers, *Genealogies of Citizenship*, 188.

40 Miller, *Cultural Citizenship*, 15.

41 City of San Antonio Cable Television Advisory Committee, minutes of 10 August 1998.

42 Miller in *Cultural Citizenship* has also pointed to the convergence of cultural identity terms in governance and consumer markets.

43 Mukherjee, *The Racial Order of Things*.

44 San Antonio Cable Television Advisory Committee, minutes of 19 April 1998.

45 See City of San Antonio and UA Columbia Cablevision of Texas, *Franchise Agreement and Ordinance No. 49433*, signed 7 September 1978.

46 City of San Antonio Cable Television Advisory Committee, minutes of 11 May 1998.

47 The Tulane Institutional Research Board requires that human subjects be anonymous in all field notes. I have chosen to use names only when cited directly in board meeting minutes.

48 San Antonio Cable Television Advisory Committee, minutes of 13 April 1998.

49 See the introduction of Brown, *States of Injury*, 3–29.

50 Mukherjee, *The Racial Order of Things*, 2.

51 Ibid., 3.

52 Ibid., 5.

53 Brown, *States of Injury*, 7.

54 Seshadri-Crooks, *Desiring Whiteness*, 21, 32–46.

55 Ibid., 37.

56 See in particular chapter three in Classen, *Watching Jim Crow*, 75–106.

57 See Hendershot, *Saturday Morning Censors*; and Mechling and Mechling, "Sweet Talk."

58 Joseph, *Against the Romance of Community*, 23.

59 Ibid., 29.

60 Hundt, *You Say You Want a Revolution*, 20.

61 After the passage of the Telecommunications Act of 1996, the economies of scale for the largest cable conglomerates grew bigger through mergers with telecommunications and publishing companies, such as AT&T/Comcast, Cox, and Time Warner/TCI. Mullen, *Television in the Multichannel Age*, 181.

62 For a history of statewide cable franchising, I have consulted Rachel Appelstein, "The Impact of Cable Franchising Laws on Public, Educational, and Government Access Television and Society," bachelor's thesis, Tulane University, May 2008.

63 Allison Perlman in "Feminists in the Wasteland," gives an excellent example of women's rights groups, such as the National Organization for Women,

which has repeatedly stepped into the realm of broadcast regulation through its own monitoring and research practices, although this was never the sole focus of the group's advocacy issues.

64 The discussion of the Davis franchise renegotiation process was quoted in Jerilyn Cochran, deputy director of Parks and Community Services, interview with the author, Davis, California, 12 April 2007. The discussion of the San Antonio franchise renegotiation process was quoted in Don Freidkin, "Paragon Disconnect," *San Antonio Current,* 4–10 February 1999, 14.

65 City of Davis, *Preliminary Report on Community Cable-Related Needs and Interests,* ed. Parks and Recreation Department (internal report, 2003), C-3.

66 Ibid., A-5. It is noteworthy, for example, that about 70 percent of the surveys were drawn from the "business community," which also had representatives in the focus groups, the telecommunications task force, and, arguably, comprised a portion of the access board members and consumer complaints. Beyond the sample size, the methods favored consumer issues in discussing television and communications. The survey questionnaire for business users addresses technology usage in terms of customer satisfaction. The focus group questionnaires expand issues of customer satisfaction to programming tastes and to the desire for more services, from paid services, such as movies on demand and interactive shopping, to public services, such as the ability to get a government permit via television. Within the focus-group evaluation, public input on producing cable programming was limited to two out of thirty questions that otherwise focused on consumption. See ibid., Appendix Attachment B.

67 Ibid., A-1.

68 Cochran, interview.

69 Kari Peterson and Steve McMahon, interview with the author, Davis, California, 12 April 2007.

70 This information came from a conference call with three San Antonio City officials, the assistant director of public utilities, Bill Mattox, the assistant city attorney, Gabriel Garcia, and the rate analyst Ben Cadena III; phone interview with the author, 4 November 2007.

71 Ibid.

72 The principle supporters of the Texas Media Empowerment Project were the United Church of Christ, which has historically represented African American communities, and the Esperanza Peace and Justice Center, which has primarily represented Mexican American and Anglo American artists and cultural producers. For more history on these groups, see Classen, *Watching Jim Crow*; and Mayer, *Producing Dreams, Consuming Youth.*

73 Patsy Robles, phone interview with the author, 4 July 2007.

74 Freedman, "Dynamics of Power in Contemporary Media Policy-Making," 912.

75 Freedman, *The Politics of Media Policy.* See also Davis, "Whither Mass Media and Power?"

76 Kirkpatrick, "Sounds Local."
77 Kirkpatrick, "Bringing Blue Skies Down to Earth," 1.
78 Brown, *States of Injury*, 194.
79 Ouellette and Hay, *Better Living through Reality TV*.
80 Turow, *Niche Envy*.
81 Ouellette and Hay, *Better Living through Reality TV*, 25–29.
82 Brown, *States of Injury*, 171.

Conclusion

1 Florida, *The Rise of the Creative Class*, 30.
2 George Yúdice makes this critique forcefully in *The Expediency of Culture*.
3 Pang, "The Labor Factor in the Creative Economy."
4 Based on a research report in 2002 by Diane Coyle and Danny Quah, "Getting the Measure of the New Economy," the Work Foundation's iSociety project, London School of Economics, quoted in Flew, "Creative Economy," 347.
5 This particular definition comes via Hartley, "Creative Identities," 114.
6 She makes this point through various recent texts. See McRobbie, "Clubs to Companies"; McRobbie, "'Everyone Is Creative'"; McRobbie, "From Holloway to Hollywood."
7 Grindstaff, "Self-Serve Celebrity."
8 Dalla Costa, *The Work of Love*.
9 Ross, *Low Pay, High Profile*, 209.
10 Maurizio Lazzarato, quoted in Terranova, "Free Labor," 40–41.
11 Ross, *Low Pay, High Profile*, 229.
12 Adkins, "Cultural Feminization."
13 Ortner, "Resistance and the Problem of Ethnographic Refusal."
14 McRobbie, "'Everyone Is Creative,'" 195.
15 Caldwell, *Production Culture*.
16 Deuze, *Media Work*.
17 Powdermaker, "Part IV: Hollywood," in Powdermaker, *Stranger and Friend*, 209–34; Born, *Uncertain Vision*.
18 Ortner, "Studying Sideways."
19 Caldwell, *Production Culture*.
20 On my own reflections on this matter, see Mayer, "Studying up and F**King Up." See also Caldwell, "'Both Sides of the Fence.'"
21 Bird, *The Audience in Everyday Life*, 6.
22 Murphy, "Writing Media Culture."
23 Mosco, *The Political Economy of Communication*.
24 Meenakshi Gigi Durham makes this point most effectively toward journalists in advocating for a reflexive use of standpoint theory in reporting practices. See Durham, "On the Relevance of Standpoint Epistemology to the Practice of Journalism."

25 Couldry, *Why Voice Matters.*

26 See, for example, Boltanski and Chiapello, *The New Spirit of Capitalism,*
    469–70, on the contradictions between authentic and commodified identi-
    ties as a site of future social critique.

27 Chakrabarty, "Universalism and Belonging in the Logic of Capital."

28 Banks, "Moral Economy and Cultural Work," 463, 469.

29 These examples can be found readily through independent Internet reporting
    on Indymedia or socialist.net.

Bibliography

Abu-Lughod, Lila. *Dramas of Nationhood: The Politics of Television in Egypt.* Chicago: University of Chicago Press, 2005.

Acosta-Alzuru, Carolina. " 'I'm Not a Feminist. I Only Defend Women as Human Beings': The Production, Representation, and Consumption of Feminism in a *Telenovela.*" *Critical Studies in Media Communication* 20, no. 3 (2003), 269–94.

———. "Tackling the Issues: Meaning Making in a *Telenovela.*" *Popular Communication* 1, no. 4 (2003), 193–215.

Adkins, Lisa. "Cultural Feminization: 'Money, Sex, and Power' for Women." *Signs* 26, no. 3 (2001), 669–95.

Ahmed, Sara. *The Cultural Politics of Emotion.* New York: Routledge, 2004.

Aldridge, Meryl, and Julia Evetts. "Rethinking the Concept of Professionalism: The Case of Journalism." *British Journal of Sociology* 54, no. 4 (2003), 547–64.

Alvarado, Manuel, and Edward Buscombe. *Hazell: The Making of a Television Series.* London: British Film Institute, 1978.

Andersen, Robin. Introduction to *Critical Studies in Media Commercialism*, ed. Robin Andersen and Lance Strate, 1–24. New York: Oxford University Press, 1994.

Andrejevic, Mark. *Reality TV: The Work of Being Watched.* Lanham, Md.: Rowman and Littlefield, 2003.

Ang, Ien. *Desperately Seeking the Audience.* London: Routledge, 1991.

Ashuri, Tamar. "Television Tension: National versus Cosmopolitan Memory in a Co-produced Television Documentary." *Media, Culture, and Society* 29, no. 1 (2007), 31–51.

Aufderheide, Patricia. *Communications Policy and the Public Interest: The Telecommunications Act of 1996.* New York: Guilford Press, 1999.

Augustín, Laura María. *Sex at the Margins: Migration, Labour Markets, and the Rescue Industry.* London: Zed Books, 2007.

Baçal de Oliveira, Selma Suely. *Reestruturação produtiva e qualificação profissional na Zona Franca de Manaus.* Manaus: EDUA, 2000.

Balibar, Etienne, and Immanuel Wallerstein. *Race, Class, Nation: Ambiguous Identities.* Trans. Chris Turner. London: Verso, 1991.

Banks, Mark. "Moral Economy and Cultural Work." *Sociology* 40, no. 3 (2006), 455–75.

Banks, Miranda. "Bodies of Work: Rituals of Doubling and the Erasure of Film/ TV Production Labor; A Production Studies Analysis of Gendered Labor in Hollywood." PhD diss., University of California, Los Angeles, 2006.

Barkin, Gareth. "The Foreignizing Gaze: Producers, Audiences, and Symbols of the 'Traditional.'" *Asian Journal of Communication* 16, no. 4 (2006), 352–70.

Barnouw, Erik. *The Golden Web: A History of Broadcasting in the United States to 1933.* Oxford: Oxford University Press, 1968.

Baudrillard, Jean. *Simulations.* Trans. Paul Foss, Paul Patton, and Philip Beitchman. New York: Semiotext(e), 1983.

Beck, Andrew, ed. *Cultural Work: Understanding the Cultural Industries.* London: Routledge, 2003.

Becker, Howard. *Art Worlds.* Berkeley: University of California Press, 1982.

——. "The Professional Dance Musician and His Audience." *American Journal of Sociology* 57, no. 3 (1951), 136–44.

——. *Sociological Work.* Chicago: Aldine, 1970.

Berlant, Lauren. *The Queen of America Goes to Washington City: Essays on Sex and Citizenship.* Durham: Duke University Press, 1997.

Bewes, Timothy. *Reification: The Anxiety of Late Capitalism.* London: Verso, 2002.

Bielby, William T., and Denise D. Bielby. "'All Hits Are Flukes': Institutionalized Decision Making and the Rhetoric of Network Prime-Time Program Development." *American Journal of Sociology* 99, no. 5 (1994), 1287–1313.

——. "Organizational Mediation of Project-Based Labor Markets: Talent Agencies and the Careers of Screenwriters." *American Sociological Review* 64, no. 1 (1999), 776–89.

Biltereyst, Daniel. "Productive Censorship: Revisiting Recent Research on the Cultural Meanings of Film Censorship." *Politics and Culture* 9, no. 4 (2008), http://www.politicsandculture.org/issue/2008-issue-4/.

Binkley, Sam. *Getting Loose: Lifestyle Consumption in the 1970s.* Durham: Duke University Press, 2007.

Bird, Elizabeth. *The Audience in Everyday Life: Living in a Media World.* New York: Routledge, 2003.

Boddy, William. *Fifties Television: The Industry and Its Critics.* Urbana: University of Illinois Press, 1993.

Boltanski, Luc, and Eve Chiapello. *The New Spirit of Capitalism.* Trans. Gregory Elliott. London: Verso, 2006.

Born, Georgina. *Uncertain Vision: Birt, Dyke, and the Reinvention of the BBC.* London: Secker and Warburg, 2004.

Braman, Sandra. "Policy as a Research Context." 2002. *Communication Researchers and Policy-Making,* ed. Sandra Braman, 52–75. Cambridge: MIT Press, 2003.

Braverman, Harry. *Labor and Monopoly Capital: The Degradation of Work in the Twentieth Century.* New York: Monthly Review Press, 1998.

Brophy, Enda, and Greig de Peuter. "Immaterial Labor, Precarity, and Recomposition." *Knowledge Workers in the Information Society,* ed. Catherine McKercher and Vincent Mosco, 177–92. Lanham, Md.: Lexington Books, 2007.

Broughton, Irv. *Producers on Producing: The Making of Film and Television.* Jefferson, N.C.: McFarland, 1986.

Brown, Wendy. *States of Injury: Power and Freedom in Late Modernity.* Princeton: Princeton University Press, 1995.

Burawoy, Michael. "Between the Labor Process and the State: The Changing Face of Factory Regimes under Advanced Capitalism." *American Sociological Review* 48, no. 5 (1983), 587–605.

Burawoy, Michael, et al. *Global Ethnography: Forces, Connections, and Imaginations in a Postmodern World.* Berkeley: University of California Press, 2000.

Burnier, DeLysa. "Encounters with the Self in Social Science Research: A Political Scientist Looks at Autoethnography." *Journal of Contemporary Ethnography* 35, no. 4 (2006), 410–18.

Butsch, Richard. *The Citizen Audience: Crowds, Publics, and Individuals.* New York: Routledge, 2008.

Caldwell, John T. "'Both Sides of the Fence': Blurred Distinctions in Scholarship and Production (a Portfolio of Interviews)." *Production Studies: Cultural Studies of Film and Television Production,* ed. Vicki Mayer, Miranda Banks, and Caldwell, 214–15. New York: Routledge, 2009.

——. "Convergence Television: Aggregating Form and Repurposing Content in the Age of Conglomeration." *Television after TV: Essays on a Medium in Transition,* ed. Lynn Spigel, 41–74. Durham: Duke University Press, 2004.

——. "Critical Industrial Practice: Branding, Repurposing, and the Migratory Patterns of Industrial Texts." *Television and New Media* 7, no. 2 (2006), 99–134.

——. "Cultural Studies of Media Production: Critical Industrial Practice." *Questions of Method in Cultural Studies,* ed. Mimi White and James Schwoch, 109–53. Malden, Mass.: Blackwell, 2006.

——. "Industrial Geography Lessons: Socio-professional Rituals and the Borderlands of Production Culture." *Mediaspace: Place, Scale, and Culture in the Media Age,* ed. Nick Couldry and Anna McCarthy, 163–90. London: Routledge, 2004.

——. *Production Culture: Industrial Reflexivity and Critical Practice in Film and Television.* Durham: Duke University Press, 2008.

Cantor, Muriel G. *The Hollywood TV Producer: His Work and His Audience.* New York: Basic Books, 1971.

Cantor, Muriel, and Cheryl Zollars, eds. *Current Research on Occupations and Professions: Creators of Culture.* Greenwich, Conn.: JAI Press, 1993.

Caputi, Jane. "The Pornography of Everyday Life." *Mediated Women: Representa-*

tions in Popular Culture, ed. Marian Meyers, 57–80. Cresskill, N.J.: Hampton Press, 1999.

Certeau, Michel de. *The Practice of Everyday Life.* Trans. Steven Rendall. Berkeley: University of California Press, 1984.

Chakrabarty, Dipesh. "Universalism and Belonging in the Logic of Capital." *Public Culture* 12, no. 3 (2000), 653–78.

Chakravartty, Paula, and Katharine Sarikakis. *Media Policy and Globalization.* New York: Palgrave Macmillan, 2006.

Chopra, Radhika. "Invisible Men: Masculinity, Sexuality, and Male Domestic Labor." *Men and Masculinities* 9, no. 2 (2006), 152–67.

Christopherson, Susan. "The Transformation of Industrial Relations in the Motion Picture and Television Industries: Craft and Production." *Under the Stars: Essays on Labor Relations in Arts and Entertainment,* ed. Lois Gray and Ronald Seeber, 113–56. Ithaca: Cornell University Press, 1996.

Clark, Danae. *Negotiating Hollywood: The Cultural Politics of Actors' Labor.* Minneapolis: University of Minnesota Press, 1995.

Clark, Jon. "Robert Merton as Sociologist." *Robert K. Merton: Consensus and Controversy,* ed. Clark, Celia Modgil, and Sohan Modgil, 13–24. London: Falmer Press, 1990.

Classen, Steven D. *Watching Jim Crow: The Struggles over Mississippi TV, 1955–1969.* Durham: Duke University Press, 2004.

Cohan, Steven. *Masked Men: Masculinity and the Movies in the Fifties.* Bloomington: Indiana University Press, 1997.

Cole, Barry, and Mal Oettinger. *Reluctant Regulators: The FCC and the Broadcast Audience.* Reading, Mass.: Addison-Wesley, 1978.

Collins, Sue. "Making the Most out of Fifteen Minutes: Reality TV's Dispensable Celebrity." *Television and New Media* 9, no. 2 (2008), 87–110.

Connell, R. W., and Julian Wood. "Globalization and Business Masculinities." *Men and Masculinities* 7, no. 4 (2005), 347–64.

Cooper, Davina. *Challenging Diversity: Rethinking Equality and the Value of Difference.* Cambridge: Cambridge University Press, 2004.

Cornea, Christine. "Introduction: Interviews in Film and Television Studies." *Cinema Journal* 47, no. 2 (2008), 117–23.

Couldry, Nick. "Media Organisations and Non-media People." *Media Organisations in Society,* ed. James Curran, 273–88. London: Edward Arnold, 2000.

——. *Media Rituals: A Critical Approach.* London: Routledge, 2003.

——. *The Place of Media Power: Pilgrims and Witnesses of the Media Age.* London: Routledge, 2000.

——. *Why Voice Matters: Culture and Politics after Neoliberalism.* London: Sage, 2010.

Cowie, Jefferson. *Capital Moves: RCA's Seventy-Year Quest for Cheap Labor.* Ithaca: Cornell University Press, 1999.

Crawford, Matthew V. *Shop Class as Soulcraft: An Inquiry into the Value of Work.* New York: Penguin, 2009.

Croteau, David. "The Growth of Self-Produced Media Content and the Challenge to Media Studies." *Critical Studies in Media Communication* 23, no. 4 (2006), 340–44.

Dalla Costa, Giovanna Franca. *The Work of Love: Unpaid Housework, Poverty, and Sexual Violence at the Dawn of the Twenty-First Century.* Trans. Enda Brophy. Brooklyn, N.Y.: Autonomedia, 2008.

Davis, Aeron. "Whither Mass Media and Power? Evidence for a Critical Elite Theory Alternative." *Media, Culture, and Society* 25, no. 5 (2003), 669–90.

Dawson, Anthony A. P. "Hollywood's Labor Troubles." *Industrial and Labor Relations Review* 1, no. 4 (1948), 638–47.

De Botton, Alain. *The Pleasures and Sorrows of Work.* New York: Pantheon, 2009.

Deery, June. "Reality TV as Advertainment." *Popular Communication* 2, no. 1 (2004), 1–20.

De Laun, Fran, and Gerald V. Flannery. "Fly, James L., 1939–1944." *Commissioners of the FCC, 1927–1994,* ed. Flannery, 60–62. Lanham, Md.: University Press of America, 1995.

Denzin, Norman. "Analytic Autoethnography; or, Déjà Vu All over Again." *Journal of Contemporary Ethnography* 35, no. 4 (2006), 419–28.

Deuze, Mark. *Media Work.* Cambridge: Polity Press, 2007.

Dornfeld, Barry. *Producing Public Television, Producing Public Culture.* Princeton: Princeton University Press, 1998.

du Gay, Paul, ed. *Production of Culture/Cultures of Production.* London: Sage and Open University, 1997.

du Gay, Paul, and Michael Pryke, eds. *Cultural Economy: Cultural Analysis and Commercial Life.* London: Sage, 2002.

Durham, Meenakshi Gigi. "On the Relevance of Standpoint Epistemology to the Practice of Journalism: The Case for 'Strong Objectivity.'" *Communication Theory* 8, no. 2 (1998), 117–40.

Elger, Tony, and Chris Smith, eds. *Global Japanization? The Transnational Transformation of the Labour Process.* London: Routledge, 1994.

Elliott, Philip. *The Making of a Television Series: A Case Study in the Sociology of Culture.* Ed. Jeremy Tunstall. London: Constable, 1972.

Elliott, Philip, and David Chaney. "A Sociological Framework for the Study of Television Production." *Sociological Review* 17, no. 3 (1969), 355–75.

Ellis, John. "Television Production." *The Television Studies Reader,* ed. Robert C. Allen and Annette Hill, 279–92. London: Routledge, 2004.

Ettema, James S. "The Role of Educators and Researchers in the Production of Educational Television." *Journal of Broadcasting* 24, no. 4 (1980), 487–98.

Ettema, James S., and D. Charles Whitney. Introduction to *Individuals in Mass Media Organizations: Creativity and Constraint,* ed. Ettema and Whitney, 1–32. Thousand Oaks, Calif.: Sage, 1982.

Ettema, James S., D. Charles Whitney, and Daniel Wackman. "Professional Mass Communicators." *Handbook of Communication Science,* ed. Charles R. Berger and Steven H. Chaffee, 747–80. Beverly Hills, Calif.: Sage, 1987.

Etzioni, Amitai. Preface to *The Semi-professions and Their Organization*, ed. Etzioni, v–xviii. New York: Free Press, 1969.

Falguni, Sheth. "Labor, Work, and Citizenship: A Study of the Meanings and the Implications of Work in Hegel, Marx, Arendt, and Kittay." PhD diss., New School University, 2003.

Ferreira, Márcio. *O desenvolvimento do capitalismo em Manaus*. Manaus: Universidade de Estado do Amazonas, 2003.

Ferreira de Melo, Lucilene, and Renan Freitas Pinto. "O migrante rural e a reconstrução da identidade e do imaginário na cidade." *Cidade de Manaus: Visões interdisciplinares*, ed. José Aldemir de Oliveira, José Duarte Alecrim, and Thierry Ray Jehlen Gasnier, 15–48. Manaus: EDUA, 2003.

Ferreira Moura, Edila, et al. *A utilização do trabalho feminino nas indústrias de Belém e Manaus*. Belém: Universidade Federal do Pará, 1986.

Fishman, Mark. *Manufacturing the News*. Austin: University of Texas Press, 1980.

Flew, Terry. "Creative Economy." *Creative Industries*, ed. John Hartley, 344–60. Malden, Mass.: Blackwell, 2005.

Florida, Richard. *Cities and the Creative Class*. New York: Routledge, 2005.

———. *The Rise of the Creative Class*. New York: Basic Books, 2002.

Fortunati, Leopoldina. *The Arcane of Reproduction: Housework, Prostitution, Labor, and Capital*, Trans. Hilary Creek. Brooklyn, N.Y.: Autonomedia, 1995.

Foucault, Michel. *The Birth of Biopolitics: Lectures at the Collège de France, 1978–1979*. Trans. Graham Burchell. New York: Palgrave Macmillan, 2008.

Freedman, Des. "Dynamics of Power in Contemporary Media Policy-Making." *Media, Culture, and Society* 28, no. 6 (2006), 907–23.

———. *The Politics of Media Policy*. Cambridge: Polity Press, 2008.

Freidson, Eliot. *Professionalism Reborn: Theory, Prophecy, and Policy*. Chicago: University of Chicago Press, 1994.

———. "The Theory of Professions: State of the Art." *Professionalism Reborn: Theory, Prophecy, and Policy*, 13–29. Chicago: University of Chicago Press, 1994.

French, John D. *Drowning in Laws: Labor Law and Brazilian Political Culture*. Chapel Hill: University of North Carolina Press, 2004.

Friedman, Walter. *Birth of a Salesman: The Transformation of Selling in America*. Cambridge: Harvard University Press, 2004.

Furchtgott-Roth, Harold W. *A Tough Act to Follow? The Telecommunications Act of 1996 and the Separation of Powers*. Washington: American Enterprise Institute Press, 2006.

Gandy, Oscar. "Audiences on Demand." *Toward a Political Economy of Culture: Capitalism and Communication in the Twenty-First Century*, ed. Andrew Calabrese and Colin Sparks, 327–40. Lanham, Md.: Rowman and Littlefield, 2004.

Gans, Herbert J. *Deciding What's News: A Study of "CBS Evening News," "NBC Nightly News," "Newsweek," and "Time."* New York: Vintage, 1979.

Garcia, Etelvina. *Modelo de desenvolvimento Zona Franca de Manaus: História, conquistas E desafios*. Manaus: Norma Editora, 2004.

Garnham, Nicholas. *Capitalism and Communication: Global Culture and the Economics of Information*. Ed. Fred Inglis. London: Sage, 1990.

Ginsberg, Faye, Lila Abu-Lughod, and Brian Larkin, eds. *Media Worlds: Anthropology on New Terrain*. Berkeley: University of California Press, 2002.

Gitlin, Todd. *Inside Prime Time*. New York: Pantheon, 1983.

——. *Inside Prime Time*. 2nd ed. Berkeley: University of California Press, 2000.

Gledhill, Donald. "The Motion Picture Academy, a Cooperative in Hollywood." *Journal of Educational Sociology* 13, no. 5 (1940), 268–73.

Gotham, Kevin Fox. *Authentic New Orleans: Tourism, Culture, and Race in the Big Easy*. New York: New York University Press, 2007.

Gray, Herman. *Cultural Moves: African Americans and the Politics of Representation*. Berkeley: University of California Press, 2005.

Grindstaff, Laura. *The Money Shot: Trash, Class, and the Making of TV Talk Shows*. Chicago: University of Chicago Press, 2002.

——. "Self-Serve Celebrity: The Production of Ordinariness and the Ordinariness of Production in Reality Television." *Production Studies: Cultural Studies of Film and Television Production*, ed. Vicki Mayer, Miranda Banks, and John Caldwell, 71–86. New York: Routledge, 2009.

Grindstaff, Laura, and Joseph Turow. "Video Cultures: Television Sociology in the 'New TV' Age." *Annual Review of Sociology*, no. 32 (2006), 103–25.

Hall, Stuart. "Encoding/Decoding." *Culture, Media, Language: Working Papers in Cultural Studies, 1972–79*, ed. Centre for Contemporary Cultural Studies, 128–38. London: Hutchinson, 1980.

Hartley, John. "Creative Identities." *Creative Industries*, ed. Hartley, 106–16. Malden, Mass.: Blackwell, 2005.

——. "Creative Industries." *Creative Industries*, ed. Hartley, 1–40. Malden, Mass.: Blackwell, 2005.

Harvey, David. *The Condition of Postmodernity: An Enquiry into the Origins of Cultural Change*. Cambridge, Mass.: Blackwell, 1989.

——. "From Space to Place and Back Again: Reflections on the Conditions of Postmodernity." *Mapping the Futures: Local Cultures, Global Change*, ed. Jon Bird et al., 3–29. London: Routledge, 1993.

Havens, Timothy. *Global Television Marketplace*. London: British Film Institute, 2006.

Havick, John, ed. *Communications Policy and the Political Process*. Westport, Conn.: Greenwood Press, 1983.

Heelas, Paul. "Work Ethics, Soft Capitalism, and the 'Turn to Life.'" *Cultural Economy*, ed. Paul du Gay and Michael Pryke, 78–96. London: Sage, 2002.

Hendershot, Heather. "Belabored Reality: Making It Work on *The Simple Life* and *Project Runway*." *Reality TV: Remaking Television Culture*, 2nd ed., ed. Susan Murray and Laurie Ouellette, 243–59. New York: New York University Press, 2008.

———. *Saturday Morning Censors: Television Regulation before the V-Chip*. Durham: Duke University Press, 1998.

Hesmondhalgh, David. *The Cultural Industries*. London: Sage, 2002.

Hesmondhalgh, David, and Sarah Baker, "Creative Work and Emotional Labour in TV." *Theory, Culture, and Society* 25, nos. 7–8 (2008), 97–118.

Hilbert, Richard A. "Bureaucracy as Belief, Rationalization as Repair: Max Weber in a Post-functionalist Age." *Sociological Theory* 5, no. 1 (1987), 70–86.

Hilmes, Michele. "Desired and Feared: Women's Voices in Radio History." *Television, History, and American Culture: Feminist Critical Essays*, ed. Mary Beth Haralovich and Lauren Rabinovitz, 17–35. Durham: Duke University Press, 1999.

———. "Nailing Mercury: The Problem of Media Industry Historiography." *Media Industries: History, Theory, and Method*, ed. Alisa Perren and Jennifer Holt, 21–33. Malden, Mass.: Wiley-Blackwell, 2009.

Hirsch, Paul. "Cultural Industries Revisited." *Organization Science* 11, no. 3 (2000), 356–61.

———. "Occupational, Organizational, and Institutional Models in Mass Communication." *Strategies for Communication Research*, ed. Hirsch, Peter Miller, and F. Gerald Kline, 13–42. Beverly Hills, Calif.: Sage, 1977.

Ho, Karen. *Liquidated: An Ethnography of Wall Street*. Durham: Duke University Press, 2009.

Hobart, Mark. "Just Talk? Anthropological Reflections on the Object of Media Studies in Indonesia." *Asian Journal of Social Science* 34, no. 3 (2006), 492–512.

Hochschild, Arlie R. *The Managed Heart: Commercialization of Human Feeling*. Twentieth anniversary ed. Berkeley: University of California Press, 2003.

Holliday, Jim. "A History of Modern Pornographic Film and Video." *Porn 101: Eroticism, Pornography, and the First Amendment*, ed. James Elias et al., 341–51. Amherst, N.Y.: Prometheus Books, 1999.

Horwitz, Robert Britt. *The Irony of Regulatory Reform: The Deregulation of American Telecommunications*. New York: Oxford University Press, 1989.

Hughes, Everett. *Men and Their Work*. Glencoe, Ill.: Free Press, 1958.

Humphrey, John. "'Japanese' Methods and the Changing Position of Direct Production Workers: Evidence from Brazil." *Global Japanization? The Transnational Transformation of the Labour Process*, ed. Tony Elger and Chris Smith, 327–47. London: Routledge, 1994.

Hundt, Reed E. *You Say You Want a Revolution: A Story of Information Age Politics*. New Haven: Yale University Press, 2000.

Husband, Charles. "Minority Ethnic Media as Communities of Practice: Professionalism and Identity Politics in Interaction." *Journal of Ethnic and Migration Studies* 31, no. 3 (2005), 461–79.

Illouz, Eva. *Saving the Modern Soul: Therapy, Emotions, and the Culture of Self-Help*. Berkeley: University of California Press, 2008.

Iton, Richard. *In Search of the Black Fantastic: Politics and the Post–Civil Rights Era*. New York: Oxford University Press, 2008.

Jenkins, Henry. *Convergence Culture: Where Old and New Media Collide*. Cambridge: MIT Press, 2006.

Jhally, Sut. "Advertising as Religion: The Dialectic of Technology and Magic." *The Spectacle of Accumulation: Essays in Culture, Media, and Politics*, 85–97. New York: Peter Lang, 2006.

Joas, Hans. *The Creativity of Action*. Chicago: University of Chicago Press, 1996.

Johnson, Richard. "What Is Cultural Studies Anyway?" *Social Text*, no. 16 (1986–87), 38–80.

Joseph, Miranda. *Against the Romance of Community*. Minneapolis: University of Minnesota Press, 2002.

——. "The Performance of Production and Consumption." *Social Text*, no. 54 (1998), 25–61.

Kenney, Martin, and Richard Florida. *Beyond Mass Production: The Japanese System and Its Transfer to the U.S.* New York: Oxford University Press, 1993.

Kessler-Harris, Alice. "Voluntary Work and Labour History: A Postscript," *Labour History*, no. 81 (2001), 129–33.

Kirkpatrick, Bill. "Bringing Blue Skies Down to Earth: The Rhetorics of Policy Translation in Negotiations for Cable Television, 1965–1975." *Globalization and Communicative Democracy: Community Media in the Twenty-First Century*, ed. Kevin Howley. Thousand Oaks, Calif.: Sage, forthcoming.

——. "Sounds Local: The Competition for Space and Place in Early U.S. Radio." *Sound in the Age of Mechanical Reproduction*, ed. David Suisman and Susan Strasser, 199–220. Philadelphia: University of Pennsylvania Press, 2010.

Krasnow, Erwin G., and Lawrence D. Longley. *The Politics of Broadcast Regulation*. New York: St. Martin's Press, 1973.

——. *The Politics of Broadcast Regulation*. 2nd ed. New York: St. Martin's Press, 1978.

Krasnow, Erwin G., Lawrence D. Longley, and Herbert A. Terry. *The Politics of Broadcast Regulation*. 3rd ed. New York: St. Martin's Press, 1982.

Laclau, Ernesto. *On Populist Reason*. London: Verso, 2005.

Landman, Jane. "Not in Kansas Anymore: Transnational Collaboration in Television Science Fiction Production." *Production Studies: Cultural Studies of Film and Television Production*, ed. Vicki Mayer, Miranda Banks, and John Caldwell, 140–53. New York: Routledge, 2009.

Lanham, Richard A. *The Economics of Attention: Style and Substance in the Age of Information*. Chicago: University of Chicago Press, 2006.

Lara Campos da Costa, Heloisa. "A respeito da lógica do poder: O controle sobre o trabalho feminino em duas empresas de Manaus." *Ciências humanas: Revista da Universidade do Amazonas* 8, nos. 1–2 (2000–2001), 1–34.

Larson, Magali Sarfatti. *The Rise of Professionalism: A Sociological Analysis*. Berkeley: University of California Press, 1977.

Lears, Jackson T. J. "The Rise of American Advertising." *Wilson Quarterly* 7, no. 1 (1983), 156–67.

LeDuc, Don R. "Transforming Principles into Policy." *Journal of Communication* 30, no. 2 (1980), 196–202.

Lerner, Daniel. *The Passing of Traditional Society: Modernizing the Middle East.* Glencoe, Ill.: Free Press, 1958.

Lerner, Daniel, and Wilbur Schramm, eds. *Communication and Change in Developing Countries.* Honolulu: East-West Center Press, 1967.

Levine, Elana. "Toward a Paradigm for Media Production Research: Behind the Scenes at General Hospital." *Critical Studies in Media Communication* 18, no. 2 (2001), 66–82.

Lichty, Lawrence W. "The Impact of FRC and FCC Commissioners' Backgrounds on the Regulation of Broadcasting." *Journal of Broadcasting* 6, no. 2 (1961–1962), 97–110.

———. "Members of the Federal Radio Commission and the Federal Communications Commission, 1927–1961." *Journal of Broadcasting* 6, no. 1 (1961–1962), 23–34.

Livingstone, Sonia, Peter Lunt, and Laura Miller, "Citizens and Consumers: Discursive Debates during and after the Communications Act 2003," *Media, Culture, and Society* 29, no. 4 (2007), 613–38.

Lotz, Amanda D. *The Television Will Be Revolutionized.* New York: New York University Press, 2007.

Lowe, Donald M. *The Body in Late-Capitalist U.S.A.* Durham: Duke University Press, 1995.

Lowe, Lisa. *Immigrant Acts: On Asian American Cultural Politics.* Durham: Duke University Press, 1996.

Lukács, Georg. *History and Class Consciousness.* Trans. Rodney Livingstone. Cambridge: MIT Press, 1971.

MacDonald, Keith M. *The Sociology of Professions.* London: Sage, 1995.

Mankekar, Purnima. *Screening Culture, Viewing Politics: An Ethnography of Television, Womanhood, and Nation in Postcolonial India.* Durham: Duke University Press, 1999.

Mann, Denise. *Hollywood Independents: The Postwar Talent Takeover.* Minneapolis: University of Minnesota Press, 2007.

———. "It's Not TV, It's Brand Management TV: The Collective Author(s) of the *Lost* Franchise." *Production Studies: Cultural Studies of Film and Television Production*, ed. Vicki Mayer, Miranda Banks, and John Caldwell, 99–114. New York: Routledge, 2009.

Marchand, Roland. *Advertising the American Dream: Making Way for Modernity, 1920–1940.* Berkeley: University of California Press, 1986.

Martindale, Don, ed. *Functionalism in the Social Sciences: The Strength and Limits of Functionalism in Anthropology, Economics, Political Science, and Sociology.* Philadelphia: American Academy of Political and Social Science, 1965.

Marx, Karl, and Frederick Engels. *The German Ideology*, 6th ed., ed. C. J. Arthur. Trans. C. Dutt. New York: International Publishers, 1977.

Mattelart, Armand, and Michèle Mattelart. *Theories of Communication: A Short Introduction*. Trans. Susan Taponier. London: Sage, 1998.

Mayer, Vicki. "Fieldnote." *Contexts: A Journal of the American Sociological Association* 5, no. 4 (2006), 58–59.

——. *Producing Dreams, Consuming Youth: Mexican Americans and Mass Media*. New Brunswick: Rutgers University Press, 2003.

——. "Soft-Core in TV Time: The Political Economy of a 'Cultural Trend.'" *Critical Studies in Mass Communication* 22, no. 4 (2005), 302–20.

——. "Studying up and F**King Up: Ethnographic Interviewing in Production Studies." *Cinema Journal* 47, no. 2 (2008), 141–48.

Mayer, Vicki, Miranda Banks, and John Caldwell, eds. *Production Studies: Cultural Studies of Film and Television Production*. New York: Routledge, 2009.

Mazzarella, William. "'Very Bombay': Contending with the Global in an Indian Advertising Agency." *Cultural Anthropology* 18, no. 1 (2003), 33–71.

McChesney, Robert. *Telecommunications, Mass Media, and Democracy: The Battle for Control of U.S. Broadcasting, 1928–1935*. New York: Oxford University Press, 1994.

McKercher, Catherine, and Vincent Mosco, eds. *Knowledge Workers in the Information Society*. Lanham, Md.: Lexington Books, 2007.

McMillin, Divya. "Outsourcing Identities: Call Centers and Cultural Transformation in India." *Economic and Political Weekly* 42, no. 3 (2006), 235–41.

McNair, Brian. *Striptease Culture: Sex, Media, and the Democratization of Desire*. London: Routledge, 2004.

McRobbie, Angela. "Clubs to Companies." *Creative Industries*, ed. John Hartley, 375–90. Malden, Mass.: Blackwell, 2005.

——. "'Everyone Is Creative': Artists as Pioneers of the New Economy." *Contemporary Culture and Everyday Life*, ed. Elizabeth B. Silva and Tony Bennett, 186–202. Durham, UK: Sociologypress, 2004.

——. "From Holloway to Hollywood: Happiness at Work in the New Cultural Economy?" *Cultural Economy*, ed. Paul du Gay and Michael Pryke, 97–114. London: Sage, 2002.

Mechling, Elizabeth Walker, and Jay Mechling. "Sweet Talk: The Moral Rhetoric against Sugar." *Central States Speech Journal* 34, no. 1 (1983), 19–32.

Meehan, Eileen. "Ancillary Markets—Television: From Challenge to Safe Haven." *The Contemporary Hollywood Film Industry*, ed. Paul McDonald and Janet Wasko, 106–19. Malden, Mass.: Blackwell, 2008.

——. "Conceptualizing Culture as a Commodity." *Critical Studies in Mass Communication* 3, no. 4 (1986), 448–57.

——. *Why TV Is Not Our Fault: Television Programming, Viewers, and Who's Really in Control*. Lanham, Md.: Rowman and Littlefield, 2005.

Menger, Pierre-Michel. "Artistic Labor Markets and Careers." *Annual Review of Sociology*, no. 25 (1999), 541–74.

Miller, Toby. *Cultural Citizenship: Cosmopolitanism, Consumerism, and Television in a Neoliberal Age*. Philadelphia: Temple University Press, 2007.

——. "From Creative to Cultural Industries: Not All Industries Are Cultural, and No Industries Are Creative." *Cultural Studies* 23, no. 1 (2009), 88–99.

Miller, Toby, et al. *Global Hollywood 2*. Updated ed. London: British Film Institute, 2005.

Mittell, Jason. *Genre and Television: From Cop Shows to Cartoons in American Culture*. New York: Routledge, 2004.

Moran, Albert. *Making a TV Series: The Bellamy Project*. Sydney: Currency Press, 1982.

Moran, Albert, and Michael Keane, eds. *Television across Asia: Television Industries, Programme Formats, and Globalization*. London: Routledge Curzon, 2004.

Moran, James M. *There's No Place Like Home Video*. Minneapolis: University of Minnesota Press, 2002.

Morley, David. "For a Materialist, Non-Media-Centric Media Studies." *Television and New Media* 10, no. 1 (2009), 114–16.

Mosco, Vincent. *The Political Economy of Communication: Rethinking and Renewal*. 2nd ed. London: Sage, 2009.

Mosco, Vincent, and Catherine McKercher. *The Laboring of Communication: Will Knowledge Workers of the World Unite?* Lanham, Md.: Lexington Books, 2008.

Moura, Edila Arnaud Ferreira, et al. *Zona Franca de Manaus: Os filhos da era eletroelectrônica*. Belém: Associação de Universidades Amazônicas, 1993.

Muir, Stewart. "Not Quite at Home: Field Envy and New Age Ethnographic Disease." *Anthropologists in the Field: Cases in Participant Observation*, ed. Lynne Hume and Jane Mulcock, 185–200. New York: Columbia University Press, 2005.

Mukherjee, Roopali. *The Racial Order of Things: Cultural Imaginaries of the Post-soul Era*. Minneapolis: University of Minnesota Press, 2006.

Mullen, Megan. *Television in the Multichannel Age: A Brief History of Cable Television*. Malden, Mass.: Blackwell, 2008.

Murdock, Graham. "Back to Work: Cultural Labor in Altered Times." *Cultural Work: Understanding the Cultural Industries*, ed. Andrew Beck, 15–35. London: Routledge, 2003.

Murphy, Patrick. "Writing Media Culture: Representation and Experience in Media Ethnography." *Communication, Culture, and Critique* 1, no. 3 (2008), 268–86.

Naficy, Hamid. *The Making of Exile Cultures: Iranian Television in Los Angeles*. Minneapolis: University of Minnesota Press, 1993.

Nakano Glenn, Evelyn. *Unequal Freedom: How Race and Gender Shaped American Citizenship and Labor*. Cambridge: Harvard University Press, 2002.

Napoli, Philip M. "The Federal Communications Commission and the Communications Policymaking Process: Theoretical Perspectives and Recommendations for Future Research." *Communication Yearbook* 25, no. 1 (2001), 44–77.

Nathan, Debbie, and Michael Snedeker. *Satan's Silence: Ritual Abuse and the Making of a Modern American Witchhunt*. New York: Basic Books, 1996.

Newcomb, Horace, and Robert S. Alley. "The Producer as Artist: Commercial Television." *Individuals in Mass Media Organizations: Creativity and Constraint*, ed. James S. Ettema and D. Charles Whitney, 69–90. Beverly Hills: Sage, 1982.

———. *The Producer's Medium: Conversations with Creators of American TV*. Oxford: Oxford University Press, 1983.

Noble, David F. *America by Design: Science, Technology, and the Rise of Corporate Capitalism*. New York: Oxford University Press, 1979.

Noriega, Chon. *Shot in America: Television, the State, and the Rise of Chicano Cinema*. Minneapolis: University of Minnesota Press, 2000.

Odendahl, Teresa, and Michael O'Neill, eds. *Women and Power in the Non-profit Sector*. San Francisco: Jossey-Bass, 1994.

Oppenheimer, Melanie. "Voluntary Work and Labour History." *Labour History*, no. 74 (1998), 1–9.

Ortner, Sherry. "Resistance and the Problem of Ethnographic Refusal." *Comparative Studies in Society and History* 37, no. 1 (1995), 173–93.

———. "Studying Sideways: Ethnographic Access in Hollywood." *Production Studies: Cultural Studies of Media Industries*, ed. Vicki Mayer, Miranda J. Banks, and John Caldwell, 175–89. London: Routledge, 2009.

Osgerby, Bill. *Playboys in Paradise: Masculinity, Youth, and Leisure-Style in Modern America*. Oxford: Berg, 2001.

Ouellette, Laurie. *Viewers Like You? How Public TV Failed the People*. New York: Columbia University Press, 2002.

Ouellette, Laurie, and James Hay. *Better Living through Reality TV*. Malden, Mass.: Blackwell, 2008.

Owen, Bruce. "A Novel Conference: The Origins of the TPRC (1998)." *Communication Researchers and Policy-Making*, ed. Sandra Braman, 364–73. Cambridge: MIT Press, 2003.

Paasonen, Susanna, Kaarina Nikunen, and Laura Saarenmaa, eds. *Pornification: Sex and Sexuality in Media Culture*. New York: Berg, 2007.

Painter, Andrew. "Japanese Daytime Television, Popular Culture, and Ideology." *Journal of Japanese Studies* 19, no. 2 (1993), 295–325.

———. "The Telerepresentation of Gender in Japan." *Re-imaging Japanese Women*, ed. Anne E. Imamura, 46–72. Berkeley: University of California Press, 1996.

Pang, Laikwan. "The Labor Factor in the Creative Economy: A Marxist Reading." *Social Text* 99 (2009), 55–76.

Pelias, Ronald. "An Academic Tourist: An Autoethnography." *Qualitative Inquiry* 9, no. 3 (2003), 369–73.

Perlman, Alison. "Feminists in the Wasteland: The National Organization for Women and Television Reform." *Feminist Media Studies* 7, no. 4 (2007), 413–31.

Peterson, Mark Allen. *Anthropology and Mass Communication: Media and Myth in the New Millennium*. New York: Berghahn Books, 2003.

Peterson, Richard A. "The Production of Culture: A Prolegomenon." *American Behavioral Scientist* 19, no. 6 (1976), 669–84.

Peterson, Richard A., and N. Anand. "The Production of Culture Perspective." *Annual Review of Sociology*, no. 30 (2004), 311–34.

Pollin, Robert. *Contours of Descent: U.S. Economic Fractures and the Landscape of Global Austerity*. London: Verso, 2003.

Poovey, Mary. "Feminism and Deconstruction." *Feminist Studies* 14, no. 1 (1988), 51–65.

Powdermaker, Hortense. *Hollywood, the Dream Factory: An Anthropologist Looks at Movie-Makers*. Boston: Little, Brown, 1950.

——. *Stranger and Friend: The Way of an Anthropologist*. New York: W. W. Norton, 1966.

Pringle, Rosemary. *Secretaries Talk: Sexuality, Power, and Work*. London: Verso, 1988.

Reed, T. V. *The Art of Protest: Culture and Activism from the Civil Rights Movement to the Streets of Seattle*. Minneapolis: University of Minnesota Press, 2005.

Reeves, Jimmie L. "Rewriting Television: A Dialogic View of Television." *Making Television: Authorship and the Production Process*, ed. Robert J. Thompson and Gary Burns, 147–60. Westport, Conn.: Praeger, 1990.

Riggs, Karen. "Preaching to the Unseen Choir." *Mature Audiences: Television in the Lives of Elders*, 97–123. New Brunswick: Rutgers University Press, 1998.

Robinson, Glen O. "The Federal Communications Commission." *Communications for Tomorrow: Policy Perspectives for the 1980s*, ed. Glen O. Robinson, 353–400. New York: Praeger, 1978.

Robinson, William I. *A Theory of Global Capitalism: Production, Class, and State in a Transnational World*. Baltimore: Johns Hopkins University Press, 2004.

Rogers, Everett. *Modernization among Peasants: The Impact of Communication*. New York: Holt, Rinehart, and Winston, 1969.

Ross, Andrew. *Low Pay, High Profile: The Global Push for Fair Labor*. New York: New Press, 2004.

——. *Nice Work If You Can Get It: Life and Labor in Precarious Times*. New York: New York University Press, 2009.

——. *No Collar: The Humane Workplace and Its Hidden Costs*. Philadelphia: Temple University Press, 2004.

Ross, Murray. "Labor Relations in Hollywood." *Annals of the American Academy of Political and Social Science*, no. 254 (1947), 58–64.

Rosten, Leo C. *Hollywood: The Movie Colony, the Movie Makers*. New York: Harcourt, Brace, 1941.

——. "A 'Middletown' Study of Hollywood." *Public Opinion Quarterly* 3, no. 2 (1939), 314–20.

Rostow, Walt. *The Stages of Economic Growth: A Non-communist Manifesto.* Cambridge: Cambridge University Press, 1960.

Salazar, Admilton Pinheiro. *Amazônia: Globalização e sustentabilidade.* Manaus: Editora Valer, 2004.

Salzinger, Leslie. *Genders in Production: Making Workers in Mexico's Global Factories.* Berkeley: University of California Press, 2003.

Sandeen, Cathy A., and Ronald J. Compesi. "Television Production as Collective Action." *Making Television: Authorship and the Production Process,* ed. Robert J. Thompson and Gary Burns, 161–74. Westport, Conn.: Praeger, 1990.

Sawyer, R. Keith. *Group Creativity: Music, Theater, Collaboration.* Mahwah, N.J.: Lawrence Earlbaum, 2003.

Scherer, Elenise. *Baixas nas carteiras: Desemprego e trabalho precário na Zona Franca de Manaus.* Manaus: EDUA, 2005.

Schiller, Dan. *Digital Capitalism.* Cambridge: MIT Press, 1999.

——. *How to Think about Information.* Urbana: University of Illinois Press, 2007.

——. *Theorizing Communication: A History.* New York: Oxford University Press, 1996.

Schiller, Herbert. *Mass Communications and American Empire.* Boston: Beacon, 1969.

Schramm, Wilbur. *Mass Media and National Development: The Role of Information in the Developing Countries.* Stanford: Stanford University Press, 1964.

Scott, Allen J. *On Hollywood: The Place, the Industry.* Princeton: Princeton University Press, 2005.

Scott, James C. *Domination and the Arts of Resistance: Hidden Transcripts.* New Haven: Yale University Press, 1992.

Seiter, Ellen, and Vicki Mayer. "Diversifying Representation in Children's TV: Nickelodeon's Model." *Nickelodeon Nation: The History, Politics, and Economics of America's Only TV Channel for Kids,* ed. Heather Hendershot, 120–33. New York: New York University Press, 2004.

Sennett, Richard. *The Craftsman.* New Haven: Yale University Press, 2008.

——. *The Culture of the New Capitalism.* New Haven: Yale University Press, 2007.

Seshadri-Crooks, Kalpana. *Desiring Whiteness: A Lacanian Analysis of Race.* New York: Routledge, 2000.

Shanahan, James, and Michael Morgan. *Television and Its Viewers: Cultivation Theory and Research.* Cambridge: Cambridge University Press, 1999.

Slotten, Hugh Richard. "'Rainbow in the Sky': FM Radio, Technical Superiority, and Regulatory Decision-Making." *Technology and Culture* 37, no. 4 (1996), 686–720.

——. *Radio and Television Regulation: Broadcast Technology in the United States, 1920–1960.* Baltimore: Johns Hopkins University Press, 2000.

Smythe, Dallas. "Communications: Blindspot of Western Marxism." 1977. *Counterclockwise: Perspectives on Communication,* ed. Thomas Guback, 266–91. Boulder, Colo.: Westview, 1994.

Somers, Margaret R. *Genealogies of Citizenship: Markets, Statelessness, and the Right to Have Rights.* Cambridge: Cambridge University Press, 2008.

Souza, Márcio. *Breve história da Amazônia.* 2nd ed. Rio de Janeiro: Agir, 2001.

Spigel, Lynn. *Make Room for TV: Television and the Family Ideal in Postwar America.* Chicago: University of Chicago Press, 1992.

Spivak, Gayatri Chakravorty. "Can the Subaltern Speak?" *Colonial Discourse and Post-colonial Theory: A Reader,* ed. Patrick Williams and Laura Chrisman, 66–111. New York: Columbia University Press, 1994.

Stahl, Matt. "Privilege and Distinction in Production Worlds: Copyright, Collective Bargaining, and Working Conditions in Media Making." In *Production Studies: Cultural Studies of Media Industries,* ed. Vicki Mayer, Miranda Banks, and John Caldwell, 54–68. New York: Routledge, 2009.

Steinert, Heinz. *Culture Industry.* Malden, Mass.: Blackwell Press, 2003.

Streeter, Thomas. *Selling the Air: A Critique of the Policy of Commercial Broadcasting in the United States.* Chicago: University of Chicago, 1996.

Symons, Howard J. "The Communications Policy Process." *New Directions in Telecommunications Policy,* ed. Paula R. Newburg, 275–300. Durham: Duke University Press, 1989.

Taylor, Frederick W. *The Principles of Scientific Management.* New York: Harper and Brothers Principles, 1911.

Terranova, Tiziana. "Free Labor: Producing Culture for the Digital Economy." *Social Text* 63 (2000), 33–58.

Thompson, Robert, and Gary Burns, eds. *Making Television: Authorship and the Production Process.* New York: Praeger, 1990.

Thynne, Lizzie. "Women in Television in the Multi-channel Age." *Feminist Review* 64, no. 1 (2000), 65–82.

Tinic, Serra. *On Location: Canada's Television Industry in a Global Market.* Toronto: University of Toronto Press, 2005.

Tovares, Raul. "Hooks, Benjamin Lawson: U.S. Media Regulator." *Encyclopedia of Television,* 2nd ed., ed. Horace Newcomb, 1134–36. New York: Fitzroy Dearborn, 2004.

Trachtenberg, Alan. *The Incorporation of America: Culture and Society in the Guilded Age.* New York: Hill and Wang, 1982.

Tuchman, Gaye. *Making News: A Study in the Construction of Reality.* New York: Free Press, 1978.

Tunstall, Jeremy. Introduction to *Media Occupations and Professions: A Reader,* vol. 8, ed. Tunstall, 1–22. Oxford: Oxford University Press, 2001.

——. *Television Producers.* London: Routledge, 1993.

Turner, Fred. *From Counterculture to Cyberculture: Stewart Brand, the Whole Earth Network, and the Rise of Digital Utopianism.* Chicago: University of Chicago Press, 2006.

Turow, Joseph. *Breaking up America: Advertisers and the New Media World.* Chicago: University of Chicago Press, 1997.

———. "Casting for TV Parts: The Anatomy of Social Typing." *Journal of Communication* 28, no. 4 (1978), 18–24.

———. *Entertainment, Education, and the Hard Sell: Three Decades of Network Children's Television.* New York: Praeger, 1981.

———. "Learning to Portray Institutional Power: The Socialization of Creators in Mass Media Organizations." *Organizational Communication: Traditional Themes and New Directions,* ed. Robert McPhee and Phillip Tompkins, 211–34. Beverly Hills, Calif.: Sage, 1985.

———. *Media Systems in Society: Understanding Industries, Systems, and Power.* New York: Longman, 1992.

———. *Niche Envy: Marketing Discrimination in the Digital Age.* Cambridge: MIT Press, 2006.

Tyler, Parker. "Hollywood as a Universal Church." *American Quarterly* 2, no. 2 (1950), 165–76.

Ursell, Gillian. "Labour Flexibility in the UK Commercial Television Sector." *Media, Culture, and Society* 20, no. 1 (1998), 129–53.

Valle, Izabel. "Globalização e reestruturação produtiva: Um estudo sobre a produção offshore em Manaus." PhD diss., Federal University of Rio de Janeiro, 2000.

Vieira, Ivânia. *O discurso operário e o espaço da fala da mulher.* Manaus: Editora Valer, 2002.

Vogler, Candace. "Sex and Talk." *Intimacy,* ed. Lauren Berlant, 48–85. Chicago: University of Chicago, 2000.

Wang, Jennifer Hyland. " 'The Case of the Radio-Active Housewife': Relocating Radio in the Age of Television." *Radio Reader: Cultural Essays in the History of Radio,* ed. Michele Hilmes, 343–66. New York: Routledge, 2002.

Weisenberger, Carol A. "Women of the FCC: Activists or Tokens?" *Business and Economic History* 21, no. 2 (1992), 192–98.

Wheeler, Mark. *Hollywood Politics and Society.* London: British Film Institute, 2006.

Whitney, D. Charles, and James S. Ettema. "Media Production: Individuals, Organizations, Institutions." *A Companion to Media Studies,* ed. Angharad Valdivia, 157–86. Oxford: Blackwell, 2003.

Wichroski, Mary Anne. "The Secretary: Invisible Labor in the Workworld of Women." *Human Organization* 53, no. 1 (1994), 33–41.

Williams, Linda. *Hard Core: Power, Pleasure, and "the Frenzy of the Visible."* Berkeley: University of California Press, 1989.

Williams, Raymond. *Keywords: A Vocabulary of Culture and Society.* Oxford: Oxford University Press, 1985.

Williams, Wenmouth, Jr. "Impact of Commissioner Background on FCC Decisions: 1962–1975." *Journal of Broadcasting* 20, no. 2 (1976), 239–60.

Willson, Margaret. "Afterword: Perspective and Difference: Sexualization, the Field, the Ethnographer." *Taboo: Sex, Identity, and Erotic Subjectivity in An-*

thropological Fieldwork, ed. Don Kulick and Willson, 251–75. London: Routledge, 1995.

Woodward, Kathleen. "Calculating Compassion." *Compassion: The Culture and Politics of an Emotion,* ed. Lauren Berlant, 59–86. New York: Routledge, 2004.

Wright, Steve. *Storming Heaven: Class Composition and Struggle in Italian Autonomist Marxism.* London: Pluto, 2002.

Ytreberg, Espen. "Formatting Participation within Broadcast Media Production." *Media, Culture, and Society* 26, no. 5 (2004), 677–92.

——. "Notes on Text Production as a Field of Inquiry in Media Studies." *Nordicom* 21, no. 2 (2000), 53–62.

Yúdice, George. *The Expediency of Culture: Uses of Culture in the Global Era.* Durham: Duke University Press, 2005.

Zimmerman, Patricia. *Reel Families: A Social History of Amateur Film.* Bloomington: Indiana University Press, 1995.

Zuboff, Shoshana. *In the Age of the Smart Machine: The Future of Work and Power.* New York: Basic Books, 1988.

Zunz, Olivier. *Making America Corporate, 1870–1920.* Chicago: University of Chicago Press, 1990.

Index

VICKI MAYER IS AN

ASSOCIATE PROFESSOR

OF COMMUNICATION AT

TULANE UNIVERSITY.

*Library of Congress
Cataloging-in-Publication Data*

Mayer, Vicki, 1971–
Below the line : producers and production
studies in the new television economy
/ Vicki Mayer.
p. cm.
Includes bibliographical references and index.
ISBN 978-0-8223-4994-5 (cloth : alk. paper)
ISBN 978-0-8223-5007-1 (pbk. : alk. paper)
1. Television—Production and direction.
2. Television supplies industry—Employees.
3. Television producers and directors. I. Title.
PN1992.75.M394 2011
791.4502'32—dc22
2010044968